The Immigration Dilemma

The Immigration Dilemma

edited by Steven Globerman

The Fraser Institute
Vancouver, British Columbia, Canada

Canadian Cataloguing in Publication Data

Main entry under title:
The Immigration dilemma

    Includes bibliographical references.

    ISBN 0–88975–150–1

    1. Canada—Emigration and immigration—
Government policy. 2. Canada—Emigration
and immigration—Economic aspects. I.
Globerman, Steven.   II. Fraser Institute
(Vancouver, B.C.)
JV7225.I44 1992   325.71   C92–091760–7

Table of Contents

Preface

by Michael A. Walker

FEW SUBJECTS ARE AS CONTENTIOUS as immigration policy. The range of opinions literally covers all of the possibilities from completely open borders on the one hand to completely closed borders on the other. To some extent, the range of opinion reflects variation amongst people in the kind of society in which they would like to live. Some prefer the polyglot, richly textured cultural experience that open borders would produce. Others seek to preserve their own traditions and regard the dilution of tradional ethnic mixes as a threat rather than an opportunity. These preferences, whether in favour of tighter or looser immigration criteria, are not something which can be subjected to scientific analysis. Hence, this book does not consider them.

On the other hand, some of the variation in opinion is due to a different perception about the facts. People with essentially the same preferences can disagree about the correct policy course because they have access to different information about the impact of immigration. The analysis provided in this book suggests that the facts are changing in the sense that historical experience and projected experience with immigration are likely to be different. The purpose of this book is to provide a broad base of information for the consideration of those who are concerned about the immigration question in the hope that a reliable and comprehensive source of facts may produce convergence of opinion about the ideal immigration policy. It considers the economic, social, legal and historical aspects of immigration and a range of professional assessment about what should be concluded on the basis of these facts.

This is a timely book in that Canada is in the process of changing its immigration policy. The Fraser Institute has been pleased to sponsor the research and to make the independent examination of a tough public policy issue possible. However, because the authors and their editor have worked independently the views expressed are those of the authors and may or may not conform to those of the members and Trustees of the Fraser Institute.

About the Authors

Roderic Beaujot
Roderic Beaujot is Professor of Sociology and former director of the Population Studies Centre at the University of Western Ontario. He is also past president of the Federation of Canadian Demographers. After a Ph.D. at the University of Alberta, he worked at Statistics Canada from 1974 to 1976 and has since been at the University of Western Ontario, teaching in the areas of Canadian population and social policy, population of third world societies, and sociology of the family. His research has been in the areas of Canadian marriage and fertility, immigration and policy. His most recent book is *Population Change in Canada: The Challenges of Policy Adaptation* (McClelland and Stewart, 1991). He currently holds a research grant to study "Production and reproduction: economic, cultural and structural accommodations for children."

Don J. DeVoretz
Dr. Devoretz obtained his doctorate in economics from the University of Wisconsin in 1968. He has been with Simon Fraser University since 1968 with visiting appointments at Duke University and the Norwegian School of Economics. In addition, Dr. DeVoretz has sat on the Academic Advisory Board of Employment and Immigration since 1987. Dr. DeVoretz' main research interests include the economics of immigration with special emphasis on the employment, income and savings effects of Canadian immigration flows. Dr. DeVoretz' research findings

have been reported both in professional journals and in *The Wall Street Journal, The Globe and Mail, Macleans,* and *The Financial Times of London.* A summary of his research findings is to be included in his forthcoming book, *Canadian Immigrants: Windfall or Downfall?*

Steven Globerman

Steven Globerman holds a Ph.D. in economics and is currently professor of economics at Simon Fraser University and Adjunct Scholar at The Fraser Institute. He has served on the Faculty of Commerce and Business Administration at the University of British Columbia, the Faculty of Administrative Studies at York University, and the Faculty of Business Administration at Simon Fraser University. He has consulted for government agencies and private sector organizations and has published over 50 journal articles and 15 books and monographs on various aspects of economics and public policy.

Larry Gold

Larry Gold is a Barrister and Solicitor in public practice in Vancouver. He graduated from the University of British Columbia law school in 1973 and was called to the Bar in 1974. He currently practices law extensively in the areas of immigration and general litigation. He is a member of the Immigration subsection of the Canadian Bar Association.

Herbert G. Grubel

Herbert Grubel is a Professor of Economics at Simon Fraser University in the Department of Economics, specializing in international trade and finance. Born in Germany in 1934, Professor Grubel was educated at Rutgers University and at Yale where he received his Ph.D. in Economics in 1962. During 1970-71 he was a Senior Policy Analyst for the U.S. Treasury Department in Washington, D.C., and in 1974-75 Professor Grubel was a visiting Research Fellow at Nuffield College, Oxford. He has held academic posts at Stanford University, the University of Chicago, the University of Pennsylvania, the University of Nairobi, the Australian National University, the University of Cape Town, the Institute of Southeast Asian Studies, and the Kiel Institute of World Economics. Professor Grubel has been the recipient of research grants from the National Science Foundation and the Canada Council. He is a member of The Fraser Institute Editorial Advisory Board. His publications include 14 books and over 100 scholarly articles in journals and books.

William Marr

Bill Marr is Professor of Economics at Wilfrid Laurier University, and has authored or co-authored several articles and books on Canadian Economic History and Canada's Immigration and its policies. His most recent research examines expenditure patterns and housing preferences of various demographic groups in Canada.

Joanna F. Miyake

Joanna Miyake is presently a researcher at The Fraser Institute and an economic graduate student at Simon Fraser University. Her current area of research interest is the economics of health care.

Alice Nakamura

Alice Nakamura is a professor of business statistics in the Faculty of Business at the University of Alberta. She received a B.A. degree in economics from the University of Wisconsin at Madison, and a Ph.D. in economics from The Johns Hopkins University. Her recent research is in the areas of labour economics and labour relations, microsimulation, and productivity measurement and analysis. She is a member of several editorial boards, on the executive for the Canadian Employment Research Forum, and the Vice President of the Canadian Economics Association.

Masao Nakamura

Masao Nakamura is a professor of finance and management science in the Faculty of Business at the University of Alberta. He received B.S. and M.S. degrees from Keio University in Tokyo and a Ph.D. from The Johns Hopkins University. His recent research interests focus on the financial and economic behaviour of firms and households in Canada, the U.S. and Japan, Japanese business practices, international business and econometrics. He has published extensively in leading economics and management journals. He is an Associate Editor for *Labour Economics: An International Journal* and a member of the Editorial Board for *Managerial and Decision Economics*.

Michael Percy

Dr. Michael Percy is a professor of economics at the University of Alberta. He has done extensive work on issues of regional economic development and resource management. Among his most recent books are *Western Canada in the International Economy* (1992) with E.J. Chambers and *Strength in Adversity: A Study of the Alberta Economy* (1990) with R. Mansell. Presently he is actively modelling the economic implications for Western Canada of alternate constitutional scenarios.

Julian L. Simon

Julian Simon teaches business administration at the University of Maryland. His newest books are *Population Matters: People, Resources, Environment and Immigration,* and *The Economic Consequences of Immigration.* Other books include *The Ultimate Resource; The Economics of Population Growth; The Resourceful Earth* (edited with Herman Kahn), *Population and Economic Growth; Basic Research Methods in Social Science; Effort, Opportunity and Wealth; Applied Managerial Economics; Issues in the Economics of Advertising; The Management of Advertising; Patterns of Use of Books in Large Research Libraries* (with H.H. Fussler); and *How to Start and Operate a Mail Order Business.*

Derrick Thomas

Since his graduation from Carelton University in 1982, Derrick Thomas has worked in one capacity or another for the Federal Government. For the past 6 years, he has been with Employment and Immigration Canada. He is currently Senior Research Officer on Social and Cultural Issues with the Strategic Planning and Research Branch of the Immigration Policy Group in Ottawa. Derrick is the author of EIC's levels consultation paper on "Immigrant Integration and the Canadian Identity." He has other publications both in print and forthcoming.

Chapter 1

Background to Immigration Policy in Canada

Steven Globerman

The policy context

IF ASKED, MOST ECONOMISTS WOULD probably agree that elimination of restrictions on the international movements of products and financial capital improves economic efficiency and, ultimately, the economic welfare of nations. To be sure, exceptional arguments can be made in support of government intervention into product and capital markets. These arguments are related to the potential for individual countries to extract higher prices for exports, or lower prices for imports, either by effectively "taxing" foreign trading partners or by enhancing the market power of domestic exporters or importers; however, it is generally acknowledged that the likelihood of retaliation on the part of other governments makes such initiatives risky and largely unattractive, since trade wars and their equivalents will make all countries poorer. Hence, multilateral free trade is still seen as the "first best" policy option by mainstream economists.[1] Interestingly, most economists do not argue for the elimination of restrictions on the international movement of people. That is, they generally support the maintenance of barriers to immigration. While there are outspoken advocates of allowing substantial increases in levels of domestic immigration, there is no visible constituency among economists for ultimately eliminating restrictions on inward immigration.[2] This seems curious in light of the propensity of economists to favour free markets in goods and capital.[3]

Arguments in support of free trade in products primarily rest upon the principle of comparative advantage. Simply put, nations will become wealthier if they specialize in what they do relatively well. In addition, free trade promotes increased efficiency by stimulating competition. Empirical evidence suggests that efficiency gains associated with increased competition can be even more important than the gains associated with specialization according to comparative advantage.[4]

Arguments in support of unrestricted movements of financial capital rest upon the principle that wealth is maximized when scarce capital is used to earn the highest attainable rate-of-return. There is also an

---

1   For a discussion of many of these issues, see Elhanen Helpman and Paul R. Krugman, *Trade Policy and Market Structure*, Cambridge: MIT Press, 1989.

2   Prominent support for liberalizing restrictions on immigration into the United States can be found in Julian L. Simon, *The Economic Consequences of Immigration*,Oxford: Basil Blackwell Ltd., 1989 and Ben J. Wattenberg and Karl Zinsmeister, "The Case for More Immigration," Commentary, April 1990, pp. 19-25. The European Community (EC) is aiming to eliminate barriers to intra-EC nationals as part of achieving its 1992 integration goals; however, immigration barriers to non-EC nationals will be maintained.

3   It might also be noted that passports did not exist prior to World War I. See Julian L. Simon, *The Economic Consequences of Immigration*, Oxford: Basil Blackwell, 1989, p. 347.

4   For a survey of evidence, see Steven Globerman, *Trade Liberalization and Imperfectly Competitive Industries: A Survey of Theory and Evidence*, Ottawa: Economic Council of Canada, 1988.

analogue to the competition argument as applied to trade in products. Namely, investments by foreign-owned firms in domestic markets can act as a stimulus to increased efficiency in those markets. In this regard, there is evidence that the presence of foreign-owned firms in Canadian manufacturing industries stimulates improved efficiency on the part of Canadian-owned firms.[5]

In principle, the migration of people is analogous to the "migration" of capital. To the extent that individuals migrate to maximize the returns to their individual skills, levels of wealth in the world will increase. Furthermore, to the extent that immigration stimulates domestic workers to achieve higher levels of efficiency, there will be a secondary wealth-enhancing impact. To be sure, if the increased wealth generated by migration is not repatriated, at least in part, to the country of emigration, the gains from international migration may be captured entirely by the immigrant and the countries of immigration. Of course, this is also true in the case of capital migration.

Ostensible similarities between migration of labour and migration of capital suggest that the public policy debate about "appropriate" levels of immigration might be informed by the lengthy debate that has surrounded foreign direct investment in Canada. Specifically, many of the reservations expressed about inward foreign direct investment have been manifested, in one form or another, in the debate surrounding immigration. For example, concerns have been expressed about the potential for inward foreign direct investment to displace domestically owned investment or to reduce the profits earned by domestically owned firms.[6] This is analogous to concerns expressed about the poten-

---

5   See Steven Globerman, "Foreign Ownership and Spillover Efficiency Benefits in Canadian Manufacturing Industries," *The Canadian Journal of Economics,* February, 1979.

6   For an overview of arguments surrounding the benefits and costs of inward direct investment, see Edward M. Graham and Paul R. Krugman, *Foreign Direct Investment in the United States,* Washington, D.C.: Institute for International Economics, 1989 and Steven Globerman, *U.S. Ownership of Firms in Canada,* Toronto: C.D. Howe Institute, 1979.

tial for immigrants to displace domestic workers and/or to depress the wages of domestic workers.

Concerns have also been expressed that foreign investors leverage subsidy and tax concessions from domestic governments as inducements to establish domestic affiliates, and that these financial transfers exceed the value of the benefits to the host economy generated by the affiliates' activities. The analogue here is to expressions of concern that immigrants are net beneficiaries of public sector tax-expenditure programs. That is, immigrants take more out of the "public purse" than they put in over the long-run.

In the Canadian context, a specific argument raised against inward foreign direct investment is that it leads to "overcrowding" of domestic industries. Specifically, the establishment of so-called miniature replica affiliates by foreign owned companies allegedly contributes to the existence of manufacturing plants that are below efficient scale and that produce too many products.[7] In effect, the argument is that inward direct investment is associated with diseconomies of scale; i.e. a larger population of firms leads to reduced efficiency. In similar fashion, some critics of immigration warn of the danger of "overcrowding" of cities associated with historical patterns of immigration which are characterized by a concentration in specific urban areas. Overcrowding, in turn, is associated with costs (externalities) imposed upon domestic residents including, for example, roadway congestion, increased classroom sizes in the schools and so forth.[8]

There have also been "non-economic" arguments against inward foreign direct investment. Specifically, concerns have been periodically expressed about the extraterritorial application of U.S. laws to the activities of U.S.-owned affiliates in Canada as a manifestation of a loss of political sovereignty associated with inward foreign direct investment. Arguments have also been raised that the presence of U.S.-owned

---

7   The miniature replica criticism of inward foreign direct investment is discussed in Science Council of Canada, *Innovation in a Cold Climate*, Report Number 15, Ottawa: Information Canada, 1971.

8   See Christie McLaren, "'We've lost control of our border,' critics say," *The Globe and Mail*, February 27, 1991, A4.

affiliates in Canada leads to the importation of U.S. culture into Canada with a subsequent loss of so-called cultural sovereignty.

Cultural impacts of immigration are a particularly noteworthy aspect of the public policy debate. Many of those cautioning about the costs of immigration to the host country raise the issue of "social friction" associated with confrontations between the imported culture of immigrants and the indigenous culture of incumbents.[9] In some instances, social frictions have been manifested in racial violence, although this has thankfully not been characteristic to date of the Canadian society.

Along with a coincidence of costs, there is also a correspondence between the theoretical benefits of foreign direct investment and immigration. For example, it is recognized that highly skilled immigrants can improve the underlying base of technological skills possessed by Canadians with spillover benefits to incumbent residents. This is analogous to the technological spillover arguments that have been applied to multinational investment. It has also been suggested that rather than leading to overcrowding, immigration will increase the size of Canada's population during a period in which any decline in population will lead to risks that Canada will be unable to support its social services network.[10] This latter argument is, in effect, tantamount to a claim that immigrants, on average, contribute more to the tax-transfer system than they take out over the course of their lifetimes. This perspective also underlies arguments for directly or indirectly subsidizing inward foreign direct investment.

Finally, supporters of liberalized immigration quotas point to the increased diversity of tastes and preferences attendant to immigration as a stimulus for new services and, in general, for increased experimen-

---

9 See Economic Council of Canada, *New Faces in the Crowd: Economic and Social Impacts of Immigration*, Ottawa: Minister of Supply and Services Canada, 1991.

10 See John Godfrey, "Hard choices on population to be faced," *The Financial Post*, May 21, 1990, p. 10.

tation and dynamism in the local society.[11] The comingling of heterogeneous points-of-view and modes of behaviour offers the promise of sparking creativity and innovation in what might otherwise be a relatively insular society. In a less dramatic way, a similar benefit has been ascribed to foreign affiliates. Specifically, the presence of foreign affiliates is suggested to broaden the attitudes of incumbents by exposing them to new ideas and practices and thereby make them more receptive to adopting new ideas from abroad.

Existing research

Given the similarity of the issues involved, the relative scarcity of research bearing upon the impacts of immigration relative to research surrounding foreign direct investment is striking. While much of the relevant literature is reviewed in the studies commissioned for this volume, it is useful to offer a brief overview of major studies, particularly Canadian studies, at this juncture.

A recent study by the Economic Council of Canada arguably represents the most comprehensive examination, to date, of the broad impacts of immigration on Canada, including the economic impacts.[12] The Economic Council of Canada (henceforth ECC) notes explicitly that the debate about immigration in Canada revolves around both the number and type of immigrants that should be allowed into the country. They stress that non-economic issues are likely to be of greater importance than economic issues in the ongoing debate. In particular, worries about the erosion of cherished traditions and values, about problems in schools swamped by pupils learning English or French as a second language and about an immigration processing system that sometimes seems out-of-control outweigh worries about job losses.[13]

---

11 See Simon, *op.cit*

12 Economic Council of Canada, *New Faces in the Crowd: Economic and Social Impacts of Immigration*, Ottawa: Minister of Supply and Services Canada, 1991.

13 Ibid., p.1.

Taking a long-term historical perspective, the ECC concludes that there is no sustained correlation between immigration and economic growth. There have been periods when per-capita income has grown rapidly while net immigration rates were quite low and other periods when the reverse was true. There have also been periods when both real incomes and immigration grew rapidly.

On a more detailed level, the ECC postulates that one major source of economic gains to immigration is related to economies of scale. Specifically, immigration could improve real income levels in Canada if a larger population size contributed to greater efficiency. Using statistical techniques, the ECC finds that for every extra million persons above Canada's current population of 27 million, Gross Domestic Product per capita would be higher by about 0.3 percent. This translates into $71 annually per present resident forever into the future and $1,894 per immigrant per annum, forever. These are all gross amounts, since costs associated with bringing in immigrants have not been netted out.[14] The ECC concludes that the foregoing benefits of immigration to present residents are rather small, although they are fairly large per immigrant. It also rejects the notion that other significant sources of economic benefits can be identified. In short, the economic argument for immigration is weak, at best.

The ECC also considers the argument that the aging of the Canadian population will cause dependency costs to rise, including health and social security costs, and that a higher rate of immigration will provide at least part of the financial wherewithal to fund these spiralling dependency costs. It concludes that a higher rate of immigration will help meet rising dependency costs, but the contribution will be quite modest. Moreover, this contribution could be more than offset by the costs of social assistance and language training that would have to be provided for the extra immigrants.

On the other hand, the ECC concludes quite strongly that immigration does not create unemployment. The main reason is that the number of firms will expand steadily to create the needed new jobs; however,

---

14   Ibid., p. 8.

sudden increases in immigration might strain market adjustment processes creating a temporary burst of unemployment.

One projection that is clear from the ECC's analysis is that Canada's ethnic mix will move from one that is overwhelmingly European in origin to one that includes substantial minorities from outside Europe as allowable immigration levels increase. Toronto and Vancouver will experience the greatest relative and absolute changes in ethnic mix. Hence, a focus on non-economic issues associated with changing ethnic mix is an important part of any overall analysis of the impacts of immigration. Whether significant social conflict will be associated with the immigration of diverse ethnic groups will depend in large measure on how well immigrants integrate into their communities. In particular, favourable attitudes towards immigration among the general population and positive intergroup attitudes more generally seem to be directly related to contact between different ethnic groups.[15] This contact ideally occurs in a way that enables people to develop mutual respect, for example, as co-workers.

The ECC commissioned a number of studies that sought to document whether racial conflict and prejudice had increased or decreased in Canada over the 1980s. The results point to a broad finding that the tolerance of Canadians for immigration generally and for visible minorities in particular is increasing.[16] Nevertheless, it cautions that a continuation of present immigration levels, or an increase in such levels, is likely to lead to some increase in the number of incidents of discrimination and ethnic conflict, if for no other reason than the larger absolute numbers of people of different ethnic backgrounds who will populate Canada in the future. The ECC therefore suggests that more action to combat prejudice is needed. Interestingly, it concludes that the more significant gains from cultural and ethnic diversity remain speculative. These include "the positive effects on native-born Canadians of emulating the industriousness of immigrants, the attraction and dynamism of cosmopolitan cities; greater export penetration by firms with multilin-

---

15   Ibid., p. 28.

16   Ibid., p. 31.

gual, multicultural salesmen and management; the beneficial effects of having to spell out human rights objectives and commitments; and the enhanced creativity and flexibility of a diverse society as opposed to one that is homogeneous."[17] This latter observation is interesting in light of claims by some that a critical benefit of immigration is the imbuing of the receiving country with entrepreneurial spirit.[18]

In the final analysis, the ECC recommends that immigration should be gradually increased above the average levels of the last 25 years. In the case of refugee claimants, the recommendation is based on humanitarian considerations. The ECC acknowledges that refugee claimants are more costly to process. Arguably, they also are less likely to "pay for themselves" in the long-run. In the case of other categories of immigrants, the recommendation is based primarily upon the ECC's opinion that it will make Canada a more interesting and exciting society, albeit that this opinion is admittedly based on little evidence and imposes some risk of more social conflict.

At least one recently completed major U.S. study offers more unqualified support for the economic benefits of immigration.[19] For example, it concludes that immigrants do not use more transfer payments and public services than do natives; rather, they use much smaller amounts in total. Taking into account taxes paid and data on transfers and services, natives are enriched each year by the net taxes paid by immigrants. The present value of a newly-arrived immigrant family discounted at a real interest rate of 3 percent was $20,600 in 1975 dollars, almost 2 years' average earnings of a native family. This is directionally in line with the ECC's assessment but suggests a larger quantitative impact.

Simon argues that though the direct effect upon industrial productivity is hard to nail down statistically, in the long run the beneficial impact upon industrial efficiency of additional immigrant workers and

---

17 Ibid., p. 31.

18 See Wattenberg and Zinsmeister, *op. cit.*

19 See Simon, *op. cit.*

consumers is likely to dwarf all other effects.[20] Part of this impact is related to economies of scale associated with a larger population and work force. Part is related to a "stimulative cross-pollenization effect that arises from encounters among people who have different ways of doing things."[21] Part is simply related to the potential for immigrants to introduce productivity-enhancing innovations that would not otherwise have taken place. This latter possibility is enhanced to the extent that immigrants have skill levels that are above the average of the general population.

Simon notes the potential for immigrants to have adverse impacts upon the productivity levels of incumbent workers. This potential is also a function of the skill levels of immigrants relative to incumbents, as well as the absolute number of immigrants. In a simple macro-model using what he considers to be reasonable parameters, Simon brings the various considerations together by way of an estimation of the difference between natives' incomes with or without immigrants. In 1975 dollars, an immigrant family increases the incomes of natives by somewhere between $15,000 and $20,000.[22] This is substantially above the estimated capitalized values of the income impact of immigrants developed by the ECC. Recall that the ECC estimates the annual increase in Gross Domestic Product per resident to be approximately $71. Using a 10 percent discount rate, this equates to a capitalized value of $710 treating the $71 as an annuity.

There is very little reliable U.S. evidence bearing upon the broader socio-cultural impacts of immigration discussed by the ECC; however, Simon interprets what evidence is available to suggest that externalities associated with overcrowded schools, job displacement and racial strife are grossly overestimated. Indeed, he interprets expert opinion as indicating that immigration has positive socio-cultural effects and recommends that U.S. immigration quotas be increased in a series of increments of one-half percent to one percent of total population at each

---

20 Ibid., p. 342.

21 Ibid.

22 Ibid., p. 343.

step. Before each quota increase an evaluation would be undertaken to identify any unexpected negative consequences, and to determine whether demand for admission ever exceeds the supply of places.

Although the major studies cited above are recent publications, they draw upon experience that may not be representative of the future impacts of immigration on the receiving country. Specifically, changing economic and political conditions inside and outside of Canada suggest that immigrants to Canada will be increasingly less skilled than earlier generations of immigrants, at least relative to the indigenous population. These changes include more aggressive "competition" for skilled immigrants from other developed countries including the U.S. and Australia, lower real after-tax disposable income levels in Canada compared to other developed countries relative to the distribution of real after-tax disposable income levels in earlier years and the increasing weight of refugee immigrants in the total immigrant population. Increased competition for skilled immigrants will directly reduce the supply of such immigrants willing to come to Canada given existing economic and social conditions in Canada. Relative decreases in real disposable income levels in Canada will also discourage immigration of skilled people to Canada, especially with Canada's relatively high marginal income tax rates.[23]

Borjas warns that the U.S. is currently attracting relatively unskilled immigrants. Although these immigrants do not greatly affect the earnings and employment opportunities of natives, he cautions that they may have an even greater long-run economic impact because of their relatively high poverty rates and propensities for participation in the welfare system and because national income and tax revenues are substantially lower than they would have been if the United States had attracted a more skilled immigrant flow.[24] In short, a cost-benefit anal-

---

23 Obviously, the impact of a more progressive tax structure in Canada would be mitigated if immigrants viewed the resulting level of public services as more than offsetting the tax consequences; however, immigrants tend to be net funders of the public sector, so this condition is less likely to maintain, the higher the marginal tax rate.

24 George J. Borjas, *Friends or Strangers: The Impact of Immigrants on the U.S.*

ysis of immigration at the margin is likely to be significantly less favourable than an analysis of the "average" experience. This caution has also been raised for Canada, although changes in Canadian immigration policy are held to be primarily responsible for the decline in the average skill level of immigrants to Canada in the 1980s. Specifically, the family reunification criterion became more important relative to the preceding "points" system which allowed immigrants to Canada to be chosen on the basis of suitability to Canada and the Canadian labour market needs.[25]

An overview of the volume

The purpose of this volume is to provide a condensed yet comprehensive overview of the major issues surrounding immigration policy in Canada. While theoretical issues are discussed in order to set the policy context, the primary emphasis is on empirical evidence bearing upon the major policy issues. Much of this evidence has been discussed elsewhere including the recent Economic Council of Canada report and other studies done by contributors to this volume. Nevertheless, there is arguably value in bringing available findings together in a single volume that is accessible to non-economists. While the basic findings and conclusions of this volume tend to support the existing literature, some of the evidence is new.

Chapters 2 through 4 provide statistical and institutional contexts within which immigration policy can be evaluated. Specifically, Chapter 2 provides a statistical overview of post-war Canadian immigration patterns. This chapter, by Professor William Marr, highlights the significant shift in source or sending areas of the world that has taken place in recent years. In the late 1950s, over 85 percent of Canada's total inflow came from Europe, with over 30 percent arriving from Great Britain. By 1981, Asia as a source area constituted about 40 percent of the flow increasing to about 43 percent by 1988.

Economy, New York: Basic Books, 1990, p. 19.

25   See R.G. Coulson and Don J. Devoretz, *Human Capital Content of Canadian Immigration 1966-1987*, Simon Fraser University, mimeo.

In Chapter 3, Professor Roderic Beaujot assesses the socio-demographic impact of immigration. He highlights the preeminent importance of immigration as a source of future population growth. While projected immigration patterns will not have a significant impact on the median age of the population, it will have an important impact on the geographic distribution of Canada's population. In particular, it will accentuate differences in regional population growth. It will also accentuate the growth of Toronto, Montreal and Vancouver. Beaujot highlights the above-average educational and labour force participation characteristics of preceding generations of immigrants but calls attention to the lower levels of education in recent vintages of immigrants, primarily reflecting the growing absolute and relative importance of family class and refugee immigrants.

Chapters 2 and 3 therefore identify an historical basis for the positive economic impacts that immigration has had in earlier periods, as well as a caution against inferring that these positive impacts will necessarily be perpetuated in the future. Chapter 4, written by Larry Gold, details current immigration law and policy in Canada from Gold's perspective as an immigration lawyer. One important conclusion is that the refugee claimant process is a potentially costly one both in terms of actual administration cost, as well as in terms of the economic impact of immigration, as refugees do not have to meet assessment criteria related to official language facility, education and vocation.

Chapter 5, written by Professor Herbert Grubel, offers a concise yet comprehensive theoretical context in which the social welfare effects of immigration can be evaluated. It stresses the need to consider the "externalities" created by immigration which can be both economic and non-economic in nature. It also reinforces the Economic Council of Canada's insight that these externalities are more likely to be "negative" the faster the rate of immigration, even if they are unrelated to the ultimate number of immigrants accepted into the country. In Chapter 6, Dr. Julian Simon provides a complementary analysis of the economics of immigration along with an overview of U.S. evidence on the important relationships identified. Simon highlights the important distinctions between immigration and trade in products. In particular, absent externalities, trade-induced shifts in prices and production benefit consumers in both countries, whereas the shifts due to international migration benefit only the migrant; however, he reads the available evidence from the U.S. as indicating that immigrants raise productivity as well as the incomes of incumbents. Immigrants are also net contributors to government finances by paying more in taxes than they receive in social services.

Chapter 7 presents an assessment of the overall macroeconomic effects of immigration using simulations performed using the RDX2 macro model. The authors, Professors Alice Nakamura, Masao Nakamura and Michael Percy describe how immigration affects macroeconomic variables such as gross national expenditure in the model along with the limitations of the methodology adopted. Simulations of the impacts of higher or lower (than experienced) levels of immigration over the period 1961-1970 were performed. They conclude that increased levels of immigration raise the predicted values of real gross national expenditure, reduce the predicted unemployment rate and increase the predicted inflation rate. The main result is that the predicted effects of immigration on key economic indicators are modest despite large experimental variations in immigration flows.

Chapter 8 complements the preceding chapter by focusing on the labour market impacts of immigration. Taking a microeconomic perspective, Professor Don DeVoretz addresses the relationship between immigration and employment, as well as between immigration and earnings. DeVoretz identifies differences between the experience of the 1967-1978 period and the post-1978 period. Specifically, between 1967 and 1978, existing policy favoured the admission of highly qualified immigrants. Armed with high educational attainment, these immigrants' earnings grew quickly with little associated job displacement and made immigrants net contributors to the treasury. After 1978, the educational attainment level of immigrants declined on average. Earnings of certain skill groups then fell below the Canadian average, and job displacement by Third World immigrants was more readily identifiable with the predominant displacement impact felt by unskilled incumbent workers. It is unclear how much of the changing nature of immigration post-1978 is due to government policy versus a changing "pool" of available immigrants.

Chapter 9 deals with the controversial issue of the impact of immigration on demand for housing and housing prices. Using different statistical approaches, Joanna Miyake, a graduate student in economics at Simon Fraser University, documents that international migration has been a significant source of increased demand for housing in Vancouver, although natural population growth and inter-provincial migration have been more significant sources of increased demand. The increased demand for housing on the part of immigrants has had a predictable positive effect on the price of housing, although the observed impact also reflects government policies constraining increases in the supply of housing.

Chapter 10 also deals with a controversial topic: the socio-cultural effects of immigration. The author, Derrick Thomas of Employment and Immigration Canada, highlights the importance of social integration as a determinant of the non-economic effects of immigration. Using various empirical measures, he concludes that immigrants to Canada have been effectively integrated into Canadian society which helps explain the relative absence of racial strife in Canada. As the mix of immigrants changes increasingly in the direction of non-traditional sources, the challenge to effective integration will grow. Clearly more money will have to be spent on language training and the like.

In summary, the contributions to this volume reinforce other studies suggesting that the historical impact of immigration has been relatively modest, especially in light of some of the exaggerated claims that have been made both in favour and in opposition to increased immigration. On balance, immigration appears to have net positive economic benefits for the receiving country, although immigration itself is no panacea for domestic economic illnesses. Moreover, future benefits may be smaller than those historically experienced, especially given a tilt toward more humanitarian criteria in Canada's immigration policies.

The social impacts of immigration also appear to have been modest in the past reflecting a relatively smooth integration process for immigrants. Again, there are grounds for speculating that the process may be increasingly less smooth in the future, as the mix of immigrants continues to shift toward non-traditional sources and towards immigrants without facility in Canada's official languages. At the least, there is a suggestion that more resources will have to be expended on facilitating the integration process. Canadians may need to confront more explicitly the implied tradeoff between economic and non-economic objectives of immigration policy.

Chapter 2

Post-War Canadian
Immigration Patterns

William L. Marr

Introduction and context

THIS CHAPTER DOCUMENTS THE NATURE and extent of immigration into Canada over the period since 1949, although some initial discussion of the role of net migration since 1851 is included in order to put Canada's recent history of international migration in a longer historical context. This provides a point departure for the chapters to follow and enables the reader to put later discussions of immigration policies, macroeconomic impacts, social and political consequences, labour market influences, and housing effects in the context of the actual immigration inflows over the last forty years.

Although this chapter emphasises immigration to Canada, it has become common practice to compare that country's immigration flows and policies to those of Australia and the United States, two other regions of migrant permanent settlement. The same will be done here at times, but in the more detailed and more specific discussions to follow only data for Canada will be used. Some comparisons among the three countries will be made at the more general level of the nature of immigration flows.

Contribution to population growth: long and short term

Table 1 presents statistics on the components of Canada's population growth over the past one hundred and thirty-five years. It makes use of the basic identity:

Change in Population = Birth – Deaths + Immigration – Emigration
= Natural Increase + Net Migration

From this identity, the ratio of net migration to total population growth can be calculated and represents one way of looking at the contribution that immigration and emigration make to Canada's increase in population. Over the entire period, about 14 percent of this population growth was caused by net migration and of course the other 86 percent was due to natural increase. This points to the important fact, which is illustrated by the immigration and emigration statistics in Table 1, that Canada has had substantial emigration as well as immigration through her history; between 1851 and 1986, Canada accepted about 11.6 million immigrants, but about 7.7 million persons also left Canada. In any discussion of the effects that immigration has on Canada's population or on social and economic structure, it is important to note net migration as well as gross migration or immigration. Clearly the net effects will be much less than what is implied by a specific level of immigration.

Table 1 illustrates the large volatility in the contribution that net migration has made to Canada's population growth. In the periods 1951-1956, 1966-1971, and 1971-1976, net migration constituted 28.9 percent, 29.8 percent, and 34.4 percent respectively of total population growth. In the post-Second World War years, the low was reached between 1961 and 1966 when net migration made up only 14.6 percent of this growth. Since 1976, net migration's contribution has gradually fallen. It is important to realize from Table 1 that Canada has had other

TABLE 2-1: Components of population growth, Canada,[a] 1851-1986

Period	Total population growth (1000s)	Births (1000s)	Deaths (1000s)	Natural increase (1000s)	Ratio of natural increase to total growth %	Immigration (1000s)	Emigration[b] (1000s)	Net migration (1000s)	Ratio of net migration to total growth %	Population at end of Census period (1000s)	Immigration as a % of population at the start
1851-1861	793	1,281	670	611	77.0	352	170	182	23.0	3,230	14.5
1861-1871	460	1,370	760	610	132.6	260	410	-150	-32.6	3,689	8.1
1871-1881	636	1,480	790	690	108.5	350	404	-54	-8.5	4,325	9.5
1881-1891	508	1,524	870	654	128.7	680	826	-146	-28.7	4,833	15.7
1891-1901	538	1,548	880	668	124.2	250	380	-130	-24.2	5,371	5.2
1901-1911	1,835	1,925	900	1,025	55.9	1,550	740	810	44.1	7,207	28.9
1911-1921	1,581	2,340	1,070	1,270	80.3	1,400	1,089	311	19.7	8,788	19.4
1921-1931	1,589	2,420	1,060	1,360	85.5	1,200	970	230	14.5	10,377	13.7
1931-1941	1,130	2,294	1,072	1,222	108.1	149	241	-92	-8.1	11,507	1.4
1941-1951[c]	2,503	3,212	1,220	1,992	92.3	548	382	166	7.7	14,009	4.8
1951-1956	2,071	2,106	633	1,473	71.1	783	185	598	28.9	16,081	5.6
1956-1961	2,157	2,362	687	1,675	77.7	760	378	482	22.3	18,238	4.7
1961-1966	1,777	2,249	731	1,518	85.4	539	280	259	14.6	20,015	3.0
1966-1971	1,553	1,856	766	1,090	70.2	890	427	463	29.8	21,568	4.5
1971-1976	1,424	1,758	823	934	65.6	841	352	489	34.4	22,993	4.0
1976-1981	1,288	1,820	842	978	75.9	588	278	310	24.1	24,343	2.6
1981-1986	1,252	1,873	885	988	78.9	500	235	264	21.2	25,354	2.1

[a] Includes Newfoundland since 1951.
[b] Emigration figures are estimated by the residual method.
[c] Data on growth components shown for 1941-51 were obtained by including data for Newfoundland for 1949-50 and 1950-51 only.

Source: *Canada Year Book,* 1990.

periods when net migration's contribution has been at the same levels as these more contemporary periods, namely the periods 1851-1861 and 1901-1911. The contemporary level of contribution has been experienced before, although the sustained contribution during the 1950s and between 1966 and 1981 is worthy of note.

Another way to put immigration in context is to see what percentage immigration over a decade was of Canada's population at the start of the decade. The data are contained in the last column of Table 1. This percentage, after being relatively high in the 1850s was much lower in the last decades of the nineteenth century, except for 1881-1891, then rose dramatically with the settling of Western Canada during the first decade of the twentieth century, fell for the next few decades, rose in the 1950s, and has shown a tendency to decline since. From the data in Table 1, the percentages are 11.0 percent, 7.8 percent, and 6.6 percent for the 1950s, 1960s, and 1970s respectively. These then compare to significantly higher percentages during several previous decades.

Tables 2 and 3 present the same components of population and its change for the years 1950 to 1989. Table 3 shows that the percentage of population change contributed by net migration varied considerably over these years, being over 35 percent in 1951, 1956, 1966, 1973, 1974 and 1975, and perhaps being negative during the relatively low immigration period of 1983 to 1985. It is also evident that the aggregate figures in Table 1 actually have a great deal of variation around those average statistics. Perhaps the most interesting aspects of net migration as a percentage of population change is its cyclical behaviour over this time period. That is, this percentage moves inversely to measures of the business cycle such as the unemployment rate, rising when the rate falls and falling when the rate rises. This pattern as it relates to the state of Canada's economy is also evident in Table 1 for the longer term. In the contemporary period, the declines in this percentage from 1957 to 1961, from 1967 to 1971, and from 1980 to 1984 are noteworthy.

Table 4 reproduces the data for immigration as a percentage of the population at the start of the year from Table 3 and includes three measures of economic activity, namely the unemployment rate, the annual growth rate of real gross domestic product, and the annual growth rate of real gross fixed capital formation. It can be seen clearly

TABLE 2-2: Components of population growth, 1950-1988

	Births	Deaths	Natural Increase	Population at Start of Year (1000s)	Population Change (1000s)	Immigration
1950	372,009	124,220	247,789	13,704	301	73,912
1951	381,092	125,823	255,269	14,005	432	194,391
1952	403,559	126,385	277,174	14,437	396	164,498
1953	417,884	127,791	290,093	14,833	437	168,868
1954	436,198	124,855	311,343	15,270	411	154,227
1955	442,937	128,476	314,461	15,681	389	109,946
1956	450,739	131,961	318,778	16,070	510	164,857
1957	469,093	136,579	332,514	16,580	482	282,164
1958	470,118	135,201	334,917	17,062	406	124,851
1959	479,275	139,913	339,362	17,468	387	106,928
1960	478,551	139,693	338,858	17,855	370	104,111
1961	475,700	140,985	334,715	18,225	346	71,689
1962	469,693	143,699	325,994	18,571	348	74,586
1963	465,767	147,367	318,400	18,919	358	93,151
1964	452,915	145,850	307,065	19,277	357	112,606
1965	418,595	148,939	269,656	19,634	364	146,758
1966	387,710	149,863	237,847	19,998	366	194,743
1967	370,894	150,283	220,611	20,364	328	222,876
1968	364,310	153,196	211,114	20,692	302	183,974
1969	369,947	154,477	215,170	20,994	294	161,531
1970	371,988	155,961	216,027	21,288	271	147,713
1971	362,187	157,272	204,915	21,559	234	121,900
1972	347,319	162,413	184,906	21,793	247	122,006
1973	343,373	164,039	179,334	22,040	317	184,200
1974	350,650	166,794	183,856	22,357	331	218,465
1975	359,323	167,404	191,919	22,688	297	187,881
1976	359,987	167,009	192,978	22,985	275	149,429
1977	361,400	167,498	193,902	23,260	243	114,914
1978	358,852	168,179	190,673	23,503	235	86,313
1979	366,064	168,183	197,881	23,738	292	112,096
1980	370,709	171,473	199,236	24,030	294	143,117
1981	371,346	171,029	200,317	24,324	247	128,618
1982	372,882	174,413	198,469	24,571	207	121,147
1983	373,689	174,484	199,205	24,778	192	89,157
1984	377,031	175,727	201,304	24,970	188	88,239
1985	379,140	178,330	200,810	25,158	190	84,302
1986	378,260	186,410	191,851	25,348	256	99,219
1987	372,080	185,260	186,820	25,604	294	152,098
1988	374,920	186,190	188,730	25,898	321	161,929
1989	381,040	191,150	189,890	26,219		190,933

Source: Department of Finance, *Quarterly Economic Review,* June 1990.

TABLE 2-3:
Components of population change, 1950-1988

	% Natural Increase to Population Change	% Net Migration to Population Change	Immigration as a % of Population at Start of Year
1950	82.3	17.7	0.54
1951	59.1	40.9	1.39
1952	70.0	30.0	1.14
1953	66.4	33.6	1.14
1954	75.7	24.3	1.01
1955	80.9	19.1	0.70
1956	62.5	37.5	1.03
1957	69.0	31.0	1.70
1958	82.5	17.5	0.73
1959	87.7	12.3	0.61
1960	91.6	8.4	0.58
1961	96.7	3.3	0.39
1962	93.7	6.3	0.40
1963	88.9	11.1	0.49
1964	86.0	14.0	0.58
1965	74.2	25.8	0.75
1966	65.0	35.0	0.97
1967	67.3	32.7	1.10
1968	69.9	30.1	0.89
1969	73.2	26.8	0.77
1970	79.7	20.3	0.69
1971	87.6	12.4	0.57
1972	74.9	25.1	0.56
1973	56.6	43.4	0.84
1974	55.6	44.4	0.98
1975	64.6	35.4	0.83
1976	70.2	29.8	0.65
1977	79.8	20.2	0.49
1978	81.1	18.9	0.37
1979	67.8	32.2	0.47
1980	67.8	32.2	0.60
1981	81.1	18.9	0.53
1982	94.4	5.6	0.49
1983	103.8	-3.8	0.36
1984	107.1	-7.1	0.35
1985	105.7	-5.7	0.33
1986	74.9	25.1	0.39
1987	63.5	36.5	0.59
1988	58.8	41.2	0.63
1989			0.73

TABLE 2-4:
Immigration and the business cycle

	Immigration	Immigration as a % of Population	Unemployment Rate	Percentage Change in GDP (1986 Prices)	Percentage Change in Gross Fixed Capital Formation (1986 Prices)
1950	73,912	0.54	3.6	7.8	7.6
1951	194,391	1.39	2.4	4.5	0.0
1952	164,498	1.14	2.9	8.3	11.2
1953	168,868	1.14	3.0	5.0	12.2
1954	154,227	1.01	4.6	-1.1	0.2
1955	109,946	0.70	4.4	9.5	10.1
1956	164,857	1.03	3.4	8.6	18.0
1957	282,164	1.70	4.6	2.5	6.3
1958	124,851	0.73	7.0	2.2	-1.3
1959	106,928	0.61	6.0	3.9	0.7
1960	104,111	0.58	7.0	2.9	-3.1
1961	71,689	0.39	7.1	3.1	-0.3
1962	74,586	0.40	5.9	7.1	4.4
1963	93,151	0.49	5.5	5.2	4.5
1964	112,606	0.58	4.7	6.7	13.2
1965	146,758	0.75	3.9	6.6	11.3
1966	194,743	0.97	3.4	6.8	10.7
1967	222,876	1.10	3.8	2.9	-0.3
1968	183,974	0.89	4.5	5.4	0.5
1969	161,531	0.77	4.4	5.4	5.4
1970	147,713	0.69	5.7	2.6	0.3
1971	121,900	0.57	6.2	5.8	7.9
1972	122,006	0.56	6.2	5.7	4.3
1973	184,200	0.84	5.5	7.7	9.9
1974	218,465	0.98	5.3	4.4	6.6
1975	187,881	0.83	6.9	2.6	5.8
1976	149,429	0.65	7.1	6.2	4.6
1977	114,914	0.49	8.1	3.6	2.1
1978	86,313	0.37	8.3	4.6	3.1
1979	112,096	0.47	7.4	3.9	8.5
1980	143,117	0.60	7.5	1.5	10.1
1981	128,618	0.53	7.5	3.7	11.8
1982	121,147	0.49	11.0	-3.2	-11.0
1983	89,157	0.36	11.8	3.2	-0.7
1984	88,239	0.35	11.2	6.3	2.1
1985	84,302	0.33	10.5	4.8	9.5
1986	99,219	0.39	9.5	3.3	6.2
1987	152,098	0.59	8.8	4.0	10.3
1988	161,929	0.63	7.8	4.4	10.2
1989	190,933	0.73	7.5	3.0	4.5

Sources: Department of Finance, *Quarterly Economic Review*, June 1990; *Historical Statistics of Canada*

that Canada's unemployment rate rose dramatically in all three of those time periods.

The expected declines in the growth rates of real gross domestic product and real gross fixed capital formation appear to lead the fall in immigration as a percentage of population by a year or two, but a relationship is still there. This counter-cyclical behaviour is partly because of potential migrants' response to the perceived costs versus benefits from moving, as well as policy makers' reactions to the state of the economy in Canada, which will be pointed out in the chapter on immigration policies. For example, when the unemployment rate rose in the early 1980s, the federal government changed the immigration regulations so that migrants in the independent and assisted relatives classes required a job to be waiting for them before they were given landing status.

With regard to this cyclical pattern, Table 4 shows the extent to which total immigration has risen and fallen with the state of Canada's economy. The relatively high rates of growth of the economy and lower unemployment rates throughout most of the 1950s along with unsettled political and economic situations in Europe plus the shortages of labour due to the decline in births and immigration in the 1930s and 1940s caused immigration to be high, reaching a peak of about 282,000 in 1957. The onset of a cyclical downturn in that year as reflected in rising unemployment rates and relatively low growth rates of real GDP and gross fixed capital formation was associated with falling immigration levels until it reached about 71,000 in 1961 and 74,000 in 1962. This was replaced by the generally buoyant mid-1960s, especially for growth rates of real fixed capital formation with immigration peaking at about 222,000 in 1967. During the later years of that decade and through the 1970s, inflows declined steadily to 1971, rose rapidly to about 218,000 in 1974, and then declined to 1978. Immigration then rose rapidly to 1980 with more prosperous conditions, but declined almost as quickly to about 89,000 by 1983 and remained at that level until 1986 as the unemployment rate remained high and real growth was relatively low. Since then, inflows have risen as the economy recovered and the federal government adopted in part the use of immigration to meet population goals associated with low fertility rates. For reference, Canada's immigration averaged about 139,000 over the 40 years that are examined here.

It has become traditional to think of the United States and Australia as the two other major countries of permanent settlement. Over the same time, the United States admitted approximately 389,000 per year, and the annual average has risen from about 251,000 in the 1950s, to 449,000 in the 1970s, and to over 580,000 in the 1980s (*Statistical Abstract of the United States*, 1989, 9). As one measure of the relative size of these flows, the number of immigrants can be expressed as an annual rate per 1,000 of the U.S. population. These rates were 1.5 in the 1950s, 2.1 in the 1970s, and 2.5 in the 1980s. In contrast, the Canadian rates were 9.9 in the 1950s, 6.3 in the 1970s, and 4.9 in the 1980s. The annual average for Australia over the period 1951 to 1988 was about 113,000 immigrants, which places Canada between the U.S. and Australia although the United States is significantly ahead in terms of absolute intake (*Year Book Australia*, 1989, 153; SOPEMI 1988 Australia). The Australian immigration statistics show the same type of volatility that was noted in the Canadian data; in the period 1951 to 1955, annual Australian arrivals averaged about 114,000 per year, and this increased during the next five years to an average of over 123,000 per year, which fell to an average of 115,000 per year from 1961 to 1965. Between 1966 and 1970, the annual average was about 160,000, the highest five-year post-war averaged. Then followed a decade of generally falling average annual inflows, which reached an annual average of about 73,000 in the period 1976 to 1980. Annual arrivals continued to fall until 1985, after which they increased to about 151,000 in 1988. The number of immigrants to Australia as a rate per 1,000 of the Australian population was 13.2 in the 1960s, 6.6 in the 1970s, and averaged 6.3 from 1981 to 1987. These are above the comparable figures noted earlier for both the United States and Canada.

Sources of immigration

Perhaps the most visible and important change in Canada's immigration since the Second World War is the significant shift in source that has taken place. Table 5 shows this change very clearly. In the late 1950s, over 85 percent of Canada's total inflow came from Europe, with about 30 percent arriving from Great Britain. Before 1961, the ten leading sending countries by birthplace were Great Britain, Italy, the United States, Poland, the U.S.S.R., Netherlands, the Federal Republic of Germany, Yugoslavia, the German Democratic Republic, and Austria (Hawkins, 260). By the late 1960s and early 1970s, significant shifts had taken place. The European percentage had fallen to about 50 percent while the percentage from Asia and South-Central America had risen to 13.7 percent and 12.5 percent respectively. But this was only the start, especially for the Asian flow.

By 1981, Asia as a source area constituted about 35 percent of the flow, with 12.3 percent from South-Central America and 8 percent from Africa. At the other end of the spectrum of change, the European area made up about 36 percent of the total. Between 1971 and 1981, Great Britain and the United States were still significant source countries in that they were in the top ten sending countries, but India, the Philippines, Vietnam, Hong Kong, and Guyana were on the top ten list (Hawkins, 260-261). Table 5 indicates that the shifts continued throughout the 1980s. By 1988, Asian source countries made up about 43 percent of Canada's total immigration flow.

TABLE 2-5:
Percentage of total Canadian immigration from various world areas

	Europe	Asia	South and Central America	Africa	Other
1956-1961	85.7	1.9	2.3	1.0	9.1
1968-1974	49.9	13.7	12.5	3.5	20.4
1981	36.0	35.5	12.3	8.0	8.2
1985	22.4	40.7	18.3	10.6	8.0
1988	25.2	43.5	13.9	13.3	4.1
1989	27.2	39.8	13.3	16.1	3.6

Source: Marr, 1975; SOPEMI 1988 Canada; special tabulations for 1989.

Although the causes of these significant shifts will be explored in later chapters of this book, it should be mentioned here that the 1960s marked a change in Canada's immigration policies where there was a deliberate effort to eliminate discrimination by racial origins or country of birth or residence. This was formally instituted with the introduction of the Points System in 1967. The so-called independent applicant was now required to obtain a certain score where points were given for possessing certain characteristics that were thought to provide a better chance of finding employment in Canada and adjusting to Canadian society; the assessment system took account of the applicant's education and training, adaptability - motivation - initiative, occupational demand and skill, age, arranged employment, knowledge of French or English, relatives in Canada, and area of destination. This Points System has remained an important part of Canada's immigration policy ever since, and, although it has undergone some modifications, many of its essential elements remain. Similar attitudes appeared in the United States and Australia during the 1960s and 1970s, so the three countries of major permanent settlement witnessed similar policy shifts. Additionally, the shift away from Europe also reflects the relative attractiveness of remaining in the home country or migrating within Europe rather than coming to Canada. As economic and political conditions improved in Europe the human capital approach to migration suggests that people will show a greater tendency to remain in the potential sending countries.

As just alluded to, similar shifts in source areas were occurring in Australia and the United States. From 1961 to 1965, about 46 percent of Australia's settler arrivals were from the United Kingdom and Ireland, and about 12 percent each were from Italy and Greece (*Australian Bureau of Statistics*, 1989, 152). By 1972, the United Kingdom and Ireland made up 45 percent of permanent arrivals, Other Europe 25 percent, Asia 9 percent, and New Zealand 3 percent (Betts, 184). By 1980, the United Kingdom and Ireland constituted 26 percent, Other Europe 18 percent, Asia 28 percent, and New Zealand 15 percent. By 1987, those from the United Kingdom and Ireland had fallen to 19 percent, Other Europe to 12 percent, while Asian immigrants had risen to 37 percent with New Zealand at about 12 percent. So the same shifts as took place in Canada were also evident in Australia. For the United States, European immigrants made up about 50 percent of the total flow in the period 1955 to 1964; at the same time, Asian immigrants were about 8 percent of the total while persons from North America were 36 percent. By 1975 to 1984, the following changes had taken place: Europeans—13 percent,

Asians—43 percent, North Americans—34 percent (and Caribbean had risen from 7 percent to 15 percent) (Miller, 1987).

Class of immigration

One of the most important issues that has concerned immigration and its policies since the 1960s has been the criteria that would apply to the various classes of immigrants that Canada admits. This will be taken up in detail in a later chapter, but a brief examination of the column head-

TABLE 2-6:
Percentage of total immigration by class, Canada

	Independent	Sponsored	Nominated Relatives
1968	55.5	20.8	23.7
1969	53.8	20.8	25.4
1970	54.1	21.9	24.0
1971	48.6	27.5	24.0
1972	47.3	27.1	25.6
1973	53.3	22.7	24.0
1974	50.4	25.2	24.4
1975	40.3	34.8	24.9
1976	32.7	41.0	26.2
1977	29.4	45.5	25.1

Source: Employment and Immigration Canada.

ings of Table 6 and the row headings of Table 7 give the reader the titles of the classes. The Independent class contains persons who expect to become self-supporting and successfully established in Canada based on their education and training, adaptability, motivation, initiative, the demand for their occupation in Canada, age, knowledge of French or English, and employment prospects; they are assessed under the Points System. The classes of Sponsored Dependents and Family Class are very similar in that they reflect the principle of the reunion of families. Close relatives are sponsored by either Canadian citizens or landed im-migrants. Nominated Relatives and Assisted Relatives are a cross be-

TABLE 2-7
Canada:
landings by class, percentage distribution

	1980	1981	1982	1983	1984	1985	1986*	1987*	1988*	1989
Family Class	35.62	39.67	41.26	54.63	49.65	45.69	45.56	39.42	31.91	31.66
Convention Refugees	0.01	0.63	1.48	4.60	6.38	7.21	7.01	5.53	5.40	5.31
Designated Class	27.50	11.02	12.49	11.07	11.01	12.67	13.67	10.43	11.22	13.95
Assisted Relatives	9.44	13.68	9.86	5.60	9.26	8.77	6.36	9.07	9.69	11.21
Retired	1.08	1.60	1.86	2.35	2.62	2.49	1.98	1.97	1.95	1.86
Entrepreneurs	0.05	0.70	1.22	2.09	4.03	5.88	6.34	6.25	7.01	6.76
Self-Employed	3.07	3.99	4.03	4.89	3.07	1.81	1.76	1.71	1.68	1.21
Investor							0.02	0.23	0.64	1.18
Independent	22.02	28.72	27.80	14.78	13.99	15.48	17.30	25.39	31.04	26.87
Total	100.00	100.00	100.00	100.00	100.00	100.00	100.00	100.00	100.00	100.00

*The percentages for these years exclude persons admitted through the Administrative Review.

Source: Employment and Immigration Canada.

tween the classes for family reunion and Independents; the Relatives classes recognize the presence of relatives in Canada, but also assess these potential immigrants by the Points System because they are likely to enter the labour force once they are in Canada. The Entrepreneurs, Self-Employed, and Investors either establish businesses in Canada or provide the financial means to do that in the expectation that jobs will be provided for themselves and for Canadians and landed immigrants. Convention Refugees are persons who, by reason of a well-founded fear of persecution, are unable or unwilling to return to their countries of birth or permanent residence; the Designated Class is composed of persons in refugee—like situations who are in need of resettlement even though they may not meet the strict definition of Convention Refugees; an example is political prisoners and oppressed persons from some South and Central American countries.

The Independent class dominated Canada's inflow until after 1974 as indicated in Table 6; the other two classes split about equally the other half of the flow. The Independent class's percentage then started to fall and the Sponsored rose, and this was a trend that carried on until after 1983. The percentages in the Independent and Assisted Relatives classes declined dramatically in 1983 and 1984 since anyone admitted in those categories required a job to be waiting for them; this was in reaction to rising Canadian unemployment. The absolute number of entrants in the Independent class declined from about 36,900 in 1981 to 12,300 in 1984; over the same period, numbers of Assisted Relatives fell from about 17,500 to less than 5,000. Such large absolute changes explain the correspondingly large changes in the percentages of Table 7. The numbers in the Family Class also declined over these years, but by much less so that class significantly increased its share of total immigration. After 1985, this restriction was eliminated, and the percentage in the Independent class especially rose to over 30 percent in 1988. Principle applicants and their dependents increased from about 12,300 in 1984 to over 49,000 in 1988; although the Family Class declined in relative importance from 1985 to 1987, the absolute numbers in this category rose from about 38,500 to over 53,000; the absolute numbers in this class did fall to about 51,000 in 1988 but increased to over 60,000 in 1989. Table 7 shows that refugees of various types (Convention Refugees plus Designated Class) have made up 15 percent to 20 percent of the total inflow in recent years;

the much higher percentage for the Designated class in 1980 reflects the large immigration of so-called boat people in that year.

Significant shifts have taken place within the Family Class over the course of the 1980s. For example, in 1980 spouses and accompanying unmarried children under 21 years of age constituted 32.3 percent of their class; by 1988, this percentage had risen to 42.4 percent. In 1980, parents of a permanent resident or grandparents (of a Canadian citizen or permanent resident) 60 years of age or over, or under 60 if incapable of gainful employment, or widowed, and accompanying family members made up 22.8 percent of the total class; in 1988, this had fallen to 14.1 percent. Finally, parents of Canadian citizens and accompanying dependents fell from 30.3 percent of the total class in 1980 to 23.8 percent in 1988.

As a point of comparison, Australia has a very similar set of admission categories as Canada, although Australia has special arrangements with New Zealand to allow a free flow between the two countries. As with Canada, Family Migration constituted over 50 percent of total Australian inflows in 1984 and 1985, and also like Canada since then this class has declined in relative importance while economic migration (labour shortages and business migration) have risen in importance. The Australian authorities introduced in 1986 a class that is similar to Canada's Assisted Relatives; in 1988, this new class accounted for about 36 percent of Australia's inflow. The percentage from the Refugee and Special Humanitarian Programme fell steadily over the 1980s; it stood at about 21 percent of the total immigration in 1984, but only about 7 percent in 1988; so refugee inflows are now less significant to the Australian total than for Canada. The intake from New Zealand ranged around 15 percent in the mid-1980s, but jumped to 19 percent of the total in 1988. So Australian inflows have recently shown some changes that are similar to Canada's, but it also has some unique aspects.

For the United States in the 1980s, family reunions of one form or another made up the majority of immigrants. From 1983 to 1986, immediate relatives of U.S. citizens and the Relative Preferences class comprised about 73 percent of the total immigrant flow; refugees were about 17 percent of this total, while the Worker Preference category made up only about 9 percent of immigrants (SOPEMI, 1989, 170). Of course high levels of immigration in any of the three countries will lead to future persons in the family reunion classes as former immigrants sponsor close relatives. This may be extenuated when migration is from so-called developing countries, as it has been over the last two decades. First, with higher fertility rates in these countries, families tend to be larger so there are more potential persons to sponsor. Second, with relatively low standards of living, there is a higher probability that those potentially sponsorable people will want to migrate. Third, with familial ideas that involve a large extended family, the notion of family reunion takes on broader dimensions than in the European situation. In any case, family reunion, as has been demonstrated, is an important aspect of immigration to Canada, Australia, and the United States.

Statements from Employment and Immigration Canada over the years suggest that it would like to see a rough balance among family migrants, refugees, and economic migrants as designated by the classes in Tables 6 and 7. If this is a goal of policy, it has not been attained in the last twenty years. Why would anyone care about this balance? Why would policy be directed to attain this balance? Presumably, one reason is that the economic characteristics of one class may differ from those of others, and a rough balance would in a sense even out some negative influences, such as higher unemployment rates in one class with lower rates in another. But is this fine tuning of immigration policy and regulation possible?

Province of destination

A few years ago a great deal of debate occurred in some parts of Canada about the concentration of population in the Windsor-Toronto-Montreal-Quebec City region of Canada. Some people were asking: Why can we not disperse people more uniformly over Ontario, Quebec, and, in fact, Canada? Today, the same question is being asked about Canada's immigrants and the foreign-born population. In both 1987 and 1988, about 55 percent of immigrants indicated that they intended to settle in Ontario (see Table 8). Two other provinces received significant numbers of immigrants, namely Quebec with about 16 percent and British Columbia with about 13 percent, but they appear to pale in significance when compared to Ontario. The figures in Table 8 indicated that this dominance has a long standing post-World War II tradition. Ontario has always dominated. In 1956, 1961, and 1971 over 50 percent of all immigrants indicated their intention to settle in Ontario. This dominance for Ontario is likely caused by that province's relatively rapid rate of economic growth and development over the last four decades, which, by a human capital approach to migration, should attract migrants, and by the fact that a concentration of former immigrants in Ontario will lead to present immigrants being attracted to the same province.

Three other facts are worth noting from Table 8:

(1) Atlantic Canada has not participated in recent inflows of immigrants to Canada,

(2) The Prairie provinces experienced a cyclical upturn followed by a downturn over the post-World War II period: generally increased percentages to the early 1980s with declines thereafter, and

(3) The Yukon and Northwest Territories have not attracted many immigrants.

In fact, Ontario has been even more of an attraction than the data on the intended destination of immigrants in Table 8 indicates. The *Report on the Demographic Situation in Canada 1988* looks at the intentions of immigrants in 1961 and in 1971 with respect to province of destination and compares them to actual provinces of residence of the foreign-born in 1986. In both cases, Ontario had in 1986 about 56 percent of those groups. On the other hand, Quebec seems to lose foreign-born population so that the figures in Table 8 overstate the resident population. For example, of the 23.6 percent who indicated in 1961 that Quebec was their province of destination, only about 18 percent resided in Quebec by 1986. Similarly, British Columbia has shown some tendency recently to lose the foreign-born through interprovincial migration over the 1980s, although this was not true previously.

It is interesting to wed the province of destination with the class of immigration. In 1988, while Ontario was the intended destination for 55 percent of all immigrants, 69 percent of Assisted Relatives and 60 percent of Independents listed Ontario as their destination; on the other hand, only 25 percent of Entrepreneurs, 28 percent of Investors, and 30 percent of Self-Employed noted Ontario. Quebec, the destination of about 16 percent of all immigrants, was mentioned by 39 percent of Entrepreneurs. So the percentages among the various classes of immigration vary a great deal across some provinces. It is also interesting to

TABLE 2-8:
**Percentage distribution of immigrants admitted
by intended province of destination, Canada, 1956-1988**

	1956	1961	1971	1981	1983	1985	1987	1988*
Nfld.	0.3	0.5	0.7	0.4	0.3	0.4	0.3	0.3
P.E.I.	0.1	0.1	0.1	0.1	0.1	0.1	0.1	0.1
Nova Scotia	1.0	1.3	1.5	1.1	0.9	1.2	0.8	0.8
New Bruns.	0.5	1.1	0.9	0.8	0.6	0.7	0.4	0.4
Quebec	19.0	23.6	15.8	16.4	18.4	17.7	17.6	15.9
Ontario	55.0	50.9	52.8	42.7	44.9	48.3	55.8	55.1
Manitoba	3.5	3.5	4.4	4.2	4.5	4.1	3.2	3.1
Sask.	1.3	1.9	1.2	1.9	2.0	2.3	1.4	1.4
Alberta	6.0	6.7	7.1	15.0	12.0	10.7	7.9	8.7
B.C.	10.8	10.2	15.5	17.1	16.2	14.5	12.4	14.3
Yukon & N.W.T.	0.1	0.2	0.2	0.2	0.2	0.1	0.1	0.1
Unknown	2.4	0.0	0.0	0.3	0.0	0.0	0.0	0.0
Total (in %)	100.0	100.0	100.0	100.0	100.0	100.0	100.0	100.0
Total (in number)	164,857	71,689	121,900	128,618	89,157	84,302	152,098	159,437

*Preliminary data.
Source: Dumas, *Report on the Demographic Situation in Canada 1988.*

note that about 12 percent of refugees list Alberta as their province of destination. The relative attractiveness of certain provinces differs significantly by the classes of immigration.

Finally, immigrants from different sending areas select significantly different provinces of intended destination. In 1987, although 45 percent from North and Central America and 49 percent from Asia listed Ontario as the province of destination, the same was done by 55 percent from Africa, 63 percent from Europe, 66 percent from the Caribbean, and 77 percent from South America (*Immigration Statistics*, 1987). For Quebec, 28 percent from the Caribbean, 25 percent from Africa, and 18 percent from Asia noted it as the intended province of destination. British Columbia was the province of destination for 17 percent from Asia and 16 percent from North and Central America, but for only 3 percent from South America and 1 percent from the Caribbean.

These last two comparisons of province of intended destination by immigration class and country of last permanent residence suggests that to some extent factors that influence class and sending area also impact on the geographical distribution of immigrants once they settle in Canada. Changes in immigration policy and regulations, as well as in the allocation of resources to handle immigration applications, are some of these factors. Both Ontario and Quebec undertake to attract immigrants to their provinces. Quebec has a special relationship with the federal government to enable that province to attract the type of immigrant that will enhance the French Canadian culture. It is not surprising that Ontario is relatively attractive to independent migrants and assisted relatives who come in part based on their abilities and employment experiences; Ontario is regarded as the economic metropolis of Canada.

Two demographic characteristics: age and sex

In terms of the interaction between immigration and other factors such as population growth and labour force impacts, the age structure and the composition of immigration by sex can have important influences. Table 9 indicates that by the late 1980s slightly over half of all immigration was in the prime labour force age group of 25 to 59, about one-fifth fell into each of the 0-14 and 15-24 age groups, and 7.3 percent was over the age of 59. But these figures hide definite cyclical patterns in some age groups.

For example, look at the 0-14 age group. It rose from 1955 to 1957 when total immigration more than doubled, and then fell to 1961 as total immigration also declined to well below its 1955 level. The percentage in this age group then increased to over 25 percent in 1966, again years of rising total immigration, although the highest year in this cycle for the total inflow was 1967 but the percentage in this age group was starting to fall. A period of decline associated with falling total immigration occurred in 1973. Then the percentage in the 0-14 age group rose dramatically to 27.2 percent in 1975, followed by a generally downward trend to 1983 and 1984 with, however, a slight rise in 1979 and 1980 when total immigration also increased. The higher inflows after 1985 have again been reflected in a rise in the percentage in the 0-14 age group. Therefore, there has been a direct relationship between total immigration and the percentage of this total in this youngest age group. Since these are children who, in most cases, are brought to Canada by their parents, the causes of this relationship are related to the reasons for fluctuations in the percentage in the age group 25 to 59 that are noted below.

In contrast, the oldest age group in Table 9, ages 65 and older, appears to run counter to total immigration. This percentage increased during the generally lower immigration years from 1958 to 1962; then when total immigration picked up after that, the percentage in the age group 65 and over fell to less than 2 percent in 1967. It then rose again to 1972 when total immigration declined. As total immigration fell to 1978, this age group's percentage rose to new heights; by 1978, 6.6 percent of total immigration was in this group. The relationship so described follows very nicely throughout the 1980s; when total immigration declines to its relatively low levels in 1983 and 1984, the percentage of this total in the age group 65 plus established a new high of 7.4 percent and 7.2 percent respectively. What is the explanation for this pattern? Immigrants over the age of 64 are likely retired and many are sponsored by their children who have already migrated to Canada. These older migrants are not very much influenced by the business cycle or the state of the Canadian economy as are of prime age labour force entrants. So when the economy worsens and that group's immigration declines, the percentage of immigrants in the 65 plus category naturally rises, and vice versa. This is not to say that the older age group is not

TABLE 2-9:
Percentage distribution of total immigration by age groups, Canada

	0-14 Years	15-24 Years	25-29 Years	60-64 Years	65+ Years	Percentage Males
1950	21.8					55.5
1951	20.3					61.8
1952	24.1					54.6
1953	22.7					54.1
1954	21.5					54.8
1955	21.5					51.7
1956	22.0	28.2	47.7	0.9	1.3	54.3
1957	23.5	26.1	48.6	0.8	1.0	54.7
1958	22.6	28.5	45.3	1.5	2.1	48.6
1959	22.6	27.8	45.7	1.6	2.3	48.1
1960	21.8	28.9	45.3	1.6	2.4	49.0
1961	21.9	28.4	44.6	1.9	3.2	44.8
1962	22.1	27.6	45.1	1.9	3.2	46.3
1963	22.6	26.8	45.9	1.7	3.0	48.5
1964	24.1	25.9	45.6	1.7	2.7	49.6
1965	25.1	25.8	45.2	1.5	2.4	50.9
1966	25.4	26.2	45.3	1.2	2.0	51.5
1967	23.2	27.5	46.2	1.2	1.9	51.7
1968	22.0	28.8	44.7	1.8	2.7	50.8
1969	21.7	29.0	45.0	1.7	2.5	49.5
1970	21.1	30.1	44.5	1.6	2.7	50.3
1971	21.8	28.7	44.6	1.9	3.1	49.6
1972	22.6	27.6	44.4	2.0	3.3	49.2
1973	21.2	28.1	46.1	1.7	2.8	51.4
1974	24.8	23.9	46.9	1.8	2.7	51.4
1975	27.2	22.4	44.4	2.5	3.6	49.3
1976	25.5	23.2	43.1	3.4	4.8	48.6
1977	23.7	23.7	43.1	3.9	5.6	47.7
1978	21.0	24.8	43.1	4.5	6.6	46.4
1979	22.2	26.2	43.1	3.3	5.3	48.9
1980	22.7	25.6	43.2	3.4	5.1	48.9
1981	22.7	25.6	43.2	3.4	5.1	50.3
1982	19.9	21.7	48.5	4.0	6.0	49.1
1983	17.5	24.7	45.7	4.7	7.4	46.6
1984	17.5	23.5	47.2	4.6	7.2	46.4
1985	18.0	23.2	48.1	4.1	6.6	47.8
1986	18.1	22.3	50.4	3.4	5.8	49.5
1987	20.3	20.0	52.4	2.7	4.6	50.6

Source: 1950-1955: *Historical Statistics of Canada* (2nd edition), A369-A384; 1956-1987: *Immigration Statistics*.

affected at all by the business cycle; Canadians may be more able to sponsor parents when economic conditions are good. However, this effect is overshadowed by the much larger numbers of immigrants in most of the other age categories. The percentage in this age group also seems to show a longer term trend over all the years in Table 9; there appears to be a tendency for this percentage to rise as demonstrated by the higher peak values as the years progress.

The prime labour force age group 25 to 59 follows the pattern of total immigration, but this is as expected given that this group makes up over 40 percent of the total. However, there are some exceptions. From 1963 to 1966 when total immigration increased, the percentage in this age group hardly changed. The same can be written about the period of falling total immigration from 1968 to 1972. The rapid rise in total immigration from 1978 to 1980 had no associated change in the percentage in age groups 25 to 59, and it was significantly higher in 1981 and 1982 when total immigration was on the decline. Since 1984 when total immigration rose the percentage in this age group has also risen.

Turning to the percentage of total immigration that is male, the last column of Table 9 shows that it is positively related to total immigration. When total immigration is rising, the percentage that is male has also increased, and vice versa. Two factors can be suggested as causes. First, the total inflow has been shown to relate closely to Canada's business cycle; since males have traditionally had higher labour force participation rates, the ups and downs of the economy that have been reflected in total immigration have to some extent also been reflected in the percentage that is male. Second, some immigration classes are more sensitive to the state of the economy than others, and some classes have higher percentages that are male than others. In 1988, the Family Class was 41 percent males and 59 percent females, while the Refugees and Designated Classes were exactly the opposite; the Independent Class was 51 percent males and 49 percent females (*Immigration to Canada: A Statistical Overview*, 15).

Finally, the different age groups that are noted in Table 9 do not have an even distribution of males and females in them. Although these percentage distributions between males and females by age group vary from year to year, in general males have recently had more than 50 percent for age groups from the mid-20s to the mid-40s, while females had more than 50 percent of the total in age groups older than that; average life expectancy would lead one to except this latter fact. The youngest age groups tend to be about equally split between males and females.

Prologue

Instead of a conclusion, it seems more appropriate to raise some key issues or questions that will be taken up in the rest of this book, issues that come directly from the patterns of immigration that have been described in this chapter.

First and foremost is the question of the average level that immigration into Canada should take. Should this be 100,000 per year, 150,000 per year, 250,000 per year, all of which would be compatible with the history of Canada's immigration as described in this chapter, or should Canada boldly move to higher levels of, say, 330,000 per year as entered in 1911 or even 400,000 per year as entered in 1913? The answer to this question depends on a number of considerations: (1) What are the objectives of Canada's immigration policies? (2) What social and economic and cultural consequences does immigration have for Canada? (3) What level of resources is Canada willing to put into attracting, processing, and settling immigrants? Several of these considerations will be addressed in this book, but some of them require statements from the federal government and, increasingly, the provincial governments before the average level of immigration can be established.

A question that is related to this first one deals with the volatile and cyclical nature of immigrant inflows, which was described earlier in this chapter. This so-called tap-on-tap-off pattern makes long-range planning more difficult and causes problems for the administration of Canada's immigration policies (Samuel, 1989). This volatility may also be unnecessary. If it is shown that various levels of immigration have only minor effects on Canada's economy and population structure, then there is little to be gained by continually changing the level of the inflow. Also, if considerations of population size and structure become more important factors in setting the level of immigration, they are by nature long term and add further to a rationale for a constant level of inflow rather than the cyclical one that is closely tied to the state of the Canadian economy.

There is a very important question that relates to the sending areas of Canada's immigration: Should Canada attempt to balance in any way the source regions? The question began to be asked in the 1970s when Asian countries became more important as sending countries and European countries less so. The answer to this question is inevitably related to changing linguistic and cultural structures. Some people react negatively to changes in Canada's ethnic composition, while others applaud these changes as a shift to a more international and cosmopolitan society. This is a question that will not be answered by hard facts alone; it involves emotions and value judgements.

Earlier in this chapter, total landings were broken down by implication into three main themes, namely family reunion (Family Class), humanitarian (Convention Refugees, Designated Class), and economic (Assisted Relatives, Retired, Entrepreneurs, Self-Employed, Investor, Independent). Just as some people seek a balance among source areas, others want to see a balance among entrants in these three themes or categories. Presumably the rationale for such a desire stems from the fact that immigrants in one of these categories display characteristics that are different from immigrants in the other two categories. For example, economic migrants may have a greater propensity to add to Canada's labour force than do persons admitted for family reunion purposes; if this latter group predominates, desired additions to the labour force may not happen. Therefore, should there be this second balance to Canada's immigration? The answer to this question is tied in part to the world refugee situation. If there are thousands of refugees around the world who want to settle in Canada, what should Canada's response be? How many should Canada admit each year? Is this an economic question, or can it be answered at the humanitarian, ethical, and political levels?

The point was made previously in this chapter that the foreign-born tend to be concentrated in only a few specific geographical locations. This has led some Canadians to associate immigration with high housing prices, depressed wages, declining industries, crime, ethnic conflict, and other "undesirable" outcomes. Is this concentration unexpected? Is it even bad? In some cases there are economic benefits to having a concentrated population; the Canadian-born have also shown a propensity to live together. What would be the economic and social advantages of having a more dispersed immigration flow?

Finally, there has been a growing recognition recently that immigration could play a role in determining the size and structure of Canada's future population. Since the late 1970s, the annual report to Parliament on immigration has linked it to Canada's demography; the creation of the Demographic Review a few years ago gave further recognition to this linkage. Many population projections, but especially those from Statistics Canada, show that if fertility rates and immigration are at relatively low levels, Canada's population will peak around 2015 and eventually start to decline, and Canada's population will age. What are the economic and social implications of these changes? Should immigration be used to try to reverse some of these changes?

The answers to these questions may mean that fifty years from now the patterns of Canada's immigration will be quite different than they have been for the last five decades.

References

Australia. Australian Bureau of Statistics. *Year Book Australia, 1989.* Canberra, 1989.

Betts, K. *Ideology and Immigration.* Melbourne: Melbourne University Press, 1988.

Canada. Department of Finance. *Quarterly Economic Review, Annual Reference Tables,* June 1990. Ottawa: Finance, 1990.

Canada. Employment and Immigration Canada. *Immigration Statistics.* Ottawa: Supply and Services Canada, various years.

Canada. Employment and Immigration Canada. *Immigration to Canada: A Statistical Overview.* Ottawa: Immigration Policy Branch, 1989.

Dumas, J. *Report on the Demographic Situation in Canada 1988.* Ottawa: Supply and Services Canada, 1990.

Hawkins, F. *Critical Years in Immigration.* Montreal: McGill-Queen's University Press, 1989.

Marr, W. L. "Canadian Immigration Policies Since 1962." *Canadian Public Policy* 1 (Spring 1975), 196-203.

Miller, M.J. *U.S. Immigration in 1987.* Unpublished paper prepared for OECD, November 1987.

Organization for Economic Co-Operation and Development. *SOPEMI 1989.* Paris: OECD, 1990.

Samuel, J. "Immigration Issues: A National Perspective." In *Policy Forum on the Role of Immigration in Canada's Future,* ed. C.M. Beach and A.G. Green. Kingston: John Deutsch Institute, 1989.

United States. Bureau of the Census. *Structural Abstract of the United States, 1989.* Washington, D.C., 1989.

Urquhart, M. C., ed. *Historical Statistics of Canada,* 2nd ed. Ottawa: Statistics Canada, 1983.

Chapter 3

The Socio-Demographic Impact of Immigration

Roderic Beaujot

The author wishes to acknowledge the assistance of Suzanne Shiel and Lorraine Schoel, and the financial support of The Review of Demography and its Implications for Economic and Social Policy, Health and Welfare Canada. The chapter is based on a report, entitled "Immigration and the Population of Canada" that was originally prepared for the Immigration Policy Group at Employment and Immigration Canada. Their permission to publish part of the report elsewhere is gratefully acknowledged.

IMMIGRATION HAS ALWAYS BEEN VERY visible in Canada's population profile. At the time of the 1986 census, almost one person out of six had been born outside of the country. In 1971, one person in three was either foreign-born or had at least one foreign-born parent. Net international migration (immigration minus emigration) accounted for 24 percent of Canada's population growth over the period 1946-1988.

Births, the other component of population growth, have undergone a long-term decline. Since 1972, Canada's fertility has been below the replacement level of 2.1 births per woman. The rate of 2.1 is the number of births needed to replace one generation by the next; two births to replace the parents and 0.1 to compensate for the small number of deaths that occur before the next generation reaches reproductive ages. Demographers speak of a population momentum wherein the inertia of a population's past growth continues for some time after fertility declines. In effect, births continue to outnumber deaths because the demographic bulge in the population age structure is at reproductive ages. Even though they are having fewer births than are needed for replacement, this generation is sufficiently numerous to ensure more births than deaths. This momentum will continue for some time. According to the latest projections from Statistics Canada, with fertility constant at 1.7 births per woman, natural increase will not stop until 2020. This is a rather amazing result, it will have taken almost 50 years for below-replacement fertility to translate itself into negative natural increase.

Demographic phenomena occur over a very long term, yet they profoundly affect society. The demographic transition involved a gradual change from high vital rates (both births and deaths) in the middle of the 19th century to low vital rates some 100 years later. For instance, in 1851 life expectancy in Canada was 41 years and fertility was 7.0 births per woman. In 1971, life expectancy had increased to 73 years and fertility was 2.2 births per woman.

Demographers are beginning to speak of a second demographic transition as births persist at below-replacement levels and the population ages significantly. In 1971 the average age of the Canadian population was 26.2 years, and in 1986 it was 31.6 years, by 2036 it will be around 45 years. These are very different population profiles. The population dynamics of a second demographic transition also imply self-reinforcing mechanisms: aging is due to low fertility, but an older population also produces fewer births. Just as population momentum has continued in spite of below-replacement fertility, so negative natural increase would tend to continue in an older population. Even if fertility were to move to above-replacement levels, the smaller numbers at reproductive ages would still imply fewer births than deaths.

Stated differently, it is unlikely that the population dynamics of the future will be the same as those of the past. In particular, immigration is likely to become the only source of population growth. As we will see, it would take a substantial level of annual immigration to compensate for the deficit in natural increase. At immigration levels comparable to the post-war average, we will no longer be talking of population growth but of population decline. While immigration is often seen as a possible compensation for low fertility, in another sense immigration may be more difficult to accommodate in an environment of population decline. When a population is growing, immigration constitutes a smaller proportion of the overall population change. Once population growth occurs through net migration rather than through natural increase, immigration will have a larger impact on the society and the structures through which it integrates new members (births and immigrants). For instance, in the period 1971-1986 there were 35 immigrants per 100 births. At levels of immigration that would maintain population growth with low fertility, the period 2021-2036 would involve 60 immigrants per 100 births. Since these population dynamics are outside of Canada's historical experience, it is difficult to anticipate their social and political consequences.

Demographic trends not only change the size and growth of the population, they also affect its characteristics. The characteristics of the population are changed in terms of age and sex structure, socio-economic composition, cultural make-up and regional distribution. This chapter will summarize the impact of immigration on these socio-demographic aspects of the Canadian population.

Demographic impact of immigration

One way to appreciate the importance of immigration in the population is by comparing annual flows to the base population. Using the data from Chapter 2, the period around the turn of the century shows an average of 2.11 annual arrivals per 100 population, compared to an average of 0.77 arrivals in the period 1951-81 and 0.44 annual arrivals per 100 population in the period 1981-88. The average figure for the whole of this century is 0.97 arrivals per 100 base population. Emigration has been more stable with an average of 0.28 per 100 base population over the period 1951-88.

Another way of measuring the impact of immigration is to compute the proportion of population growth that is due to net migration. For the whole of this century, the net immigration of 4.5 million persons comprised 22 percent of the total population growth. The relative contribution of immigration to population growth was highest between 1901 and 1911, when it reached 44.1 percent. Over the period 1946-88, net migration accounted for 24 percent of population growth.

These measures of the impact of immigration do not take into account the further impact through children born to immigrants while in Canada. At the 1971 census, the "birthplace of parents" question enabled us to determine that 33.8 percent of the entire population were first or second generation in Canada (Kalbach and McVey, 1979:179). It is also possible to simulate population change by isolating the effect of births and deaths on the population. Applying birth and death rates observed over the 1951-1981 period to the 1951 population, the population would have changed from 14.0 million in 1951 to 20.4 million in 1981 (Le Bras, 1988:9). In effect, the 1981 population was 24.3 million. This implies that 38 percent of the actual growth was a function of immigration and births to these immigrants over the period 1951-81.

Another way of assessing the demographic impact of immigration is through projections into the future. Three projections are used here in order to highlight the potential impact of this component of population change (Figure 1). All three projections use a constant fertility of 1.7 births per woman. They differ on immigration which is 200,000 arrivals per year in the first projection, 140,000 in the second and zero in the third. Emigration is introduced as a rate, which amounts to 0.25 departures per 100 population (except in the third projection where emigration is zero). Annual net migration is approximately 120,000, 60,000 and zero in the three projection series under discussion.

In the 40 year period 1946-86, Canada's population increased by more than 100 percent, from 12.3 to 25.4 million persons. Over the next 40 years, the total increase would be much lower: 33 percent under the high immigration assumption, 23 percent under the low assumption and only 10 percent with zero net migration. The comparison to zero migration implies that in the high projection 69 percent of population growth from 1986 to 2026 would be a function of net migration and births to migrants. In the low projection, 55 percent of population

Figure 3-1:
Total population size, 1946 to 1986 and projections to 2036

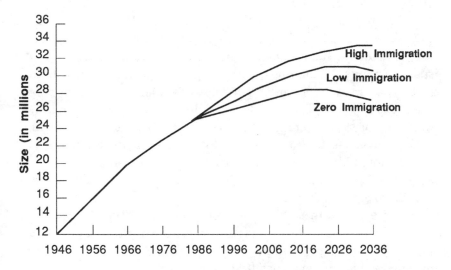

Note: Projections are based on fertility assumption of 1.7, immigration of 200,000, 140,000 and zero persons per year and emigration of 0.25, 0.25 and 0.0 persons per 100 population per year.

Sources: Postcensal annual estimates of population by marital status, age, sex and components of growth for Canada, provinces and territories. Statistics Canada, catalogue no. 91-210 (annual); and Statistics Canada, Demography Division, Special Tabulations.

growth is due to migration. There are also sizeable differences in the total populations. Compared to the zero immigration scenario, the population in 2026 would involve 5,700,000 more people under high immigration and 3,200,000 more under low immigration.

Three turning points are particularly interesting in these projections. The first is the point at which net migration becomes equal to net natural increase. This occurs in 1998 and 2009 for the high and low assumptions respectively. After that date, more than 50 percent of population growth is due to net migration. The next turning point is where natural increase becomes negative, after which immigration constitutes over 100 percent of population growth. Given that the same fertility assumptions are used, this point does not vary extensively: 2018 for zero immigration, 2020 for the low immigration and 2022 for the high immigration assumptions.

The final turning point is that at which population growth itself stops. This occurs in 2017 for zero migration, 2025 for low immigration and 2034 for the high immigration assumptions. After that, we must speak of population decline rather than growth. In approximate terms, each 60,000 more in net migration delays population decline by 8 or 9 years. Other projections have estimated that it would take an annual net migration of 163,000 (or immigration of 212,000) to prevent population decline under a fertility assumption of 1.7 births per woman (Avery and Edmonston, 1988). Other calculations show similar results. To maintain a population of 25 million with fertility of 1.7 requires a net immigration of 125,000 per year (Taylor, 1988).

Figure 2 sets these projections against the background of past demographic changes. The graph that is scaled along the left axes measures annual population growth in given periods. Growth has declined in each period since 1951-56, and would continue to decline, at least in the long term, even under the high immigration scenario. The graph that is scaled on the right axes indicates the proportion of total growth that is due to net immigration. Especially noticeable here is the sharp increase in the relative contribution of immigration to future population growth.

Age structure

The impact of immigration on the age structure can best be appreciated by comparing the median age of immigrants on arrival to that of the Canadian population (see Chapter 2). The median age of arriving immigrants has been about a year younger than that of the receiving population over the period 1945-71, changing to two years younger by 1981 and four years younger by 1986.

These measures imply that immigration has a rather minor impact on the age structure. In effect, simulating population change as a function only of births and deaths since 1951 produces a 1981 population with an average age that is only 0.5 years older than the actual average observed in that year. Stated differently, the 1951-81 immigration would

Figure 3-2:
Average annual growth and proportion of population growth that is due to net migration, 1901-11 to 2031-36

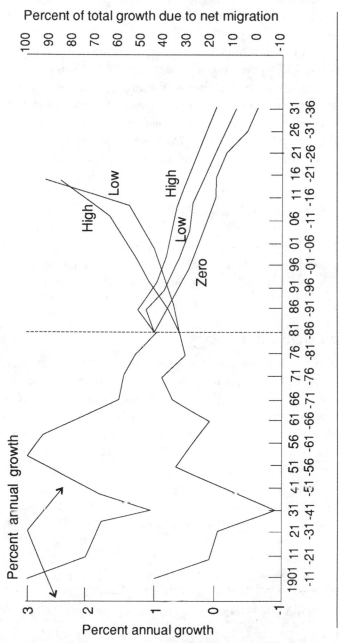

Notes: 1. Projections are based on fertility assumption of 1.7, immigration of 200,000, 140,000 and zero persons per year and emigration of 0.25, 0.25 and 0.0 persons per 100 population per year.

2. Since the proportion of growth due to net migration is over 100 percent in the periods 2021-36, the data are not shown.

Source: Statistics Canada 92-120: 13; Beaujot et al., 1988: 2; Beaujot and Rappak, 1988b: 47; Statistics Canada, Demography Division: special tabulations.

have reduced the average age of the 1981 population by a half year (Le Bras, 1988: 12).

Similar results are obtained with projections into the future. The population projections defined earlier produce median ages in 2036 of 44.7 years under high immigration 45.7 under low immigration and 46.9 years under zero migration. The population aged 65 and over in 2036 is 24.6 percent, 25.7 and 27.0 percent under high, low and zero migration assumptions. Clearly, the immigration assumptions have a rather small impact on the age structure (Figure 3). This is especially true compared to the long term effect of lower births. The median age of the Canadian population will increase by some 13 to 14 years between 1986 and 2036. In comparison, the high versus low immigration assumptions only change the median age by one year.

Another useful indicator of the age structure is the median age of the population at labour force ages. In 1986, the median age of the population aged 15-64 was 34.8 years. By 2036, this median would increase to 41.1, 41.3 and 41.9 years respectively under the high, low and zero migration assumptions. Once again, the aging of the labour force will be significant, but it will not be much affected by the level of immigration.

Geographic distribution

Immigration, and to a lesser extent the subsequent internal migration of the foreign-born, has an important impact on the geographic distribution of Canada's population. In particular, these trends tend to accentuate the differences in regional population growth.

From the data presented in Chapter 2, it can be seen that the arrivals of the post-war period have largely been to the advantage of the relative size of the populations of Ontario and British Columbia, and to the disadvantage of the Atlantic Provinces and Quebec. For instance, among the Canadian-born, Ontario is only 17 percent larger than Quebec, but adding the foreign-born makes Ontario 39 percent larger. The foreign-born population of Ontario was four times as large as that of Quebec in 1986 (Beaujot and Rappak, 1990:115).

The geographic concentration of immigrants also accentuates the growth of the metropolitan areas, particularly Toronto, Montreal and Vancouver. In the mid-1980s these three cities were the intended desti-

Figure 3-3: Projected age profile of the population in 2036, showing effect of different immigration assumptions.

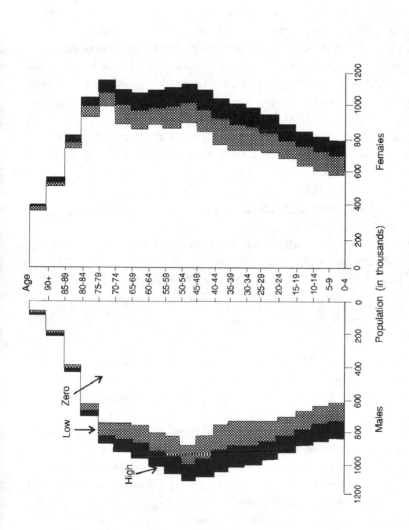

Note: Projections are based on fertility assumption of 1.7, immigration of 200,000, 140,000 and zero persons per year, and emigration of 0.25, 0.25 and 0.0 persons per 100 population per year.

nation of over 60 percent of immigrants, with Toronto alone accounting for 25 percent of arrivals (Hersak and Thomas, 1988). The Review of Demography (1989:34) concludes that immigrants of the post-war period have largely not gone to places outside of the major urban centres, nor to the major urban centres east of Montreal. Rather than being a national phenomenon, immigration has focused on the large cities: Montreal and the large cities west of Quebec. It is especially Toronto and Vancouver that have significantly higher proportions of post-war immigrants than their relative share of the Canadian born population. For Quebec, immigrants are highly concentrated in Montreal. Noting that 80 percent of Quebec's arrivals settle in that one city, Termote (1988) projects that at 40,000 arrivals to the province per year, Montreal's population would increase significantly. After considering births, deaths and departures, over a 40 year period this level of immigration would add 1,150,000 to Montreal's population (compared to a 1986 total population of 1,750,000).

Given that immigrants are likely to settle mostly in metropolitan areas, and to follow the "pathways" established by earlier cohorts, immigration will probably continue to accentuate the inequalities in Canada's regional population distribution. For the most part, immigration cannot be seen as a means of demographic redistribution to areas of lower population concentration.

Socio-economic impact

The propensity of different groups to sponsor relatives and the characteristics of the relatives they sponsor have become the major determinants of the socio-economic and socio-cultural composition of the current flow (Simmons, 1988).

The research that has been done on the family class indicates that they have a reasonable level of socio-economic integration. A survey of 1400 family class immigrants who arrived in the period 1981-84 finds that, while the majority did not manage to enter their intended occupations, and their levels of unemployment were higher than the Canadian average, their earnings and working conditions were on average better than those in their home country (Samuel, 1988a). Despite not being selected on job-related criteria, the family class immigrants have demonstrated considerable ability to penetrate the Canadian occupational structure.

The refugee class is the smallest among the three major classes. With the arrival of the Indo-Chinese "boat people," the refugee class almost equalled the independent class in 1979 and 1980. Until 1972 refugee admissions involved specific groups who were mostly from European-based cultures. The total admissions over the period 1946-87 amounted to 483,000 or 8.6 percent of total immigrants (Nash, 1989:114, 125; Dumas, 1984:114). With the arrival of refugees from Tibet, Ghana and Indo-China came the realization that it was possible to integrate "any kind of refugee" (Lanphier, 1988). Refugee intake has now become a permanent feature of immigration. Another new feature of refugee admissions involves persons coming directly to Canada to seek asylum. Until the early 1980s refugees were almost all chosen for settlement in Canada from points of first asylum outside of the country.

Since refugees are not specifically coming for economic reasons, and they are consequently less likely to have transferable skills, it is understandable that their economic integration is uneven. The 1972 Asian expellees from Uganda are an example of a very successful group. After one year, their average income exceeded the Canadian average (Samuel, 1984). In contrast, the Indo-Chinese group has suffered relatively high levels of unemployment and low occupational mobility, partly because they arrived just before the recession of the early 1980s (Neuwirth et al., 1985). On the other hand, the experience of refugees over the last quarter century indicates that the vast majority have adjusted well economically (Samuel, 1984).

Level of education

Most of the analyses of the socio-economic characteristics of immigrants are based on census data, where it is not possible to distinguish the various "immigration classes." While there is much diversity among immigrants, as there is in the Canadian-born population, immigration has tended to increase the socio-economic profile of the Canadian population. This is especially visible with regard to education, where immigrants are on average selected for higher levels of education and skills. The relative advantage of immigrants compared to the Canadian-born was highest in the immediate post-war period, when Canadians were suffering from a poorly developed educational system. For instance, in the 1971 census 23.1 percent of the 1961-69 immigrant cohort aged 25-64 had some university education, compared to 10.5 percent of the Canadian-born population. As of the 1986 census, 25.3 percent of the foreign-born had some university education compared to 20.4 percent of the Canadian-born, at ages 25-64 (Beaujot and Rappak, 1990).

The educational advantages of immigrants are stronger for men. Since women are more likely to arrive as dependents, they are less "selected" on educational characteristics. In effect, women immigrants have higher proportions than the Canadian-born at both high (some university) and low (primary school or less) levels of education.

With the increased educational profile of the Canadian-born population and the greater importance of the family and refugee classes in immigration, the more recent immigrants do not have such an advantage with regard to education. In the 1980-84 cohort, 17.0 percent of immigrants at ages 25-64 had less than nine years of education compared to 14.8 percent of the Canadian-born. The average levels of education of future immigrant cohorts will depend considerably on the relative mix of immigrant classes. It would appear that the human capital disadvantages of the 1980-84 cohort are a function of the reduced independent class admissions, which followed on the economic recession of the early 1980s. With higher levels of immigration, it is easier to maintain a larger proportion of independent arrivals, whose educational qualifications tend to be higher.

When looking at the most recent immigrants, it is also important to note that some will pursue further education in Canada. This is especially the case for immigrant children. Analyses based on the 1971 census found that immigrants who came to Canada as children or young adults took more advantage of educational opportunities than did the Canadian-born of the same age cohorts (Rao et al., 1984:96).

Labour force participation

The 1971, 1981 and 1986 censuses have documented higher rates of labour force participation on the part of immigrants than on the part of the Canadian-born. In 1981, this applied to all immigrant cohorts except those who had arrived in the year and a half preceding the census (Beaujot et al., 1988:39). The greater labour force participation of immigrants especially applies to women. For both women and men, the labour force participation increases with a longer period of residence. Figure 4 illustrates the 1986 data on proportions working full-time for 40 or more weeks, within given age groups. Immigrant cohorts arriving before 1980 are more likely to be working full-time, especially in the case of women, than their Canadian-born counterparts. For instance, among immigrants who arrived in 1975-79 and who were at ages 25-34 in 1986, 74.2 percent of men and 54.9 percent of women were working full-time. The comparable figures for the Canadian-born population at these ages were 71.8 and 52.7 for men and women respectively. The 1980-84 cohort is a major exception to the general pattern, with lower proportions working full-time. Once again, the different position of this recent group may be a function of the smaller relative size of the independent class.

On the whole, the unemployment rates of immigrants are comparable to that of the Canadian-born. In one study, the unemployment experiences of principal applicant immigrants who arrived in 1975 were followed over the period 1977-81. (Robertson, 1986). It was found that immigrants had a slightly higher "incidence" of unemployment, but the "spell frequency" and "duration" were very similar to the Canadian average. It was concluded that after a relatively short (two to three year) period of adjustment, unemployment patterns of immigrants are very similar to the Canadian average.

Given the strong labour force participation on the part of immigrants, it should not be surprising to find that immigration has made a rather important contribution to labour force growth. For instance, over the period 1966-86 the labour force grew by 74 percent or by 5,547,000 persons. Of the labour force growth in these 20 years, 1,292,000 or 23 percent were immigrants who had arrived in the interim.

Over the next 20 years, the labour force would increase by 1,838,000 persons (12%) with zero net migration and by 3,094,000 persons (25%) with net migration of 100,000 per year (Denton and Spencer, 1987:197). With zero net migration, the labour force reaches its peak in 2006, then declines. An immigration level of 100,000 per year postpones the decline by 10 years. Clearly, the labour force will expand at a much slower rate now that the baby-boom generation is past the prime ages for labour force entry.

Figure 3-4: Proportion working full-time, by age, for immigrants and Canadian-born, 1986

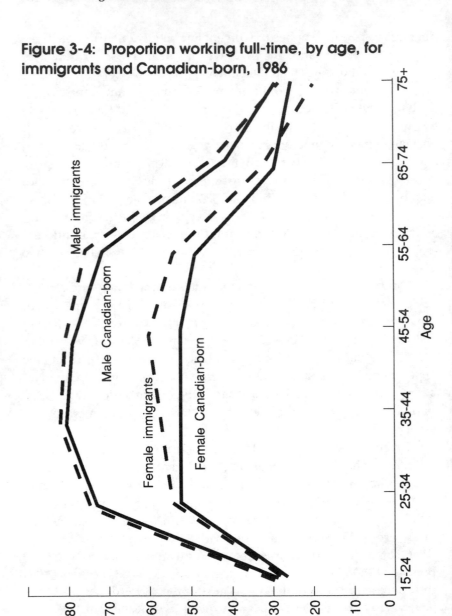

Note: The proportion working full-time is the proportion of a given age-sex group that worked full-time for 40 or more weeks in 1985.

Source: Statistics Canada, special tabulations for the 1986 census.

Occupations

The occupational distribution of immigrants does not differ greatly from that of the Canadian-born labour force (Figure 5). Both male and female immigrants are more concentrated in the service, processing, product fabricating and assembling occupations. Male immigrants are also more concentrated in the managerial, professional and technical occupations. In effect, the foreign-born are over-represented in the faster growing occupations of the 1970s (Marr, 1986). The occupational distribution of immigrants in Canada contrasts sharply with the immigrant populations of most European countries, where the bulk of arrivals are labourers and unskilled workers (Dumas, 1984:99). This generalization is somewhat less applicable to women, who are more likely to arrive as dependents rather than as principal applicant immigrants, and who are disproportionately represented in the clothing industry (Seward, 1990). Nonetheless, except for some groups of immigrant women, there is little evidence of labour market segmentation by immigration status (Basavarajappa and Verma, 1990; Beaujot et al., 1988:43).

Clearly, immigrants are involved in various parts of the economy (McInnis, 1980). After reviewing several studies on this question, Richmond and Zubrzycki (1984:85) conclude that "the most striking feature of the distribution of the foreign-born in the labour force is the degree of similarity to the native-born." The distribution of immigrants across Canada's occupational structure facilitates their integration into the society. If they were concentrated at the top it would cause resentment, concentration at the bottom would introduce "ghetto mentalities."

Income

In summarizing the economic situation of immigrants, Richmond (1988:122) writes: "while not proportionally represented in the power elites, there is growing evidence that European immigrants and their children have been economically successful and upwardly mobile in the post-Second World War period." However, Richmond continues, "although it may be premature to draw firm conclusions, the preliminary evidence concerning immigrants from Third World countries, particularly visible minorities, is not as encouraging." Let us briefly review the evidence on these questions (see also Beaujot et al., 1988).

Figure 3-5a: Percentage distribution by major occupation groups, sex of the immigrant, and Canadian-born labour force, Canada, 1986

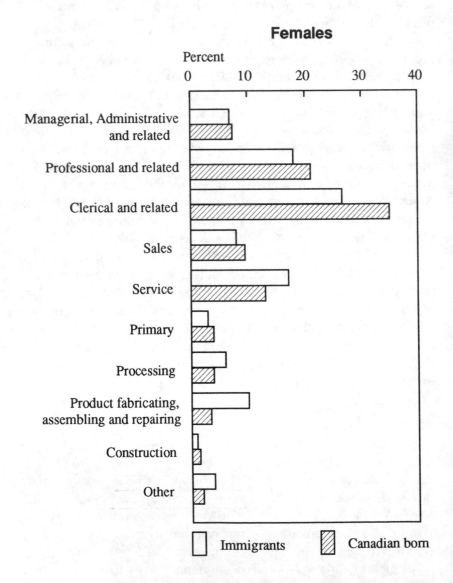

Statistics Canada. 1989. *Dimensions, Profile of the Immigrant Population.* (1986 Census of Canada). Catalogue no. 93-155. Ottawa: Statistics Canada.

Figure 3-5b: Percentage distribution by major occupation groups, sex of the immigrant, and Canadian-born labour force, Canada, 1986

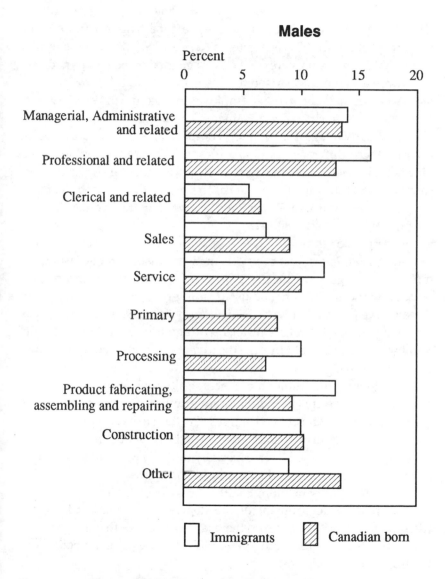

Statistics Canada. 1989. *Dimensions, Profile of the Immigrant Population.* (1986 Census of Canada). Catalogue no. 93-155. Ottawa: Statistics Canada.

As a total group, immigrants have average levels of income that compare favourably to the Canadian-born. Among men, immigrants had average total incomes that were 7.7 percent above the Canadian-born average in 1970, 12.0 percent above in 1980 and 11.8 percent above in 1985. For women, the average figures are basically identical in 1970, while immigrants are 6.7 percent above the Canadian-born in 1981 and 5.6 percent above in 1985 (Beaujot and Rappak, 1988:139). These results imply that immigrants increase the average total income in Canada.

Restricting the comparison to persons working full-time for 40 or more weeks in the year, average employment incomes in 1970, 1980 and 1985 indicate a five percent advantage for immigrant men and a one percent disadvantage for women, compared to the Canadian-born. Overall, these differences are small, especially in comparison to the difference between men and women in employment incomes for persons working full-time. For instance, among the Canadian-born, these differences amount to a 35 percent disadvantage for women in 1985 (Beaujot and Rappak, 1988:141).

Since part of these differences may be due to differences in the profile of the two groups, comparisons were made after adjusting for differences in age and education. On average employment income, for persons working full-time, adjusted immigrant income averages are three to five percent below the Canadian-born in 1980 and 1985. Thus removing their advantages in terms of age and educational profile, immigrants have a slight income disadvantage compared to the Canadian-born (See Figure 6).

Considering the employment income situation of the different immigration cohorts, it is found that immigrant men who arrived before 1975, and women who arrived before 1970, tend to have higher average incomes in 1985 than the Canadian-born of the same age and sex groups. Immigrants who arrived later, especially the 1980-84 cohort, have average incomes below that of the Canadian-born.

After age and education, length of residence is clearly the single most important determinant of the degree of economic adaptation (Richmond, 1988:62). However, there is also evidence that the period of adaptation is longer for more recent immigrants, especially those arriving from Third World countries.

Figure 3-6: Average employment income compared to the Canadian-born, after adjusting for age and education, for persons aged 15-64 working full-time for 40 or more weeks, by immigration cohort and sex, showing traditional and new immigration groups, 1986.

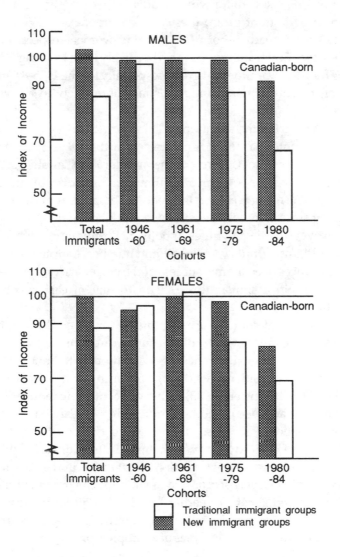

Extensive comparisons were made to contrast the traditional immigrant group from Europe and the United States, and the new immigrant group from other parts of the world. For instance, it is found that, in the 1975-79 cohort, the mean employment income of the traditional immigrant group represents 98.7 percent of the Canadian-born average for men and 93.3 percent for women (adjusting for age and education). In the new immigrant group these averages represent 77.8 and 83.3 percent of the Canadian-born for men and women respectively. For men, the new immigrant group is also less likely to be working full-time than the traditional immigrant group, especially for the 1975-84 arrivals. However, recent women immigrants are more likely to be working full-time.

In summarizing the situation of Third World immigrants, it is first important to note that those who arrived in the 1960s or earlier succeeded as well or better than most other immigrants (Lanphier, 1979:38-39). The comparison of various immigrant cohorts by period of immigration also suggests a rather encouraging account of economic adjustment since incomes rise with longer periods of residence in Canada. However, these were times of buoyant economic growth, and the Third World immigrants were smaller in number. Lanphier concludes that "the chances of economic success of the newer arrivals on the same scale and within a similar time period to that of earlier cohorts is unrealistic."

Once statistical controls are introduced for other "human capital variables," these differences by place of origin are significantly reduced. For instance, the initial differences in occupational attainment by place of last permanent residence were large for immigrants who arrived in 1969-71 and 1976 (Ornstein, 1983). However, controls for education, age, year of arrival and occupation before coming to Canada introduced "drastic reductions" in these differences to the point that "human capital type variables largely overwhelm the effects of nationality."

Another encouraging observation is that the second generation has shown very strong levels of economic adaptation. Richmond and Verma (1978:34) conclude that "Canadian society has provided significant opportunities for upward mobility for children of immigrants, irrespective of ethnic origin." The analyses of a sample from Toronto also show that the second generation has the highest level of socio-economic attainment (Rhyne, 1982).

The immigration monograph from the 1971 census had documented interesting progress among the immediate post-war immigrants (Richmond and Kalbach 1980:109-118). In particular, the 1946-60 immigrant cohort tended to be below the Canadian-born average total incomes by ages and sex in 1961. However, the immigrants made greater progress over the decade, and the 1971 census showed that these 1946-60 arrivals had now mostly surpassed the average incomes of their Canadian-born counterparts of the same age and sex groups. Comparing the censuses of 1971, 1981 and 1986, there are few instances of this type of progress. Given immigrant cohorts tend to be either above or below the Canadian-born at each census. Typically, those who arrived before 1970 or 1975 are above the Canadian-born while subsequent cohorts are below the Canadian-born. The multivariate analyses that were done on the 1971 and 1981 censuses also confirm that recency of arrival has a more negative impact on incomes in 1980 than in 1970 (Beaujot and Rappak, 1988).

There are several possible reasons why the rate of economic adaptation (measured in terms of average differences with the Canadian-born) has become slower: the quality of immigrants may have declined (e.g. less knowledge of the official languages at arrival), the quality of the Canadian-born population may have increased (e.g. more development of education and training), economic structures may involve greater difficulty in accommodating immigrants (e.g. greater importance of seniority in wage structures, greater weight of the service sector where familiarity with the society may be more important), and more discrimination (towards immigrants who are more different from the receiving population, making it harder for employers to accurately assess their qualifications). In other words, the economic adaptation of immigrants is dependent on their characteristics (selectivity, age, education, language, etc.) and the nature of the receiving society (levels of skills, needs for labour, extent of closure toward outsiders). The experience of a given cohort of immigrants will be largely a function of their quality and the economic situation at the time of their arrival. We have seen that the more recent cohorts are less selective, even in terms of education and labour force status. This in turn would be a function of the reduced relative size of the "independent class," and the greater importance of family and refugee classes in the more recent arrivals. Obviously, we should not expect that persons selected on the basis of family reunification and humanitarian concerns would necessarily achieve levels of economic performance comparable to that of the receiving society.

Low income status

As well as comparing groups through their average income, it is useful to consider variations around this mean. A particularly useful measure is the proportion of a given group that has been attributed "low income status." This status is a relative concept, based on the proportion of total income that is needed for the essentials of food, clothing and shelter. Using average expenditure on these essentials, various "income cut-offs" are established depending on family size and size of the place of residence.

In the data from the 1971 and 1981 censuses, low income was less common among immigrants than in the Canadian-born population for "economic families." However, for "unattached individuals," the foreign-born had a higher incidence of low income (Beaujot et al., 1988:79-85). In the 1986 census data, immigrants have relative disadvantages both for economic families and unattached individuals (Table 1). In addition, low income status increases with recency of arrival. Compared to the traditional immigrant group, the new immigrant group arriving since 1970 tends to be at a greater disadvantage.

Among economic families with both husband and wife present, 11.3 percent of cases with immigrant husbands had low income status compared to 10.1 for the Canadian-born. The proportions with low income increase rather uniformly with recency of arrival. For both the traditional and new immigrant group, cohorts arriving since 1970 have higher proportions at low income than the Canadian-born average.

Among the other (i.e. non husband-wife) economic families, the proportions at low income again increase rather uniformly with recency of arrival. Cohorts arriving since 1975, plus women arriving in the 1970-74 and all immigrant categories aged 65 and over have higher proportions at low income than the Canadian-born of the same age/sex groups. In the cohorts arriving since 1970, the proportions at low income

Table 1—Percent of given groups with low income status, by period of immigration, Canada, 1986

	Husband/ Wife	Other Families Reference Person		Unattached Individuals	
	Families	Male	Female	Male	Female
Canadian-born	10.1	18.2	43.6	33.0	40.9
Arrived before 1946	6.3	10.6	15.9	35.7	47.8
TIG	6.1	10.5	15.8	35.3	47.9
NIG	10.1	12.0	20.0	49.3	47.4
Arrived 1946-60	7.5	13.0	26.5	28.5	42.9
TIG	7.3	12.9	26.5	28.5	42.9
NIG	9.3	15.2	26.3	28.8	42.9
Arrived 1961-69	9.6	14.6	35.1	28.1	40.5
TIG	9.8	14.8	36.1	28.4	42.1
NIG	9.0	14.1	33.1	27.3	36.2
Arrived 1970-74	12.1	21.1	49.2	32.3	43.1
TIG	11.1	16.9	43.6	30.9	43.6
NIG	13.0	24.0	52.3	33.9	42.6
Arrived 1975-79	16.2	26.0	52.8	35.3	52.0
TIG	11.9	19.1	49.6	30.6	50.0
NIG	19.2	28.7	54.1	38.9	53.6
Arrived 1980-84	25.6	38.5	58.2	46.0	62.3
TIG	16.2	24.2	51.1	33.1	55.8
NIG	32.1	41.2	60.3	53.2	67.3

Note: TIG: Traditional immigrant group
NIG: New immigrant group

Source: Special tabulations from the 1986 census.

are almost uniformly higher for the new than for the traditional immigrant group. For instance, at age 35-44 in the 1975-79 cohort, the proportions with low income status amount to 28.6 percent of the new immigrant group and 18.4 percent of the traditional immigrant group (19.5 percent of the Canadian-born) for families with a male reference person, and 56.1 percent of the new immigrant group compared to 44.7 percent of the traditional immigrant group (45.5 percent of the Canadian-born) for families with a female reference person. In effect, in the majority of comparisons the traditional immigrant group has lower proportions at low income than the Canadian-born, even in the last two immigrant cohorts (Beaujot and Rappak, 1988: 151).

For persons who are not in economic families, unattached male immigrants have higher proportions at low income than the Canadian-born in the 15-24 and 65+ age categories, plus among the 1980-84 immigrant cohort and for ages 25-34 and 55-64 in the 1975-79 cohort. Thus at ages 35-54, immigrants have lower proportions at low income, except for the most recent 1980-84 cohort. The patterns are similar for female unattached individuals, although they are somewhat more likely to have low income, compared to the Canadian-born. For instance, all comparisons for the 1975-79 and 1980-84 immigrant cohorts involve higher proportions at low income than the Canadian-born of the same age groups. The difference between the traditional and new immigrant groups are significant. It is essentially for cohorts arriving since 1970 that the new immigrant group is at a greater disadvantage in terms of low income status for unattached individuals.

Clearly, the receiving society needs to pay continual attention to the opportunity profile of its newest arrivals from abroad. Only if this profile is interpreted positively will immigration itself be seen positively both by immigrants and the receiving society.

Socio-cultural impact of immigration

Immigration obviously produces a population that is not completely native-born. The foreign-born have comprised 15 to 16 percent of the total population of Canada over the period 1951-86. These proportions of foreign-born are comparable to those found in Australia (22 percent) but considerably higher than in the United States (6 percent).

The long-term impact of the immigration, fertility and mortality levels of the 1981-85 period would produce a Canadian population that is about 20 percent foreign-born. An immigration level of 275,000 arrivals per year produces, in the long term, a population that is about 30 percent foreign-born, with current fertility levels (Ryder, 1985:6). These proportions are considerably higher than comparable data for Europe. For instance the proportions of persons from outside of Europe amount to only 2.2 percent of the entire population of the 12 countries of the European Economic Community. The highest proportion is in Germany with 5.5 percent (Levy, 1988:4). Given the low birth rates in Europe, immigration needed to keep the population from declining would produce a population where the "share of aliens and their descendants" would be some 30 to 34 percent of the total population in the middle of the next century (Lesthaeghe et al., 1988:11).

Place of origin and visible minorities

Chapter 2 has analyzed the change in the source countries of immigration. There is much diversity in the places of origin of Canada's immigrants. The annual *Immigration Statistics* lists a total of 184 countries of birth. We often pay special attention to the top ten sending countries but in 1980-85, these top ten countries accounted for only about half of all immigrants. This is rather different from European countries where immigrants are predominantly from one source: Algerians in France, West Indians in the United Kingdom or Turkish people in Germany. Since racial criteria were lifted in immigrant selection, the origin of immigrants to Canada has become very diversified. This reduces the formation of "ghettos" involving persons from a given place of origin.

Nonetheless, immigrant "networks" are an important part of the migration process. Policies favouring the family class and sponsored relatives encourage a migration chain from a specific place of origin and often to a specific place of destination. In effect, the propensity of immigrants from various places of origin to sponsor the arrival of their relatives is a major determinant of the ethnic composition of the current flow (Simmons, 1988).

While the foreign-born can be divided into various places of origin, it is useful to distinguish the traditional immigrant group from Europe and the United States, and the new immigrant group from other parts of the world. Among persons enumerated in the 1986 census, the new immigrants amounted to 5.0 percent of the pre-1961 arrivals, compared to 50.3 percent of the 1970-74 cohort and 65.1 percent of the 1980-86 arrivals. Altogether, the new immigrant group amounted to 11.1 percent of the total foreign-born in 1971 and 30.6 percent in 1986.

Immigration also plays the key role in terms of increasing the visible minority component of the Canadian population. Defining visible minorities as people who are neither Aboriginal nor of European ethnic origin, some 4.7 percent of the 1981 census population can be so classified (Samuel, 1987). In this component, 15 percent were Canadian-born and 85 percent were born abroad. As another indicator, the population born in Asia, Latin America and Africa increased from 336,000 in 1971 to 1,152,000 in 1986, a total increase of 340 percent. In comparison, the population born in Europe declined by 7 percent in this period. Nonetheless, the population born in Asia, Latin America and Africa represents only 30 percent of the total foreign-born in 1986, or 4.6 percent of the total population.

Based on the 1981 census, Samuel (1988b) estimated that the visible minority component would increase from 5.6 percent of the total Canadian population in 1986 to nine to ten percent by 2001. Using the 1981-85 immigration trends, the visible minority component would reach a stationary figure of about ten percent of the total Canadian population (Beaujot and Rappak, 1988:105). This is probably a maximum figure since, especially over time, persons of various visible minorities become considerably less visible. Intermarriage being strong among Canada's various ethnic groups, it can be argued that Canada is becoming a multi-ethnic society where "pluralism" rather than "visible minorities" is the more appropriate term. These figures are considerably lower than those for the United States where 20.1 percent of the 1980 population was Black, Hispanic or Asian, with projected levels in the range of 25 to 28 percent by the year 2000 (Samuel, 1988b).

Language

Immigration has clearly benefited the English more than the French language in Canada. That is especially true outside of Quebec where there is less French among immigrants than in the Canadian-born population. The trends outside of Quebec are stable over time: the overwhelming majority of immigrants and their descendants come to associate with the English language as their main language, among the official languages.

At the time of arrival, about a third of immigrants speak neither English nor French (Beaujot, 1989: 48). In the 1980-86 cohort, 49 percent had home languages other than English or French at the time of the 1986 census. However, over time the majority come to associate with one or the other of the official languages. In order to highlight this tendency, we have adopted the concept of "predominant language" which combines the responses on language spoken at home and knowledge of official languages. Persons who speak English or French at home were assigned this language as their predominant language. Persons speaking "other" languages at home were also assigned to English or French predominant language if they could speak "only" that language among the official languages. In effect, we are measuring which among the official languages is a given person's predominant language. Using these definitions, the immigrants living outside of Quebec were 92.5 percent English, 0.6 percent French and 6.9 percent other in the 1986 census (Beaujot and Rappak, 1988:112).

Quebec receives the majority of French speaking immigrants to Canada. In effect, of the foreign-born who were classified as predominantly French among the official languages, 90 percent were in Quebec in 1986. Nevertheless, the French comprise less than 6 percent of the total foreign-born in Canada. For cohorts that arrived before 1970, immigrants who stayed in Quebec contributed more to the English than to the French language. Since 1970, immigrants have been more likely to associate with the French language, especially the younger immigrants and those who do not know English at the time of arrival (Veltman, 1988). However, persons of third languages are more likely to retain these languages in Quebec. In 1986, 38.3 percent of immigrants living in Quebec were predominantly English, 37.6 were French and 24.1 percent were other.

The general linguistic trends in Canada involve decreases in the official language minorities, that is English in Quebec and French in the rest of Canada. Outside of Quebec, immigration contributes to the trend as there is less French among immigrants than in the native-born population. In Quebec, immigration enhances the English minority because there is more English among immigrants than in the native-born, and a sizeable proportion of third language migrants continue to transfer to the English language. Immigration therefore plays an important role in Canada's changing distribution by official languages. While this distribution changes very slowly over time, immigration is the main element producing an increase in the relative size of the English language in Canada (Lachapelle, 1988). Partly because of anglophone control over economic opportunity, at least in provinces other than Quebec, immigrants and their descendants are primarily oriented to the anglophone society in Canada (Reitz, 1980).

Summary and conclusions

In contrast to many other advanced industrial countries, Canada has a long history of policies and programs through which immigration has contributed significantly to population change. Over this century, net international migration has accounted for some 22 percent of total population growth. This does not count the further impact through births to immigrants. Simulating the change over the period 1951-81 implies that 38 percent of the growth was a function of immigration and births to these immigrants over the period. In 1986, 16 percent of the population of Canada was foreign born, which is higher than the major industrial countries except Australia and Israel. The average foreign born for the industrial countries with populations over one million is 6 percent or less than half the Canadian level (Lachapelle, 1990). Immigration has little impact on the age structure, and it reinforces the trends in growth of the largest cities, but it also counters the trends toward slower population growth.

As a function of both a baby boom and an immigration boom, the population of Canada more than doubled over the period 1946-91. Immigration contributed to almost a quarter of this population growth. Over the next forty-five years, population growth is likely to stop completely. If population growth is to be maintained, there are obviously only two approaches that are possible, and each has their specific difficulties.

The immigration approach sustains demographic and labour force growth, and provides a slight counter to population and labour force aging. However, immigration needs to be well planned, preferably in a long-term context, including appropriate integration programs for the new arrivals, preferably maximum distribution of immigrants over space, as well as various efforts to build a harmonious multi-cultural society. The "immigration solution" therefore requires a number of services, and various adaptations, especially in education. Chesnais (1989) contrasts these "desiderata" to what is often instead largely unorganized arrivals to select large cities, that follow on short-term labour force needs or on pressure from the world outside.

The "fertility solution" is also costly both to parents and to the society. At the level of the society, there is a need to deal with the incongruities between individual and social interests. At the level of individuals, there is the competition between parenthood and other work and life style options. It is also necessary to support families that may be very different in terms of size, structure and needs. The fertility approach therefore requires resource transfers to the benefit of children, posing conflicts with the needs of the elderly.

Given this balance of costs, a case can be made for entertaining both alternatives. The immigration solution presents advantages in terms of sustaining population growth and especially introducing flexibility in the labour force. Judging from past experience, it would appear that immigration levels in the range of 150,000 to 250,000 persons per year can be advantageously accommodated. At the same time, arrivals from the outside can be more easily accommodated if fertility is sustained, ensuring that immigration does not change the basic socio-cultural character of the population more than is considered acceptable. Children are costly in a variety of ways and require various kinds of sacrifices, but they are ultimately the most important investment in the future of the society.

While the demographic side of immigration is relatively easy to assess, the economic implications are harder to delineate. However, properly controlled immigration is likely to present a net economic benefit, if only because the majority arrive at the most productive stages of the life cycle. Without having to invest in their education, the receiving country benefits from their various talents and abilities. The receiving society is probably best served if immigrants have a socio-economic profile that is not too different from that of the society to which they are arriving. In effect, we have seen that the socio-economic profile of the foreign born is not that different from the Canadian born. The 1980-85 cohort may have been an exception due to the lower proportion of the independent class. It would appear that a balance between the family, independent and refugee classes is more likely to present an average profile that, at least after a few years, is not that different from the Canadian born.

While immigration probably involves net economic benefits, the social impact may not be as positive (Bourbeau et al., 1986). Immigration changes the regional distribution and the linguistic composition in ways that can be interpreted negatively. Termote (1988) finds that an immigration of 40,000 per year to the province of Quebec would increase the size of Montreal by some 1,150,000 over 40 years. Lachapelle (1988) concludes that immigration has been the main factor reducing the relative weight of the French in Canada, while Paillé (1989) is concerned about the relative impact of immigration and fertility on the future linguistic composition of the Island of Montreal. It is in view of social impacts that the Parliamentary Standing Committee recommended slower immigration growth over the period 1991-92 (Blackburn, 1990). This Committee expressed concerns with respect to social relations, concentration of immigrants and immigrant integration. It was felt that "a degree of stability at this time would give our settlement services an opportunity to try to catch up with demand, our schools a chance to upgrade their teaching of English or French to the many immigrant children who know neither, and our large cities a chance to ensure successful integration of their many recent arrivals."

The question is always to know how to control the size and composition of immigration, and how to organize the economic and social integration of immigrants, in order to assure that the society is not changed more than is deemed acceptable. This assessment also needs to recognize the valuable role that immigration has played in Canada's past. Under the proper conditions, immigration can continue to represent contact with other cultures, openness to the world, and a dynamic approach to the future.

Bibliography

Avery, Roger and Barry Edmonston, *Canada's Stationary Population Equivalent: the Effect of Variations in Population Conditions.* Paper presented at the meetings of the Population Association of America, New Orleans, April 1988.

Basavarajappa, K.G. and Ravi B.P. Verma, "Occupational Composition of Immigrant Women." Pp. 297-314 in S.S. Halli, F. Trovato and L. Driedger, *Ethnic Demography.* Ottawa: Carlton University Press, 1990.

Beaujot, Roderic, *Immigration and the Population of Canada.* Report prepared for Strategic Planning and Research, Immigration Policy Group, Employment and Immigration Canada, 1989.

Beaujot, Roderic P., K.G. Basavarajappa and Ravi B.P. Verma, *Income of Immigrants in Canada* (Catalogue No. 91-527). Ottawa: Statistics Canada, 1988.

Beaujot, Roderic and J. Peter Rappak, *The Role of Immigration in Changing Socio-Economic Structures.* Report prepared for the Review of Demography and Its Implications for Economic and Social Policy, 1988.

Beaujot, Roderic and J. Peter Rappak, "The Link between Immigration and Emigration in Canada, 1945-1986." *Canadian Studies in Population* 16(2): 201-216, 1989.

Beaujot, Roderic and J. Peter Rappak, "The Evolution of Immigrant Cohorts." Pp. 111-140 in S.S. Halli, F. Trovato and L. Driedger, *Ethnic Demography.* Ottawa: Carlton University Press, 1990.

Blackburn, Jean-Pierre, *Interim Report on Demography and Immigration Levels.* Report of the Standing Committee on Labour Employment and Immigration, Issue No. 40, 1990.

Bourbeau, Robert, Norbert Robitaille and Robert Choinière, "Impact de l'immigration sur la structure de la population canadienne et sur sa répartition géographique." Report prepared for *The Review of Demography*, 1986.

Chesnais, Jean Claude, "L'inversion de la pyramide des âges en Europe: perspectives et problèmes." *General Conference of the International Union for the Scientific Study of Population.* Vol 3: 53-68, 1989.

Denton, Frank T. and Byron G. Spencer, "Changes in the Canadian Population and Labour Force: Prospects and Implications." *Canadian Studies in Population* 14:187-208, 1987.

Dumas, Jean, *Report on the Demographic Situation in Canada 1983.* (Catalogue No. 91-209). Ottawa: Statistics Canada, 1984.

Hersak, Gene and Derrick Thomas, "Recent Canadian Developments Arising from International Migration." Working Paper, Policy Analysis Directorate, Immigration Policy Branch, Employment and Immigration Canada, 1988.

Kalbach, W.E. and W.W. McVey, *The Demographic Bases of Canadian Society.* Toronto: McGraw-Hill, 1979.

Lachapelle, Réjean, "L'immigration et le caractère ethnolinguistique du Canada et du Québec." Statistics Canada: Direction des études analytiques, Documents de Recherche No. 15, 1988.

Lachapelle, Réjean, Workshop on contemporary demography in Canada and Quebec. Conference celebrating the 25th anniversary of the Département de Démographie, Montreal, September 1990.

Lanphier, C. Michael, *A Study of Third-World Immigrants.* Discussion Paper No. 144. Ottawa: Economic Council of Canada, 1979.

Lanphier, C. Michael, "Irreversible Shift: Refugee Intake and Canadian Society." Paper presented at the meetings of the Canadian Population Society, Windsor, June 1988.

Le Bras, Hervé, "The Demographic Impact of Post-war Migration in Selected OECD Countries." OECD Working Party on Migration, 1988.

Lesthaeghe, R., H. Page and J. Surkyn, "Are Immigrants Substitutes for Births?" Vrije Universiteit Brussel, Interuniversity Programme in Demography Working Paper 1988-3.

Levy, Michel Louis, "Europe et démographie." *Population et Sociétés* No. 230, 1988.

Marr, William, "Are the Canadian Foreign-Born Under-Represented in Canada's Occupational Structure." *International Migration* 14:769-775, 1986.

McInnis, R. Marvin, "A Functional View of Canadian Immigration." Paper presented at the Annual Meetings of the Population Association of America, Denver, 1980.

Nash, Alan, "International Refugee Pressures and the Canadian Public Response." Institute for Research on Public Policy, *Discussion Paper* 89.B.1, 1989.

Neuwirth, Gertrud, et al., *Southeast Asian Refugee Study*. A Report on the Three Year Study of the Social and Economic Adaptation of Southeast Asian Refugees to Life in Canada, 1981-83. Unpublished manuscript, 1985.

Ornstein, Michael D., *The Work Experience of Immigrants to Canada: 1969-1976*. Downsview, Ontario: Institute for Behavioural Research, York University, 1983.

Paillé, Michel, *Nouvelles tendances démographiques dans l'Ilse de Montréal*. Quebec: Conseil de la langue française, 1989.

Rao, G. Lakshmana, Anthony H. Richmond and Jerzy Zubrzycki, *Immigrants in Canada and Australia. Volume One. Demographic Aspects and Education*. Downsview, Ontario: Institute for Behavioural Research, York University, 1984.

Reitz, Jeffrey G., "Immigration and Inter-ethnic Relationships in Canada." Pp. 337-362 in R. Breton et al. (eds.). *Cultural Boundaries and the Cohesion of Canada*. Montreal: Institute for Research on Public Policy, 1980.

Review of Demography, *Facing the Demographic Future*. Ottawa: Review of Demography, 1989.

Rhyne, Darla, *Generational Differences Between the Canadian Born and Immigrants in Metropolitan Toronto*. Downsview, Ontario: Institute for Behavioural Research, York University, 1982.

Richmond, Anthony H., *Immigration and Ethnic Conflict*. New York: St. Martin's Press, 1988.

Richmond, Anthony and Warren Kalbach, *Factors in the Adjustment of Immigrants and Their Descendants*. Ottawa: Statistics Canada, 1980.

Richmond, Anthony H. and Ravi P. Verma, "Income Inequality in Canada: Ethnic and Generational Aspects." *Canadian Studies in Population* 5: 25-36, 1978.

Richmond, Anthony H. and Jerzy Zubrzycki, *Immigrants in Canada and Australia. Volume Two. Economic Adaptation*. Downsview, Ontario: Institute for Behavioural Research, York University, 1984.

Robertson, Matthew, "A Longitudinal Perspective on the Unemployment Experience of Principal Applicant Immigrants to Canada: 1977-1981." *Canadian Studies in Population* 13: 37-56, 1986.

Ryder, Norman B., *A Population Policy for Canada*. Manuscript. Toronto: University of Toronto, 1985.

Samuel, T. John, "Economic Adaptation of Refugees in Canada: Experience of a Quarter Century." *International Migration* 22: 45-55, 1984.

Samuel, T. John, "Visible Minorities in Canada." *Contributions to Demography, Methodological and Substantive: Essays in Honour of Dr. Karol J. Krotki*. Edmonton: Population Research Laboratory, 1987.

Samuel, T. John, "Family Class Immigrants to Canada, 1981-1984: Labour Force Activity Aspects." *Population Working Paper No. 5*. Ottawa: Employment and Immigration Canada, 1988a.

Samuel, T. John, "Immigration and Visible Minorities: A Projection." *Canadian Ethnic Studies* 20(2): 92-100, 1988b.

Seward, Shirley B., "Immigrant Women in the Clothing Industry." Pp. 343-363 in S.S. Halli, F. Trovato and L. Driedger, *Ethnic Demography*. Ottawa: Carlton University Press, 1990.

Simmons, A.B., *How Social and Economic Trends in Other Countries Affect the Composition of New Immigrants to Canada*. Report for the Review of Demography and Its Implications for Economic and Social Policy, 1988.

Termote, Marc, "Ce que pourrait être une politique de migration." *L'Action nationale* LXXVIII-5 (May): 308-322, 1988.

Taylor, Chris, "The Role of Immigration in Determining Canada's Eventual Population Size." *Population Working Paper No. 11*. Ottawa: Employment and Immigration Canada, 1988.

Veltman, Calvin, *L'impact de l'immigration internationale sur l'équilibre linguistique québécois*. Report prepared for the Review of Demography and Its Implications for Economic and Social Policy, 1988.

Chapter 4

Immigration
Law and Policy

Larry Gold

Introduction

THIS PAPER PROVIDES AN OVERVIEW of the legal and administrative processes surrounding immigration into Canada.

Since the initial writing of this chapter, the Minister of Immigration has tabled legislation making substantial changes in the law and procedure.[1] In respect to the refugee system, the initial inquiry procedure has been eliminated, powers of appeal have been reduced, and immigration officers have been given increased powers to turn back prospective refugee claimants. In addition, refugee claimants will not be able to work until their claims have been completed (unlike the current system wherein they are able to receive employment authorizations after their

---

1   Given the substantial changes in the Act since this chapter was written, the interested reader is advised to consult the new legislation.

initial inquiry). If a claimant is successful, the waiting period in respect to sponsorship of immediate family has been reduced or eliminated. All refugee claimants are to be fingerprinted, and the system for expelling unsuccessful claimants as well as those who break the law streamlined.

The changes in the Act are to include a system whereby independent applicants will be allowed to come into the country only if they are prepared to live for at least two years in an area where their skills are required. In addition, changes to business class applications and family sponsorships are anticipated.

Church groups, some provincial governments, and legal groups have made representations to the federal government voicing concerns over various aspects of the proposed legislation, namely, as it relates to the refugee system and the perception that the federal government is attempting to reduce the number of refugees seeking status in Canada in violation of its international obligations. The Minister of Immigration to date has resisted attempts to delay or alter the legislation and it is scheduled to be in place by January 1, 1993. It seems a certainty that there will be legal challenges to portions of the legislation as it may conflict with the Canadian Charter of Rights.

Overview of this chapter

The purpose of this chapter is to provide an overview of the provisions of the Immigration Act and Regulations as well as the role of the lawyer in the immigration process. At common law, prior to statutes dealing with immigration, the Crown had an unfettered discretion to determine the rights of the alien. This common law position was described by Lord Denning of the English Court of Appeal in the case of Regina v. Governor of Pentonville Prison, ex parte Azam[2]

> At common law no alien has the right to enter the country except by leave of the Crown; and the Crown can refuse without giving any reason ... If he comes by leave, the Crown can impose such conditions as it thinks it, as to his length of stay, or otherwise. He has no right whatever to remain here. He is liable to be sent

---

2   [1973] 2 All E.R. 741

home to his country at any time if, in the opinion of the Crown, his presence here is not conducive to the public good . . .

The federal government as represented by the Minister of Employment and Immigration is the authority that determines the rights of the alien in Canada. Much of the discretion and arbitrariness in the decision-making process has been removed by statute, namely the Immigration Act,[3] and Immigration Regulations wherein the rules and policies are well defined. In law, those who carry out the function of implementing the rules and policies are required to do so in a fair, non prejudicial manner.

Canadian citizens and with few exceptions permanent residents of Canada have an absolute right to enter this country, all others can enter only upon satisfying immigration officials of their right to do so. Those who choose not to voluntarily leave after their admission is refused at a port of entry have the right to an enquiry and to be represented by legal counsel. If they do not retain their own lawyer (5.30.2) of the Act provides for the appointment of a designated counsel to represent them. The designated counsel is paid from a fund established by the Federal Government and administered across Canada by Peat Marwick and Associates. If the refusal is upheld, there is a further right to appeal to the Federal Court of Appeal, upon leave to appeal being granted by that court.

The Immigration Act further provides that all those who seek admission to Canada either on a temporary or permanent basis are subject to standards of admission that do not discriminate in a manner inconsistent with the Canadian Charter of Rights and Freedoms. The necessity for immigration officials to act in a reasonable manner extends to those cases where the alien has not presented himself at a port of entry, but remains outside the country. In the cases of Rattan v. Canada (Minister of Employment & Immigration),[4] the Immigration Appeal Board over-ruled an immigration officer's decision not to allow a wife who was a Canadian citizen to sponsor her husband's landing in

---

3   1976-1977 Statutes of Canada C.52 and Amendment thereto.

4   (1987), 1 Imm. L.R. (2d) 317 (Imm. App. Bd.)

Canada because their marriage took place in India under circumstances that may have made the marriage invalid under Indian law. The Board ruled that the relevant law to apply was Canadian marriage law, as at the time of their marriage, they intended to come to Canada to live. As their marriage would have been legal in Canada, the immigration officials had erred in denying the sponsorship application. The Federal Court of Appeal in the case of Canada (Minister of Employment & Immigration) v. Porter allowed an appeal of a visa officer's refusal to grant permanent resident status to a family member on the basis that although the application was out of time, the delay was caused by the Minister's representative.

The legal principles to be appreciated from cases such as these is that, although the Minister has absolute discretion in carrying out the government's policies, the Minister must exercise that discretion, and act, in a manner that is fair, reasonable, judicious and consistent with the law and intention of the policies as set out in the Act and Regulations.

Objectives of immigration policies

Section 3 of the Act sets out the objectives of immigration policies, rules and regulations. As stated therein the policies, rules and regulations shall be designed and administered in such a manner so as to promote the domestic and international interests of Canada recognizing the following needs, (a) demographic goals as established by the federal government (b) enrichment and strength of Canadian culture taking into account the federal and bilingual character of Canada (c) facilitation of revision of Canadian and permanent residents with family abroad (d) co-operation of various levels of government and non-government agencies in order to facilitate and encourage the adoption of immigrants (e) facilitation of visitor entries to promote tourism, trends, commerce, science and international understanding (f) assuring those seeking to come to Canada are not discriminated against and are subject to the same standards as set out in the Charter of Rights and Freedoms (g) recognition of Canada's humanitarian obligations with respect to refugees, displaced and persecuted (h) fostering a strong and viable economy (i) protection of the health safety and good order of Canadian society (j) promoting international order and justice by denying Canada as a base for those who are likely to engage in criminal activity.

Levels of immigration and priorities

There is no absolute quota as to the number of immigrants allowed into Canada each year. There are, however, levels that are established and immigrants are processed in priority with these levels in mind. In October 1990, the Minister of Immigration announced a substantial increase in the number of immigrants to be allowed to come to Canada. By 1992, the annual number will be 250,000 which is 50,000 greater than the 1990 level. Refugees are not included in that number. Prior to the recent announcement made by the Minister, parents were allowed to sponsor unmarried children regardless of age and dependency. Pursuant to the recently announced changes, a child may be sponsored only if it is dependant. The immigrant child who is dependant on his family will be admitted. Those who are not dependent will not be admitted. The new policy is being established in order to allow the immigration of more independent applicants who possess skills that are required in Canada. [5]

The Immigration Regulation, Section 3 set out the priorities for processing immigrants. Consistent with the aforementioned stated objectives of reunification of Canadian citizens and permanent residents with their families abroad and the need to fulfil Canada's international legal obligations with respect to refugees, the first priority is given to family class immigrants and convention refugees.

The balance of priorities in order are business immigration of investors, entrepreneurs and self-employed individuals, persons who are qualified for and are willing to engage in a designated occupation, individuals who have arranged employment in Canada and are able to meet the necessary criteria associated with that employment, retired persons, people who are able to satisfy certain occupational requirements and meet other criteria and, lastly, all other immigrants not referred to previously.

---

5   *The Globe and Mail*, October 26, 1990.

First priority — family class and refugees

Family class sponsorship under the new regulations allows all Canadian citizens and permanent residents who have resided in Canada for at least three years, if they are eighteen years of age, to sponsor an application for landing made by relatives. The category of relative includes spouses, unmarried children if under 19 (only if dependant), and married or unmarried children over 19 if dependent. It also includes parents, grandparents, orphaned brothers, sisters and extended family under 19 years who are unmarried. Note that those who are sponsored can also include on their application their own dependents. The relevant regulation provides for the allowance of one sponsorship of a relative (undefined in the regulations), regardless of age or relationship. Relative sponsorships are separated into two categories. The first are those close relatives, being those in a direct linear relationship, namely spouses, unmarried children (pursuant to recent changes these children must be dependant) and parents and grandparents.

In all cases except for inland refugee claims, the application by the immigrant to come to Canada should first be made at an immigration office outside the country. The individual sponsoring a family member must establish his status in Canada, prove his relationship with the person being sponsored (this is usually achieved by way of official documentation to prove the relationship) and satisfy immigration officials that the sponsor is able to provide lodging, care and financial assistance to the person who is being sponsored. There is a minimum income requirement that the sponsor must establish and the sponsor must sign an undertaking of financial responsibility. The necessary income level is dependent on the population size of the area that the sponsor resides in, the number of dependents that the sponsor is responsible for and the number of relatives being sponsored. For example, in Vancouver, the low income figure as at December 1990 for an undertaking of assistance is $15,253.00 for a family of two persons seeking to sponsor one individual. The figures are adjusted every six months. When determining whether to approve the sponsorship, the officials will also review debt obligations. A visa will not be issued to any relative who is inadmissible for reasons that will be outlined later in this chapter. Nor will a visa be issued where immigration officials form the opinion that the sponsor will not be able to fulfil his undertaking.

Assisted relatives are relatives such as aunts, uncles, nieces, nephews, brothers and sisters. In this category, the sponsor can assist the immigration of these relatives to Canada by providing a financial undertaking. However, there is an additional requirement that assisted relatives score 55 units of assessment criteria. This assessment criteria awards specific units based on matters such as knowledge of English or French, age (10 units for individuals between 21 years and 44 years, subtract two for each year in excess of 44 or less than 21 years), education and vocation. The lawyer's role, if any, in respect to the family sponsorship and assisted relative category is generally limited to assisting in the preparation and obtaining of proper documentation. If the sponsorship application is unsuccessful, a lawyer may be retained to review the circumstances to ensure that the decision was not made on a wrong principle or for reasons contrary to law or policy, in which case, the decision may be appealed. The sponsor is liable to support the sponsored relative for a period of one to ten years. In the event that the relative requires social assistance during the period of financial undertaking, the province paying the assistance can take legal action against the sponsor to recover the monies.

Family class including assisted relative class was the largest single category of immigrants to Canada in 1989, comprising 81,670 immigrants given permanent resident status. This compares with 12,660 entrepreneurs, 2,146 investors and 51,000 independents. [6] The effect of the recently announced changes to the regulations will be to stabilize the number of family class immigrants and to increase the number of independent immigrants.

Refugee claimants

There is no area of immigration law that is as complex, controversial, costly or contentious as the law as it relates to refugees. Hence, this section will consider the relevant legislation and practice in some detail.

Canada, as a signatory to the 1951 Convention Relating to the Status of Refugees, has undertaken to shelter those who are unable to safely

---

6   Statistics provided by Immigration Canada Statistics Division.

reside in their own country. "Convention Refugee" is defined in the Immigration Act, S2, as a person who by reason of a well founded fear of persecution for reasons of race, religion, nationality, political opinion or membership in a particular social group, is outside his country of his nationality and, by reason of this fear, is unable or unwilling to avail himself of the protection of that country or, not having a country of nationality, is outside the country of his former habitual residence and is unable or, by reason of such fear, is unwilling to return to that country.

Prior to January 1, 1989, pursuant to the Immigration Act of 1976, the refugee process created a huge backlog of refugees because the system was unable to meet the demand. Under that process, a refugee would be examined by a senior immigration official under oath, a transcript of the proceedings would be prepared and forwarded to Ottawa to the Refugee Advisory Committee appointed by the Minister, the transcripts would be reviewed and a recommendation as to acceptance or rejection made to the Minister. In 1985, the Supreme Court of Canada struck down this process in the case of Harbajnir Singh v. the Minister of Employment and Immigration.[7] The court in that decision ruled that the Canadian Charter of Rights and Freedoms applied to all people inside Canada, even if their status had not yet been determined. The clause of the Charter that the Court dealt with in that case was Section 7, which states "everybody has the right to life, liberty, and security, and the right not to be deprived thereof except in accordance with the principles of fundamental justice."

After determining that Section 7 applied to the refugee process, the court went on to review the procedures of the then existing refugee system. The court held that the procedure adopted by the Minister did not provide adequate opportunity for the claimant to state his case and that the opportunity for less than a full hearing was being provided. This decision resulted in a slowing of the ability to process refugees. At the same time, increasing numbers of people were coming to Canada and claiming refugee status. Because Canada would not send prospective refugees back to their countries of origin, without first hearing their claim, refugee claimants were allowed to stay and obtain employment

---

7   [1985] 1 S.C.R. 178

while their claims were being processed. Many thousands of people came to Canada often from countries that prima facie did not create refugees.

At the commencement of the backlog clearance process, in the early spring of 1990, the Immigration Commission estimated that there were approximately 85,000 backlog cases. Some individuals in the refugee backlog had been in Canada for up to four years without determination of their cases. The estimate of the numbers of claimants in the backlog was subsequently increased to 120,000.[8]

The federal government, in a stated attempt to maintain the integrity of the immigration policies of Canada, decided that it would be inappropriate to grant amnesty to those who came here not as legitimate refugees, but in order to bypass the "normal" immigration process. The decision not to grant a general amnesty was partially predicated on the philosophy that if there were a general amnesty, it would encourage another flow of illegitimate claimants, who would again clog the system and wait for the next amnesty.[9] After refusing a general amnesty, a process was legislated for dealing with the backlog. This process was set to begin in January 1989 but was delayed in various regions.

The first step in clearing the backlog involves the claimant being interviewed by an immigration official, who determines if there are reasons to grant immediate landing on humanitarian and compassionate considerations. The immigration officials have guidelines for this determination. Originally, the guidelines for the initial interview were restricted so that landing was to be granted only in situations where a refugee claimant could have been sponsored as a member of the family class, or if he was a high profile sporting or cultural figure from certain countries.

On March 5, 1990, the Federal Court of Canada Trial Division in a case call Yhap v. Canada (Minister of Employment and Immigration) struck down the restrictive criteria used for the review process and

---

8   *The Vancouver Sun*, August 15, 1990.

9   Minister of Employment and Immigration, the Honourable Barbara McDougal Press Release, December 28, 1988.

required that the Minister apply the broader criteria developed by the Immigration Commission. These criteria include family relationships (not only blood relatives, but de facto family), severe consequences if returned to their country of origin, public policy (which remains essentially undefined) and consideration for those who have established close ties to Canada and have severed ties with their own country. As a result of the Yhap decision it was necessary to re-interview all those who had been rejected during their initial interview. As of September 1990, according to figures from the Immigration Department, approximately 10% of the claimants interviewed were accepted as a result of the interview. It has been the writer's experience and based upon information from those who conduct the interviews that landing is not to be granted to those who are able and have not been self-supporting for a substantial portion of their stay in Canada. As of March 1990 only 1,000 of the 23,000 interviewed were granted immediate landing as a result of their interview. As these interviews are highly discretionary and reasons for rejection are not usually given it is difficult to know why so few have been accepted.

If the claimant is not accepted, they are scheduled for an inquiry before an adjudicator and a member of the Immigration and Refugee Board. If one of the panel determines that the claimant has a credible basis and there is no reason not to grant landing, the claimant may apply for landing and it will be granted. The test for "credible basis" is very broad and means any credible or trustworthy evidence upon which the refugee division might determine the claimant to a convention refugee.

In order to decrease the backlog the government as an incentive has agreed that those who leave voluntarily will receive a letter guaranteeing an interview with a Canadian visa officer abroad, and further assurance that they will be given every consideration as to their experiences in Canada. This means that the Canadian visa officer, will look to the applicants work history, language skill, general roots and adaption to Canadian society.

It has been estimated that clearing the current backlog will cost the Canadian taxpayers in excess of $175,000,000. One might question whether utilizing the backlog program rather than invoking a general amnesty has in fact protected the integrity of our system. As political situations change in the various countries from where the claimants originated, so has their status in Canada. For example, an individual, who came to Canada from an east bloc country in 1987, claiming refugee status on the basis of religious or political persecution, would have had, at that time, a good prospect of having his or her claim accepted. That same person in the backlog will have little chance of acceptance, as the relevant time for determining the potential of such persecution is not when refugee status is claimed, but when the claim is heard.

In many cases, those who entered into the backlog process came to Canada with valid claims at the time of their arrival, but due to the government's inability to process their claims in a timely fashion, events may have changed the circumstances surrounding their claims. In the interim, many claimants have lived and worked in Canada for several years and have established family relationships. Although the human-itarian and compassionate considerations in the Act are meant to recog-nize their economic and emotional connection to Canada, many are now being forced to leave the country because of the change of conditions in their country of origin. Moreover, the relevant interviews are informal, and in practice, reasons for the decision not to land claimants are not necessarily given. One might question a policy that forces people to leave Canada who have proven their ability to adapt to Canadian life, have resided in Canada as productive residents and who at the time of their arrival may have been legitimate refugees. The issue of how to handle the refugee backlog is perhaps the most contentious legal issue confronting the public policy process today.

The new refugee process

At the same time as the backlog system described above was developed, an entirely new refugee process was established in Canada pursuant to Parliamentary Bill C-55. Under the terms of this Bill, the refugee process was to be altered so as to deal with the problems associated with the original backlog, while meeting the challenge of being a more judicious system. In particular, the refugee claimant was to be dealt with on an expedited basis.

Most refugee claims originate at a port of entry. The claimant informs an immigration officer of his or her intentions to make a refugee claim and to reside permanently in Canada. In almost all cases, the claimant is not in possession of a visa to enter Canada. Provided the claimants are not a danger to society and it appears that they will attend the inquiry they will be released. Otherwise they will be held in service custody. The refugee process is first initiated by the claimant completing a personal information form. The form is reviewed by a case officer. If there exists a prima facie case, that the claimant is credible (based upon the written story contained in the information form, and the country where persecution is claimed) his file will be forwarded to the refugee division for a full hearing before the refugee board. If the claim appears to be non-credible, an inquiry will be held before an adjudicator and a member of the refugee board. At the inquiry level the claimant must only establish that they are eligible to make a refugee claim, and that there is some credible evidence upon which a refugee board might determine the claimant to be a convention refugee. If the claimant fails at the inquiry, he or she will be excluded from Canada. If found to be credible, the claim will be forwarded to the refugee division for a full hearing.

The refugee hearing is held before two members of the Immigration and Refugee Board, an independent board established under the new refugee system. At both the inquiry and the hearing the onus is on the claimant to establish the essential elements of their claim. Although both the inquiry and board hearings are quasi judicial in nature, it is not a requirement that those hearing the claims have any legal training.

To be successfully determined a convention refugee, the claimants must through their own evidence, subject to cross examination, establish their claim both on objective and subjective criteria. In addition to the *viva voce* evidence of witnesses, other evidence in the form of documents are often introduced. This documentary is comprised most often of reports from international human rights organizations such as Amnesty International and America's Watch. The refugee division maintains documentation centres in each of Canada's major cities and compiles profiles on countries that are most often the focus of refugee claims.

The decision at both the inquiry and hearing levels may be appealed to the Federal Court of Appeal on arguments of law or law and fact, upon leave being granted by the Court. A body of jurisprudence from the courts has tended to widen the tests to be applied in the determination of convention refugee status. As these decisions are from Courts of superior jurisdiction the legal principals they enunciate are binding on the boards and upon the inquiry panels.

If the refugee claim is refused, a humanitarian and compassionate review is held in Ottawa prior to the exclusion of the claimant. The claimant may be landed on the basis of the humanitarian and compassionate review. There are certain countries to which Canada will not, or is reluctant to, deport individuals, because of the dangers that they may face if returned. This often results in claimants going through the refugee process, being found not to be refugees and then remaining in Canada, because Canada will not deport them. These countries include China, Sri Lanka and most often El Salvador and Guatemala.

In 1985, there were 4,617 refugee claims received by the Refugee Advisory Committee. In 1989, there were in excess of 21,000[10] refugee claims made from 100 countries, and it is estimated that for 1990 there will be approximately 40,000.[11] The budget established to deal with the refugee system is approximately $80,000,000. A refugee claimant arriving in Vancouver in January 1989 could have expected his/her full hearing to have taken place within four to six weeks. The same claimant arriving in September 1990 would not have his full hearing for at least 6 months as a new backlog slowly develops. The delay in the major eastern centres is even greater. Further steps are being implemented to increase the efficiency of the system.

Designated class

In addition to refugees who pass through the inland refugee system, Canada processes refugees through visa officers located in foreign countries. This group not only includes convention refugees, but also includes Indochinese Designated Class, Political Prisoners and Oppressed Persons Designated Classes. In order to comply, the individual must not only fit the criteria for the particular class under which he seeks to enter Canada but also must convince the visa officer that he will become successfully established in Canada.

---

10 Statistic supplied from Immigration and Employment Canada.

11 Statistic supplied from Immigration and Employment Canada.

The criteria to determine successful establishment are set out in a Schedule to the Immigration Regulations and include such matters as age, education, vocational preparation, occupational demand and knowledge of English and/or French. There is a further provision for groups of five or more or corporations to sponsor people in the above classes by undertaking to assume financial responsibility for them in Canada. According to statistics released by Employment and Immigration Canada, there were 26,564 designated class immigrants who came to Canada as permanent residents in 1989.

Business immigration

Business immigration is designed to attract investment and experienced business people to Canada. The program is divided into three separate categories; the entrepreneur, the investor and the self-employed. The courts have seldom become involved in the decisions made in respect to business immigrants. However, in the case of Muliada v. Minister of Employment & Immigration,[12] the Federal Court of Appeal ruled that the decision of a visa officer could not stand. In that case, the visa officer, in the course of rejecting an entrepreneur's application, failed to give the applicant a reasonable opportunity to correct a negative assessment of his business plan and indicated that the decision to reject the applicant was made by a provincial official, rather than the visa officer himself, who was the party that is empowered under the law to make such decisions. Part of the visa officer's decision was based on the requirement that "a significant number of jobs be created" when, in fact, no such requirement was contained in the definition of "entrepreneur." This decision illustrates the necessity, for those who carry out administrative functions, to consider only those matters that are mandated to them by policy or legislation and that they alone must make any decisions, which only they are empowered to make.

---

12 (1986), 18 Admin. L.R. 243 (Fed. C.A.)

Entrepreneur

The entrepreneurial category was designed for the purpose of encouraging successful business immigrants. The entrepreneur is an individual who has owned, operated or controlled a successful business enterprise and who desires to immigrate to Canada to establish a new business or purchase or make a substantial investment in an existing Canadian business. The key is that the business will create employment or continue employment for at least one Canadian citizen or permanent resident, other than the immigrant and his family. It is a requirement that the entrepreneur be involved in hands-on management of the business. Prior to the fall of 1989, it was required that the entrepreneur provide a business plan as part of the acceptance procedure. This is no longer a requirement. Immigration officials are most interested in past business performance and current ability to make an investment. The amount of money required for this category is not stipulated. It is anticipated that the entrepreneur may not have an exact business plan in mind when he comes to Canada. The entrepreneur is expected to provide a curriculum vitae describing industrial, managerial or business experience and a statement of financial resources, including funds for immediate use and those for later transfer. If available, a general description of the potential business venture of interest and the name of the province of intended residence should also be provided.

It is anticipated that the entrepreneur will come to Canada with a view to examining business opportunities and meeting with provincial officials to examine prospects and potential available programs. The most usual form of admission for the entrepreneur is a conditional landing, pursuant to which the entrepreneur and his dependents will have two years to establish the intended business venture. While the conditions are in place, the progress of the entrepreneur is monitored by immigration officials. According to statistics released by Employment and Immigration Canada for the period January 1, 1990 to June 30, 1990, the three countries from which most entrepreneurs came to Canada were Hong Kong (1820), Taiwan (593), and Korea (442). The U.S. accounted for only 85 entrepreneurs.

Immigrant investor program

The immigrant investor program was established in 1986 to allow investors, who themselves had been successful in amassing a net worth of at least $500,000 (Canadian), to come to Canada upon investing in this country in approved investments. Since that time, 3,510 investors have come to Canada. These investors are not expected to be involved in the management of their investments. The system is a three tier system and the amount required for investment is dependant upon the province wherein the investment is made. The minimum investment criteria were recently increased as was the time that the investor must keep his monies invested. The first tier requires that $250,000 be invested. This minimum requirement applies to provinces that have received less than 10 percent of the business immigrants in a calendar year. Currently these provinces are the Atlantic Provinces, Alberta, Saskatchewan and Manitoba. Tier two requires an investment of $350,000 and for tier three, the investor must have a net worth of $750,000 and he must invest $500,000.[13] The investments usually involve more than a single investor and may consist of either equity or debt financing.

The difference between tier two and tier three investments relate to the security that the investor may take on his investment. In respect to tier two investments, the business itself may offer security in the form of mortgages and guarantees provided that they are given by the business venture itself. Tier three investments may be guaranteed by third parties, thereby substantially reducing the risk. Most of these investment opportunities are offered through prospectus type offering memoranda. The provinces determine what sorts of investments are acceptable and determine requirements of, and approve the content of, the offering memorandum. The federal government makes the final determination as to the acceptability of the investor as an immigrant.

Quebec has its own unique policy in respect to monies invested in that province. The required former holding period for other provinces of three years has been abridged in that a $250,000 investment results in the government of Quebec returning a fully negotiable $200,000 bond,

---

13 *Canada's Immigration & Citizenship Bulletin*, October 1990.

resulting in only $50,000 of the investor's funds being at risk.[14] According to the most recent figures established by Employment and Immigration Canada, during the period January to June 1990, of the 1,628 investors who were given permanent resident status, 803 came from Hong Kong.

Self-employed

These immigrants will establish their own business in Canada, in which they will be the only employees. The business must contribute to the economic, cultural or artistic life of Canada. This category contemplates farming, artists and owners of small community businesses. The applicant will be required to obtain 70 units of assessment criteria in total but will be awarded 30 units if in the opinion of a visa officer the applicant will be successful in the establishment of his occupation.

Qualified employment in designated occupations

The balance of the categories except for the Retired Applicants are grouped as Independent Applicants. Those who apply under qualified employment have job skills, and experience in areas of employment that are required in Canada. The applicant will be awarded 10 units of assessment for employment, but will be required to obtain an additional 60 units of assessment.

Arranged employment in Canada

Applicants in the category have been offered employment in Canada. In order for them to be accepted, the Visa Officer must determine that the employment will not take jobs from Canadians, and that the employment must be such that it offers the continuity, standards and conditions sufficient to attract and retain Canadian Citizens and permanent residents. The applicant must be qualified for the employment and

---

14   *Vancouver Business Report,* July/August 1990.

in addition to the 10 units that will be assessed for the employment an additional 60 units will be required.

Retired persons

Under this category the applicant will not be taking employment in Canada and would be able to demonstrate that he\she is self-supporting. Other criteria include the ability to adjust to Canadian society and roots in Canada such as the presence of friends and family in the chosen area of residence.

Minimum of 5 assessment units

The sixth category is for those who can obtain at least 5 units out of a possible 10 units in respect to demand for their occupational skills. They would be required to obtain a total of 70 units of assessments.

Immigration Canada publishes a list of occupations open to prospective immigrants and the number of points assessed in respect to each occupation. Examples on the list for 1990 are as follows:

(a)	Chemist	1 point
(b)	Social Worker	10 points
(c)	Dental Hygienist	10 points
(d)	Economist	1 point

General category

This last category deals with those who would not get into any of the above categories.

Denying entry

Even though an individual may be admissible under the rules allowing for admission to Canada established in the various admission categories discussed above, Section 19 of the Immigration Act overrides their admission by setting out certain criteria for excluding people from admission to Canada.[15] This section sets out ten separate categories

---

15 C.A., Doc. No. A-357-87 April 14, 1988.

which form the basis for inadmissibility. Included in the categories of inadmissibility are those with mental or physical disorders that may, in the opinion of a medical officer, result in their being dangerous to the public health or safety or that might reasonably be expected to cause them to make excessive demands upon health or social services, those who are unable or unwilling to support themselves or have been convicted of a serious criminal offence, those who are reasonably suspected of being war criminals and those who are likely to carry on subversive activities against democratic government or engage in acts of violence.

Section 27 of the Immigration Act provides for the revocation of permanent resident status and resulting deportation in the event that the original landing of the individual would not have been granted due to the application of certain of the exclusions contained in section 19 or the additional criteria set out in Section 27. This section contemplates situations that were unknown to the immigration officials at the time permanent resident status was granted. Section 27 provides for the deportation of, inter alia, those who have been convicted of an offence in Canada, whereby a sentence of 6 months has actually been imposed or a sentence greater than 5 years may have been imposed, those who originally gained landing by way of false documents, fraudulent or improper means or misrepresentation of any material fact and those who wilfully fail to support themselves or any member of their dependent family.

In respect to status revocation and deportation, the process is carried out by way of an inquiry before an adjudicator. The adjudicator performs a function similar to that of a judge in a court of law. The inquiry under the Immigration Act is an administrative process. It is quasi judicial in nature and the individual who is the subject of the inquiry must be informed of his or her right to be represented by legal counsel. A recent decision of the Supreme Court of British Columbia has made it mandatory for legal services to be provided by legal aid in the event that the individual cannot pay for such services.[16] The adjudicator

---

16 This decision is being appealed as the effect of it is to require the provincial government to pay lawyers for a process that is completely under federal jurisdiction.

must provide reasons for the basis of his decision. The hearing itself is in the nature of a trial with rights to examine and cross-examine witnesses. The claimant is a compellable witness; however rules pertaining to the admissibility of evidence are far less formal than in a court of law. The final ruling of the adjudicator from an inquiry may be appealed to the Federal Court of Appeal on questions of law or mixed law and fact, provided that the court grants leave to appeal.

The Citizenship Act governs the permanent resident's right to obtain Canadian citizenship. In order to become a citizen, the individual must establish that he or she has been admitted as a permanent resident and has not given up that status, and that he or she has, within the 4 years immediately preceding the application, accumulated at least three years of residence in Canada. Whether the permanent resident has given up his or her status is dependent on intention. Pursuant to Section 24 of the Immigration Act, a permanent resident who spends more than 183 days out of any 12 month period outside Canada is presumed to have abandoned permanent resident status. The onus is then on the individual to establish that there was no such intention. Actual physical residence is not necessarily required, provided that it is found that there was an intention to remain a resident of Canada.

In determining intention, the courts will look not only to the actual amount of time the permanent resident has spent in Canada, but to roots established in Canada. These include such indicia as a continuing residence, family connections, bank accounts, frequency of trips to Canada and participation in Canadian programs and institutions. The issue of residence is particularly important to immigrants from places like Hong Kong where the individual's business dealings are still in the Orient and the permanent resident spends long periods outside of Canada on business.

Federal and provincial jurisdictions

Although the powers in respect to immigration were granted to the federal government under the terms of the British North America Act, the Immigration Act and Regulations (as discussed above) recognize provincial interests in immigration policy. The objectives section refers to both the bilingual character of Canada and the need to facilitate the adaption of permanent residents to Canadian society by promoting cooperation between the Government of Canada and other levels of government. It is a requirement that the Minister of Immigration, prior to setting levels in respect to the number of immigrants that are to be admitted to Canada, consult first with the provinces concerning regional demographic needs and labour market considerations. It is a further requirement that the Minister present to Parliament the manner in which demographic considerations have been taken into account. Under the terms of the Immigrant Investor Program, which were discussed above, the provinces and the federal government share joint jurisdiction. The federal government determines the general rules as to the program and who qualifies thereunder, while the provincial governments determine the acceptability of the actual investments. Provincial securities regulations apply in respect to such ventures.

In the case of family class sponsorships, provincial authorities have the exclusive right to approve applications to sponsor minors who are adopted outside Canada, as well as orphans and abandoned children who the sponsor intends to adopt. In certain cases where the provincial and federal governments have entered into agreement, the provincial authorities have the right to determine if a family sponsor residing in that province has the capability of fulfilling a financial undertaking in respect to the sponsored relative.

The Province of Quebec and the Government of Canada entered into a special immigration agreement in 1978, called the Canada–Quebec Agreement. The agreement was brought about as a result of the perceived needs of Quebec to maintain its special cultural needs, one of the ways being by having some control over the immigrants coming to that Province. For those independent applicants who are seeking to come to Quebec, or are seeking to come to Canada and have relatives in Quebec, or are French speaking or are married to a French speaking person, the applications are assessed by Quebec officials in respect to the potential of their successful establishment in Canada. This is an important criteria in the immigration selection of independent applicants. Quebec is allowed to utilize its own grid in assessing these applicants. In cases where an individual would not be processed due to failure to pass the federal criteria, he may still be admitted if he is acceptable to that province.

Chapter 5

The Economic and
Social Effects of
Immigration

Herbert G. Grubel

The first draft of this paper was written during the Summer of 1990 while I was Deutsche Bundesbank Visiting Professor of Finance at the Free University of Berlin. I thank Steve Globerman, Don DeVoretz, Charles Campbell, Doug Collins, Alan Jessup and seminar participants at Simon Fraser University for helpful discussions and comments.

DISCUSSIONS ABOUT POLICIES TOWARDS IMMIGRATION need a solid analytical basis to bring clarity to the likely effects of possible actions. This study attempts to provide such a basis by reviewing existing economic models which analyze the effects of immigration on output, employment, income distribution and the welfare of the population in the country of immigration.

At the outset it should be noted that this study does not discuss the effects which migration has on the welfare of emigrants or of the population in the country of emigration. This is done in order to save space and because the primary concern of this paper is immigration policies. Nevertheless, three brief points can readily be made about the problems facing migrants and the countries of emigration.

First, there is a strong presumption that migrants raise their expected future level of welfare if they move abroad voluntarily. If this were not true, they would stay at home and accept the economic, political or racial problems they encounter there rather than face the uncertain hardships and benefits from foreign residence. Second, the citizens of the country sending emigrants experience welfare effects which are analogous to those experienced by the citizens of the receiving country. All of the arguments and evidence discussed below can therefore readily be applied to the study of the effects of emigration on the welfare of residents left behind.

Third, current and past cumulative immigration into Canada are and have been large relative to the internal growth rate of the population and the total stock of Canadian born. Therefore, it is reasonable to apply the analytical structure of non-marginal flows developed below. However, the people coming to Canada represent a very small proportion of the population growth in the countries of emigration, particularly of some of the large developing countries of Asia. For this reason, the emigration flows have empirically minute effects on issues that are of central concern to Canadians, such as income distribution, the optimum growth rate and level of population and other externalities.

An immigrant has hands and a mouth

One of the most fundamental economic propositions about the effects of immigration is summarized by the idea that immigrants are both producers and consumers, or in a popular vein, each brings along hands and a mouth. This fact has two important implications for issues of great concern to the people in the country receiving the immigrants. First, it means that immigrants occupy jobs but they also add to demand for labour. When they spend their income from work they create the jobs which they fill. Second, it means that the population in the country of immigration does not suffer a reduction in income. To the contrary, the presence of new workers and consumers gives rise to the opportunity for welfare-raising additional trade and specialization among the residents of the country of immigration.

Marginal productivity theory of wages

The preceding proposition is obviously very important since it suggests that immigration must always lead to increased welfare among the residents in the country of immigration. In following sections we discuss conditions under which this proposition needs to be modified. However, because of the importance of the basic idea, it is worth considering in some detail the arguments which lead to this conclusion.

The cornerstone of the economist's model of immigration is the marginal productivity theory of wages. It states that the earnings of labour in a competitive economy are equal to the contribution which this labour makes to the output of society. The reasoning which underlies this conclusion can easily be understood with the help of the following thought-experiment.

Consider that a firm hires a given worker at a wage rate of $5 per hour. If the contribution of the worker to the output and income of the firm is worth less than the wage due, the firm loses money. It cannot pay for the capital it has borrowed and cannot provide profits for the owner in compensation for the risk involved in operating the firm. Eventually the firm goes out of business and the worker is unemployed. In the real world, firms take many precautions to avoid hiring workers at wages above their contribution to output. If a mistake is made in hiring, a worker's poor performance results in dismissal. The main point of the analysis is that competition among firms tends to assure that workers' wages are no higher than the worker's productivity.

The same forces of competition tend also to assure that wage rates are not below the productivity of workers. Consider that a person is hired for $3 per hour but contributes $5 to the net income of the firm. Word will spread about the qualities of this individual. Friends and colleagues talk about them and routine business contacts with competitors result in the exchange of first-hand information. Competitors tend to offer this individual more than $3 in order to obtain for themselves the difference between the wage rate and productivity. The incentives for such hiring by competitors cease to operate only when the wage rate is $5 and equals productivity. Often such individuals with wages below their productivity do not have to change jobs since their own employers tend to raise their wages in order to prevent them from leaving and to avoid the cost of hiring and training a replacement.

The marginal productivity theory of wages does not result in the predicted outcome at all times, not least because it takes time to establish workers' true productivity. There may also be conspiracies among employers to avoid competition for each others' workers. Individual workers may be reluctant to change jobs because of the costs and risks associated with such a move. Unions and government regulations may prevent the operation of market forces. The social value of a worker's output may be larger or smaller than the wage earned because the work or output has effects on the welfare of others which are not reflected in the market transaction. In the technical language of economics such non-market effects are called externalities. They will be discussed further below.

In spite of the many possible ways in which the marginal productivity theory of wages may fail to work, it provides the best, logically consistent and empirically supported explanation of the determination of wage rates of workers in free market economies like Canada. Most important, it provides the basis for the fundamental propositions about the effects of immigration noted above. First, immigrants do not take away jobs from the resident Canadians since their purchases create exactly the need for the jobs which they fill. Second, since immigrant workers earn a pay equal to their contribution to output of the country, when they spend their pay, they leave unaffected the income of the original residents of the country of immigration. Third, the original residents benefit to the extent that they can extend their opportunities for exchange and specialization in production.

Effects on income distribution

The preceding analysis and conclusions assumed implicitly that immigration is small enough so that it does not depress the wage rates earned by the workers in the country of immigration. In the following we discuss the case where the stock of past immigrants is so large that it results in a lowering of wages.

Consider Figure 1 in which the horizontal axis measures the quantity of labour in the country of immigration. The vertical axis measures the marginal product of labour, which is assumed to be equal to the wage rate W. The line AA' reflects the marginal productivity of labour. It slopes downward because, given the stock of capital in the economy and the ubiquitous law of diminishing returns, the marginal product of labour decreases with the addition of workers. The case of increasing returns to scale is discussed below in the context of arguments over optimum population growth rates and levels.

Figure 5-1: Non-Marginal Immigration

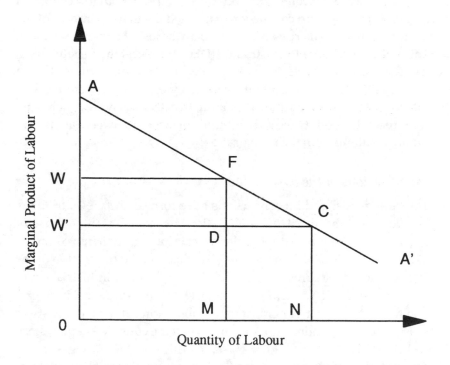

In the initial situation, the country's stock of labour is 0M and the wage rate is 0W. The total output of the economy is represented by the sum of the marginal productivities of additional units of labour and thus consists of the area 0AFM. The area 0WFM is the total income of labour. The remaining output is WAF and goes to the owners of capital. Now consider the addition of MN immigrant labour working with the given stock of capital. The wage rate falls to 0W'. Total output is now 0ACN, of which 0W'CN goes to labour and W'AC goes to the owners of capital.

For the debate over the merit of immigration, perhaps the most important conclusion of the preceding analysis is that the wage rate of the original workers falls and their total income decreases by the area W'WFD. This effect in a sense underlies the opposition of labour to large-scale immigration. This fear focuses on the loss of jobs which is the surrogate for the need to exchange high- for low-paying jobs.

The second conclusion from this analysis is that the output lost by the resident workers accrues to the owners of capital. This explains why business tends to welcome additions to a country's labour force through immigration. The third conclusion of the model is that the income of the owners of capital is increased by more than the loss of income by labour. This net gain is equal to the triangle DFC. It reflects the benefits from increased opportunities to trade created by the immigrants. It also underlies the case for immigration made by economists who focus on the increase in total output. It is clear that this analysis attaches no welfare implications to the redistribution of income between labour and capital resulting from the immigration.

Modifications of the basic model

The basic model and its conclusions have formed the views of many people about the merit of immigration, most importantly those of organized labour which opposes large-scale immigration into countries like Canada. It is based on the empirical fact that the proportion of the total labour force represented by immigrants in many industrial countries is substantial. According to Beaujot (1990) in Canada, net immigration has added about 24 percent to the labour force during the postwar years. Therefore, under the assumption that the country's capital stock had remained the same, Figure 1 is realistic and the immigrants are certain to have lowered wages of resident Canadians below the level they would have been without the immigration.

The preceding model of immigration has been discussed widely in the literature. This discussion focuses on the income redistribution effects and considers these to be equivalent to a social cost, an externality, on the grounds that welfare is lowered through a redistribution of income from labour to capital. Berry and Soligo (1969) is the most widely cited source of the analysis, though as Simon (1989) notes, there have been earlier articles by Yeager (1958) and Borts and Stein (1964), making essentially the same points. Usher (1977) and Simon (1976) used this model to estimate the size of the income redistribution and welfare effects of immigration. In essence, they made a case against immigration by arguing that immigrants "obtain benefits from capital they do not pay for, and thereby either reduce the amount of available capital per native or force natives to pay for capital to equip the immigrants." (Simon (1989), p. 143).[1]

The conclusion that immigration results in an undesirable and welfare-decreasing redistribution of income between capital and labour can be challenged on several grounds. All of these challenges introduce into the analysis essential elements of realism lacking in the basic model. The remainder of this section is devoted to this task.

The role of human capital and ownership

First, there is the question about the magnitude of the cost of the income redistribution effect in a world in which the capital stock of industrial countries consists to a very large extent of human capital in the form of education, skills and health of the labour force. An estimate by Jorgensen and Fraumeni (1987) suggests that in recent years as much as 70 to 80 percent of total US wealth consists of human capital and it is almost certain to be near this level in other developed countries like Canada.

The important role of human capital implies that the income redistribution caused by immigration largely raises the returns to this factor of production. This means in practice that immigration raises primarily the demand for and the wages and productivity of skilled labour rather than the income of owners of physical and financial capital. The wage rate depressing effects of immigration therefore tend to be concentrated on unskilled labour competing directly with immigrants. Since this segment of the Canadian labour force is rather small, the welfare effects are smaller than is suggested by the basic model. Moreover, the higher

---

1   In a personal letter, Simon pointed out that, in contrast with Usher, he does not consider this effect to be quantitatively important.

incomes of skilled workers should also be considered to have a positive effect on welfare in the views of those who deplore shifts of income from labour to capital in the standard model.

The welfare implications of the basic model are also modified by the fact that in modern industrial societies the bulk of physical and financial capital is owned by workers through pension funds and private savings. Increased returns to capital raise the wealth and income of these workers rather than those of a class of wealthy capitalists and rentiers.

In sum, the important role of human capital and the wide holding of capital in modern industrial countries like Canada implies that the redistribution of income from workers to capital raises the relative income of a very large segment of the population. However, the unskilled workers, who are also likely to own little capital through pensions, still suffer a reduction in income. Much public disagreement about the merit of immigration depends on observers' more or less subjective assessment of the welfare implications of this effect on unskilled workers. It should also rest more than it does on the assessment of the validity of the basic model from which the conclusion is derived, for there are two important modifications that need still to be made.

Immigrants bring capital

The second modification of the basic model involves the fact that migrants tend to bring along human knowledge and other capital. This extension of the analysis is shown in Figure 2, which repeats all of the elements of Figure 1 but adds a line labelled CC'. This function represents the marginal productivity of labour under the assumption that the stock of capital has been increased as a result of the immigration. Such capital growth implies that every worker is equipped with larger amounts of capital.

The size of the outward shift in the function shown in Figure 2 is such that the immigration of MN workers has left unchanged the marginal productivity of labour, original inhabitants and new immigrants combined. More precisely, it implies that the immigration induced into Canada the inflow of an amount of capital per worker just equal to the average capital per worker which would have existed without the new labour. Under this special assumption and for reasons obvious from the diagram, the wage rate of resident Canadians is not lowered by the immigration. As a result, there are none of the negative welfare effects due to income redistribution caused by immigration in the basic model.

Figure 5-2: Immigration with Capital

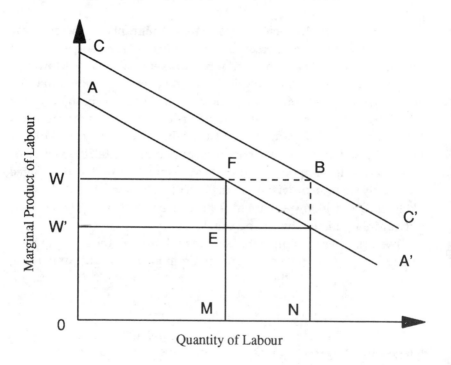

Of course, in the real world the income distribution and welfare effects depend on the actual amounts of capital brought along by the immigrants. In principle, these amounts can still result in lower wages and the implications of the basic model remain, though with less strength. The amounts could also be so great that the marginal productivity of labour is raised and there are gains for resident, unskilled workers.

There are some empirical insights available about the inflow of capital induced by immigration. Grubel and Scott (1977) estimated that the highly skilled immigrants who came to North America during the 1960s and 1970s have tended to bring along human capital just about equal in value to the average quantity of human and physical capital of a single worker in Canada or the United States. The Canadian policy which grants immigration visas to entrepreneurs able to invest at least $500,000 almost certainly raises the overall capital labour ratio in that country.

The traditional, so-called economic immigrants of the postwar years in Canada have tended to have high skill levels and some personal savings, so that the stock of capital per worker probably was lowered very little, if at all. As an example, DeVoretz (1990) has shown that the knowledge capital brought to Canada by Norwegian immigrants has raised greatly the productivity of workers engaged in fish-farming on the B.C. coast, in effect shifting outward the productivity schedule in Figure 2, just like the inflow of financial or human capital. However, for later analysis it is important to note that immigrants under the refugee and family reunion provisions of the Canadian Immigration Act are not likely to bring along amounts of human and other capital to shift outward the function by a substantial amount.

In sum, the extension of the basic model through the incorporation of the inflow of capital along with immigrants affects substantially the conclusions reached in the simpler analytical framework. The immigration of skilled and wealthy workers substantially reduces and can even eliminate the negative effect of immigration on the wages of resident unskilled workers and the distribution of income. Empirical studies suggest that this has been the case during most of Canadian history.

Induced international capital flows

The third and probably the most important modification of the basic model involves the introduction of international capital flows responsive to increased returns to capital. For analytical clarity it is important to distinguish these inflows from those discussed in the preceding section. The former are motivated by market-induced increases in the returns to capital in the country of immigration whereas the latter are tied directly to the immigration itself and would take place even if the rate of return on capital are not raised.

This extension of the model is strangely absent from the literature since in models of international finance and macro-economics, much is made of the near perfect interest elasticity of capital flows and the same assumptions can readily be applied to the present problem. With unchanged technology, constant returns to scale and an infinitely elastic supply, immigration attracts capital in an amount sufficient to keep the rate of return to investment at its initial, world level. In equilibrium after immigration and the induced capital inflows, the wage rate also remains unchanged. In effect, the capital flows endow every migrant with the same amount of capital as is used by the original residents of the country of immigration.

In Figure 2 the equilibrium with perfect international capital markets is shown by the outward shift of the marginal productivity schedule from AA' to CC'. It is due to the immigration of MN workers and leaves unchanged the wage rate at OW. In this situation, the owners of the foreign capital earn income equal to the area ACBF.

The capital inflows may be considered to have some effects on welfare. For one, nationalists in many countries object to the foreign ownership of domestic capital while Grubel (1974) has argued that the taxes paid by the foreign owners of the capital raise income in the host-country. For another, adjustments in the exchange rate may be needed to maintain balance of payments equilibrium. These exchange rate changes can involve a lowering in the terms of trade and thus a reduction in the country's welfare. However, these are separate issues, which cannot be discussed here. The most important result of the model represented by Figure 2 is that the incomes of resident workers are unchanged at 0WFM. At the same time, the immigrant workers earn a wage rate equal to that of the resident workers and a total income represented by the area MFBN.

It should be noted that the traditional model can be extended even further by considering the existence of land as a third factor of production, measured along the horizontal axis of a new diagram. The vertical axis and downward sloping function then represent the marginal productivity of immigrant labour equipped each with a quantity of capital equal to that of the resident population. In this model the immigration and capital inflow results in the traditional triangle gains from free factor movements. Most important, the usual problem of income redistribution between the owners of factors of production also takes place. In this case, the owners of land benefit at the expense of workers and the owners of capital.

In assessing the qualitative importance of this income redistribution effect, the following points are relevant. First, physical land is in finite supply on earth. However, the economically relevant supply of land services is very expandable. The intensity of land use by agriculture, industry and housing can and is being increased through the application of more and better capital. Land use for housing, for example is intensified by increasing density and raising the average height of buildings. In addition, in many countries like Canada land at the margin of economic use is taken into cultivation and converted from agricultural to other uses. Capital required for this process can be supplied through international flows accompanying immigration. The increased supply of land services affected by this process shifts outward the marginal productivity schedule of labour and capital. It thus reduces, probably significantly, the effect of immigration on the relative price of land.

Second, through widespread private ownership of housing, farms, and industrial land through corporations, the benefits of increases in the value of land are distributed widely. Losers in the redistribution of income are those who do not own land, predominantly the poor, the young and the immigrants themselves. Third, ideologically the issue of redistribution of income towards the land-owning classes does not have the same strong political bite as does income redistribution from workers to capitalist. Modern industrial countries like Canada never had an aristocratic, landed class and land ownership has always been the right and successful economic goal of people from all walks of life.

In sum, in a model which reflects the modern world of near perfect international capital movements, the welfare implications of the income redistribution effects of immigration disappear. Each migrant in effect automatically attracts a stock of capital from abroad to maintain the original wage rate and incomes of the resident workers. A further extension of the traditional model considering land as the factor in fixed supply restores the problem of income redistribution effects due to immigration. However, for a number of reasons, these effects may be considered to be less important quantitatively and ideologically than those between capital and labour considered in the traditional model.

The role of government taxation and spending

The preceding analysis abstracted from the existence of government taxation and spending programs. These programs represent one of the most important characteristics of modern industrial societies. They also are at the heart of concerns by many about immigration policies in countries like Canada. In particular, there appears to be a widely held view that immigrants raise the tax burden on residents since they are more likely to be recipients of welfare benefits and to pay on average fewer taxes than the residents of the country of immigration. How valid is this view?

Basic principles

The analysis of the effects of immigration on the tax burden of residents requires a brief discussion of the basic principles of three types of government spending programs. First, there is the provision of services which contain some elements of income redistribution but which for all practical purposes involve the substitution of government for private financing. The most important of these types of programs is education. The average family in a country like Canada pays taxes instead of private tuition to finance the education of the average number of children it has attending public rather than private schools and institutions of higher learning. The young of any generation which receive the free education eventually become tax-payers and repay their debt by financing the educational needs of the next generation. The provision and financing of government pensions involves exactly the same principles.

Seen from this perspective, the effect which immigrants have on the tax burden of residents depends crucially on the question of whether the immigrants are above or below the average of the resident population with respect to the taxes they pay and the number of children that require educational expenditures and the length of time during which they contribute to and receive public pensions.

The second major set of government spending programs involves insurance against major hazards like unemployment, illness and general misfortunes resulting in the need for welfare payments. In the case of these programs the general principles noted above also are applicable. The payment of benefits to the average person must be equal to the taxes paid by the average resident in a country. Therefore, the crucial issue in the case of these programs is also the average propensity of immigrants to pay taxes and draw on the benefits of the programs.

The third set of government spending programs involves the provision of what is known as public goods. These consist of public security generated by the work of the police, armed forces and the judiciary. They also include transportation facilities such as roads, harbours, canals and airports for which no user-fees are charged. The basic principles about average contributions and claims are relevant for this class of government spending as in the preceding cases.

However, there is one important difference. In the case of all of the social insurance and pension programs the cost of providing government services to additional persons is near the average. In the case of public goods, on the other hand, the cost can be very low or zero. The best example of the latter case is defence. It is often cited by those who favour immigration, like Simon (1989). The strength of the security provided by defence forces to the average resident is the same regardless of the number of locally born and immigrants in the country, at least over a wide range of possible population levels.

On the other hand, in the case of practically all other public goods marginal costs are very low or zero only in the short run. In the longer run, capital projects for public goods and educational programs wear out and are expanded in response to crowding or scaled down if there is excess capacity. Since the analysis of the welfare effects of immigration should be concerned with the long run, this latter model appears to be the most relevant and we may conclude that immigrants do not provide residents with a free ride by paying for public services at unchanged levels. In the longer run they claim in services what they pay for.

Empirical evidence

There has traditionally been a strong presumption that immigrants are particularly healthy, able and well-trained individuals. The decision to leave a familiar society and face the hardships of living in a new country was not for the physically and mentally weak. Surviving the travels has tended to weed out the infirm. In addition, the immigration policies of most industrial countries during the late 19th and early 20th century reinforced these natural tendencies by refusing immigration permits to the unskilled, sick and disabled. Individuals with these natural and government-reinforced characteristics would be expected to do better economically than the average in the country of immigration. They also would be expected to be in less need of the benefits of social insurance programs.

These presumptions are reflected in almost all historic studies of the economic characteristics of immigrants to North America and Australia. There are several contributions to this volume which discuss this evidence. Nevertheless, it is worth noting here that Simon (1989) provides a summary of several studies in this tradition. Akbari (1989) has found the same for Canada in recent years. Immigrants have had lower than average incomes for short periods after arrival in the new country. Thereafter, their incomes have tended to exceed those of the resident populations, making for above-average life-time incomes. Taxes tend to be proportional to income and therefore these immigrants have tended to make above average contributions to government revenues.

The same studies also note that demands on social insurance programs by these immigrants have historically been lower than average. This is due partly to the fact that earnings and wealth of the immigrants have been above average. It is also explained to some extent by the fact that most of the immigrants in these historic studies have come from societies where traditional values of self-reliance were strong and social stigma were attached to drawing on public assistance.

The preceding empirical findings may not hold true in the future. In recent years, the immigration policies of countries like the United States, Canada and Australia have changed dramatically. Historically, the policies were designed to attract skilled labour from countries of Western Europe with relatively homogeneous cultural and linguistic characteristics contributing to their successful economic performance as found in the studies noted above.

In recent years, a complex set of political pressures have resulted in the adoption of new immigration policies alleged to be non-discriminatory and humanitarian. As a result of these policies to be discussed further below, since the middle 1970s about 75 percent of all Canadian immigrants have been refugees from persecution or close members of a family already in Canada. The bulk of these immigrants have come from countries with cultural and linguistic characteristics different from those of Canada. The economic performance of these immigrants can be studied in depth and with sufficiently large numbers only gradually, as the relevant statistical base is generated. Preliminary information collected by DeVoretz and Fagwers (1990) suggests that immigrants of the new type may have less than average incomes and have a greater propensity to draw on government programs than do the immigrants admitted under the traditional programs.

Traditional externalities

Costs imposed on residents by immigrants which are not reflected in measured market incomes, so-called externalities, underlie many of the public discussions over immigration policies. There are economic externalities like the effects of too many people on pollution and congestion and the quality of life generally. But there are also arguments about the benefits which are generated by large populations. In recent years increasing importance has been attached to what might be called social externalities. These are due to frictions among groups of residents and immigrants over discrimination and rights in housing, jobs and government grants. They also concern changes in a country's social and cultural characteristics.

These externalities will be analyzed in some detail in the remainder of this study. The current section deals with the mostly economic externalities related to population growth and levels. The following section takes on the difficult and emotionally laden subject of the social externalities.

Economic externalities—optimum population growth rates

Immigration affects the growth rate and ultimately the steady state level of the population in the country receiving the immigrants. There are several distinct types of externalities associated with different population growth rates. The first concerns the cost of government programs providing pensions, education and health care. Low or negative growth results in what is known as a costly dependency ratio. This ratio reflects the number of unproductive young and retired people who must be supplied from the output of those of working age through high levels of taxation. This taxation creates disincentives for work and investment. Immigration can be used to reduce the dependency ratio.

The second type of externalities associated with population growth involves economic adjustment costs. The nature of these costs is familiar to many from the experience of firms and similar organizations. When growth takes place, outstanding individuals can be promoted more quickly and without the need for the demotion of others. More generally, economic growth results in the more rapid introduction of new and technologically advanced machinery. As a result the average age of the economy's capital stock is lowered and its productivity is raised. Immigration can be used to increase economic growth and the opportunity to reap positive externalities of this type of externality.

The preceding suggests that positive is better than negative population growth. But what positive growth rate provides the optimum amount of benefits? We know that there is some high rate at which external diseconomies occur as a result of increasing costs from the rapid construction of social overhead facilities and private investments. In the absence of any evidence on this subject, most analysts rely on the judgement of historians who found that annual population growth rates of around one to two percent appear to have been associated with rapid economic growth without stress in Canada.

In many industrial countries, including Canada, the reproduction rate of residents is low and implies a decline in population growth during the early part of the 21st century. One estimate published in Government of Canada, Health and Welfare Canada (1989), shows that at the fertility rate of 1.7 existing in Canada during the 1980s, the population will reach a peak of 28 million in 2011. Thereafter, a slow decline sets in. After 100 years it leaves Canada with a population of about 19 million. Eventually, the population approaches zero.

The same official publication discusses the different development of the population if the fertility rate is assumed to remain the same but there is an annual net immigration of 80,000 into Canada. Under these assumptions immigration at this level does not prevent the decline of the population in the longer run since the immigrants are assumed to have the same fertility rates as Canadians have currently once they are in the country. However, the rate of decline is smaller than in the case without immigration and a stable population of 18 million is reached in the long run.

Population growth projections are hazardous since little is known about the determination of fertility rates. It may well be that Canadians would begin to have more children once population begins to decrease and the trends in the above projections will be reversed. The point of the projections is not to predict the future but to analyze the implications of recent trends for future population levels with and without immigration.

On this point the analysis is clear and persuasive. Its implications are also well understood by the public. This knowledge may well explain why in opinion surveys the aging population is considered to be the third most important factor, after unemployment and skill shortages, which should be used in setting the future level of immigration (see Reid (1989, page 10)).

Economic externalities—optimum population stock

One important problem feeding back on the choice of an optimum rate of population growth is the fact that there is also an optimum stock of population. We have seen above that with immigration at 80,000 per year the population of Canada is projected to settle at a long run level of 18 million. Other rates of immigration will result in different levels.

Analytically, the optimum stock of population is defined to exist when welfare of the population is maximized. Unfortunately, students of the question of optimum population come up with widely differing views. There is little doubt that in Canada a population consisting of a single family alone would have a low standard of living since it would have to produce all of its goods without the benefit of specialized production and trading with other Canadians and the rest of the world.

Higher levels of population bring economies of scale in production and the use of social overhead facilities. They also bring economies of agglomeration which make cities such great centres of science, technology and culture. The more people, the more geniuses there are bringing extraordinary benefits to society through their activities. On the other hand, high population levels also bring costs associated with congestion, pollution and diminished quality of life.

Because of the existence of these positive and negative influences, most people believe that there is a level of population at which additions bring gains in terms of higher productivity equal to the losses due to higher cost of dealing with crowding. At such a stock of population, productivity and living standards would be highest and population would be at its optimum level.

The widely cited and influential study by Simon (1989) did not address the question of optimum population in the way it was posed in the preceding paragraph. However, one can interpret his analysis as suggesting that he departs radically from the received wisdom and suggests that there is no such optimum level for any one country and for mankind as a whole. Or at least he may be interpreted as saying that the optimum involves such a large population that concern with it is irrelevant in the present and foreseeable future.

Simon's view is based on his interpretation of the history of population growth and the scientific and economic developments accompanying it. He believes that the growth of science and productivity are endogenous to the level of population. The more people there are the more scientific and technological knowledge is produced to overcome the problems of crowding and the scarcity of resources. This knowledge has historically permitted the industrial world to enjoy ever higher living standards. It has also resulted in great cultural achievements and higher quality of life.

Simon provides impressive evidence on the fact that science and technology have raised living standards through lowering the cost of almost all goods and services in terms of hours of labour required to acquire them, be it copper, energy or medical care of constant quality. Using life expectancy and general health as proxies for quality of life, improvements have gone along with greater population in all industrial countries.

In Simon's view, the current popular concern over pollution, global warming and other man-made catastrophes, is misplaced since progress has been made and will continue to be made to deal with these problems. In many ways, the environment in most industrial countries is cleaner and safer than it has been since the onset of the industrial revolution. At the historic and expected rate of growth of scientific knowledge it is therefore almost certain that what may be conceived to be insuperable problems of crowding, pollution and lack of natural resources will be resolved in, as yet, unknown ways by the advances in science and technology produced in growing quantity by the large populations.

Simon's conclusions may be too optimistic and are not shared by all analysts. It is conceivable that at some future point mankind will run into diminishing returns to the production of knowledge or even know everything there is to know. However, at the end of the 20th century and in the foreseeable future the prospect of this happening is not very high.

For countries like Canada the problems associated with reaching the optimum stock of population appear to be at least several generations away. This conclusion is explained by the low fertility and historic rates of immigration discussed above. Therefore the potential problems due to going beyond optimum population levels should carry very little weight in decisions about the future levels of immigration. Instead, the spectre of absolute declines in population should be one of the dominant considerations.

Social externalities

Social externalities are analogous to economic externalities. They represent effects on the welfare of some created by the actions of others which are not reflected in market prices. In the case of immigration, positive social externalities accrue to resident populations as a result of the social, intellectual and cultural enrichment of life brought about by the activities of immigrants from different cultures. The most outstanding examples are the benefits of variety of food, artistic endeavours and intellectual stimuli which immigrants from non-European cultures have brought to Canada.

Negative social externalities arise when the resident population of a country is forced by immigrants to change its culture, value systems and social structures to accommodate the new citizens. These changes are considered to be a cost. The nature and existence of the relationship between Canadian immigration and the need to make adjustments is explained by one of the contributors to this volume, Derrick Thomas (1990):

> The new ethnic and cultural composition of immigrations clearly has implications both for the integration of newcomers and for the Canadian identity. Third World immigrants diverge more radically from Canadian norms in terms of their economic, social and cultural experience than do immigrants from the traditional source areas. Many Third World immigrants also differ racially from the host population, making them visibly and permanently different from the existing majority in at least this respect. *Clearly, Canada's image of itself will change. Its culture and perhaps its social structures will also be transformed. The challenge will be to ensure that these changes occur smoothly and in a way that involves everyone—immigrants and Canadian-born"* [emphasis added].

The discussion of social externalities of immigration is a highly emotional undertaking. Nevertheless, the subject is important to many Canadians, as is revealed by casual study of the media. Certainly, any study analysing the welfare effects of immigration would be incomplete if it did not raise the issue, present some facts and summarize the different points of view.

Some facts

The type and potential magnitude of both positive and negative social externalities in Canada can readily be discerned from Figure 3.[2] Data on

---

2   The immigrants from the region "Other" have mainly been from Australia, New Zealand and the United States. Immigration from the latter country was particularly large during the war in Vietnam, when it made up a significant proportion of the total.

the regional origin of Canadian immigrants are available in published form only for the years shown at the bottom of the figure. The numbers for 1956 to 1961 and 1968 to 1974 are averages. The remaining figures represent linear interpolations between the years for which the data are available. Important for the present purposes of analysis are major trends rather than precise annual figures, so that the inaccuracies of the graphic are not important.

Figure 5-3: Origin of Canadian Immigrants and Total Number of Immigrants

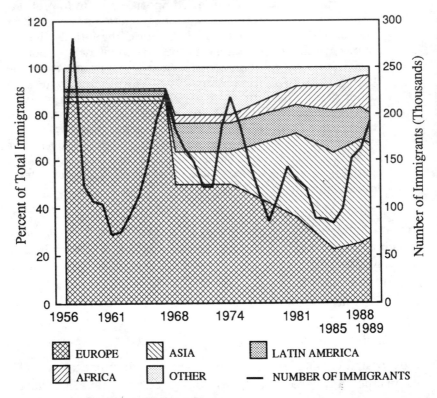

Source: Marr (1976); SOPEMI 1988 Canada
Special Tabulation for 1989; Canada Yearbook.

It may also be worth noting that the pattern of the late 1950s roughly also characterized the preceding centuries of Canadian immigration. It shows that the total annual number of immigrants has fluctuated widely between 1956 and 1989, with only a slight downward trend. Most important for the present purposes of analysis, the share of immigrants coming from different regions of the world has shown a strong and clear trend during this period.

As can be seen from the figure, during the years 1965 to 1961 about 95 percent of all Canadian immigrants originated in Europe and the United States (shown in the category "Other"). During the same period, the rest of the immigrants came from Asia, Latin America and Africa, the officially called "non-traditional" sources. The share of immigrants from these non-traditional regions has been rising since the early 1960s and reached a peak of 70 percent in 1985. The share remained at this level during the rest of the decade when a slight increase in immigration from Europe was matched by an equal sized decrease of immigration from "Other" countries.

It is important to put into perspective the influence which the changed composition of immigration flows tends to have on the characteristics of the Canadian stock of population. Let us assume that future gross immigration levels will be 250,000 per year, as was announced as the official policy in 1990, that the proportion of non-traditional immigrants remains at the recent level of about 70 percent and that immigrants once in Canada will have the same fertility rate as the rest of the population. Under these conditions, Canadians with a non-traditional family background by the year 2020 will represent only about 8 to 10 percent of the total. This result is due to the fact that annual net immigration of 200,000 represents only .5 percent of the total population. Of course, to the extent that immigrants from non-traditional origins tend to concentrate regionally, they can represent large proportions of certain areas or population centres even if they make up only a relatively small share of the total.

Problems of measuring social externalities

Unfortunately, it is impossible to use scientific methods to establish the magnitude of likely positive and negative externalities. In chapter 10, Thomas reviews the evidence which sociologists have generated. In general, such sociological studies show that immigrants in Canada have tended to integrate readily and that therefore negative and positive externalities are small and short-lived. However, there is some question about the validity of generalizing about such adjustment because in the past the ethnic minorities were very small in number whereas in the future they will be large enough to afford the construction of their own schools, places of worship and recreation and to reach a critical mass needed for the maintenance of their original culture and social value-systems.

Moreover, uncomfortable questions about the general validity of sociological findings concerning the history of immigrants' integration tendencies are raised by the persistence of problems in relations between the English-speaking majority and the natives and French-speaking minorities in Canada. In the United States, India, Lebanon, Ireland, Israel and many countries of Western Europe social, economic and religious frictions between ethnically different segments of the population continue in spite of great efforts by governments over many years to eliminate them. What have been the causes of the difficulties encountered in these countries and to what extent are they relevant to Canada in the future when there will be large numbers of non-traditional immigrants?

At any rate, Thomas notes that the analysis of the social effects of immigration lends itself to a pessimistic interpretation. This view is held by a vocal group of Canadians[3] who are urging the government of Canada to change the immigration policy such that the proportion of migrants from non-traditional sources is reduced to the levels prevailing until the 1970s and that the prominence of immigrants from Europe be restored.[4]

Persons who view the external costs of immigrants from non-traditional sources to be very large also argue rationally that if sufficient numbers of immigrants from traditional sources cannot be found, it is

---

3   See for example Collins (1979) (1987) ████████████████

4   No one knows what number of Europeans, including those from Eastern Europe, are potential immigrants into Canada. Before the opening of the Iron Curtain Collins (1979) argued that Australia faced an excess supply of immigrants from Europe, many of which would have applied for immigration to Canada.

better to reduce the overall level of immigration and accept whatever economic costs in terms of suboptimal population growth and levels this may imply. Thomas also describes the optimistic view of the social cost and benefits of having large numbers of immigrants from non-traditional sources. This view is articulated consistently by the politicians in charge of the Department of Immigration of the government of Canada. It is backed by many official departmental publications, most of which are authored by outside consultants. Most important, it is reflected in the current policies of the government of Canada.

Politics and the risks of different policies

In free countries like Canada, the government uses the political process to resolve conflicts between the views of different population groups about the desirability of certain policies. In the ideal model of democracy, therefore policies of the government reflect "the will of the people." Accordingly, the existence of the present policies favouring non-traditional immigrants implies that optimists about the social costs of such immigration represent the majority of Canadian voters.

However, two points need to be made in modification of this conclusion. First, the importance of special interest group politics has grown in recent decades with the lowering of the cost of communication and travel. Such special interest groups lobby politicians for the enactment of policies favourable to their cause in return for financial contributions and the assured delivery of votes in districts where they represent the margin of victory. At the same time, the rest of the voters are not influenced by the special interest group legislation since the costs are diffuse and often not known. According to the interest group model of government, existing policies do not necessarily reflect the will of the people as they do in the traditional models of democracy.[5] Immigrants in Canada are known to have organized effectively to lobby for the

---

5   Many scholarly works support the theory and empirical evidence on the working of special interest groups and the effect they have on economic and social policies. One of the best known of these is by Olson (1965). Brimelow (1986) discusses the relevance of the model to Canadian immigration policies developed during the 1970s.

immigration policies now in effect and some legitimate questions have been raised about the extent to which they reflect the will of the majority of Canadians.

Second, the attitudes of voters are shaped by information about the likely costs and benefits of policies. The information about the positive net benefits of non-traditional immigration in Canada are based on sociological studies undertaken when levels were low. This fact gives rise to the problem that if net benefits turn out to be negative after non-traditional immigration has continued for some time, Canadian society has to pay these costs for a long time in the future. The residents causing these difficulties cannot be expelled and reversal of the policies brings benefits only after a long lag, even if the political process makes it possible to have such a reversal. Policies which maintain the traditional composition of immigrants, on the other hand, avoid the risk of having to face the longer run costs. From these considerations follows the need to discuss whether the social benefits of non-traditional immigration exceed those of traditional immigration by a sufficient amount to outweigh the risk of the high costs associated with the former policies.

Summary and conclusions

The analysis of this study considered the economic and social effects of Canadian immigration. It showed that the economic effects of immigration on the welfare of resident Canadians tend to be positive. In Canada's market economy immigrants may be expected to earn their marginal product and thus contribute as much to output as they claim through their earnings. They do not cause unemployment and affect welfare positively as they increase the opportunity for economic exchange. The effects of immigration on income distribution considered important in the past are minimal in a world of integrated capital markets. The redistribution of income to the owners of land is likely to be small because of the ease with which the economic services of land can be augmented.

Government programs of taxation and spending can result in the redistribution of income from residents to immigrants, but only to the extent that immigrants have above average claims on services and pay below average taxes. Under the system of selecting immigrants according to their human capital and the ease of integration into the social environment, in Canada costs for the resident population did not arise. Under the new system of permitting immigration on humanitarian grounds and in disregard of likely ease of social integration, such costs are more likely to develop.

Economic externalities which are created by immigration tend to be related to optimum population levels and growth rates. While the positive and negative influences of these levels and growth rates can readily be described, they are impossible to measure and are valued differently by different individuals. Given recent trends in the fertility of resident Canadians, population growth will become negative in a few decades. Immigration levels can be chosen to obtain any desired rate of population growth and stocks. Current fertility rates and the actual level of the population suggest that by most common-sense criteria, the welfare of Canadians will be higher if immigration levels are chosen such as to assure a longer run population growth rate of around two percent per year.

Among the most important welfare effects of immigration are social externalities. These externalities manifest themselves through the possible creation and persistence of distinct groups of ethnic, racial and cultural minorities in Canada, bringing benefits as well as costs to society. Some Canadians believe that current policies favouring the immigration of non-traditional immigrants will result in positive net social benefits, others believe that these policies will create large net social costs. No universally accepted methods exist for deciding the correctness of the views of optimists and pessimists. Nevertheless, the issue is important to many Canadians and deserves further study.

One approach to this study considers the wisdom of parliament and the people who elect it to make immigration policies. A widely held view is that government policies in a democracy reflect the views of the people. Therefore, the existing policies favouring non-traditional immigrants signal that the majority of Canadians see the net benefits of such immigration to be positive. However, the special interest group model of policy making in modern democracies and the asymmetric risks of the two types of immigration policies suggest that the naive model of democratic policy formation is imperfect. At the very least, these arguments suggest that the problems of social externalities deserves further study and public discussion.

References

Akbari, Ather S. (1989) "The Benefits of Immigrants to Canada: Evidence on Tax and Public Services," *Canadian Public Policy*, XV, 4, 424-35.

Beaujot, Roderic (1990), "Immigration and the Population of Canada," *Research Abstract*, Ottawa: Employment and Immigration Canada, March 1989.

Berry, Ronald R. and Ronald Soligo (1969), "Some Welfare Aspects of International Migration," *Journal of Political Economy*, September/October.

Borts, George H. and Jerome Stein (1966), *Economics in a Free Market*, New York: Columbia University Press.

Brimelow, Peter (1986), *The Patriot Game*, Toronto, Ontario: Key Porter Books.

Collins, Doug (1979), *Immigration: The Destruction of English Canada*, Richmond Hill, Ont.: BMG Publishing Company.

_____ (1987), *Immigration: Parliament vs. the People*, Toronto: Citizens for Foreign Aid Reform.

Campbell, Charles M. (1989), *A Time Bomb Ticking: Canadian Immigration in Crisis*, Toronto: The Mackenzie Institute.

DeVoretz, Don and S. Fagwers (1990), "Some Evidence on Immigrant Quality Decline: Foreign born versus Resident-Born Earnings Functions 1971-1986," presented at the Canadian Economics Association meetings, Victoria, B.C.

Government of Canada: Health and Welfare Canada (1989), *Charting Canada's Future: A Report of the Demographic Review*.

Grubel, Herbert G. (1974), "Taxation and the Rates of Return from some US Asset Holdings Abroad," *Journal of Political Economy*, May/June.

Grubel, Herbert and Anthony D. Scott (1977), *Brain Drain: Determinants, Measurement and Welfare Effects*, Waterloo, Ont.: Wilfred Laurier University Press.

Jorgenson, Dale and Barbara Fraumeni, "The Accumulation of Human and Non-Human Capital 1948-84," Cambridge: Harvard University, Discussion Paper.

Marr, W.L. (1975) "Canadian Immigration Policies, Since 1962," *Canadian Public Policy*, 196-203.

Olson, Mancur (1965), *The Logic of Collective Action*, Cambridge, Mass.: Harvard University Press.

Reid, Angus (1989), *Immigration to Canada: Aspects of Public Opinion*, Report Prepared for Employment and Immigration Canada by Angus Reid Group Inc., October.

Simon, Julian (1976), "The Economic Effect of Russian Immigrants on the Veteran Israeli Population: A Cost-Benefit Analysis," *Economic Quarterly*, August (in Hebrew).

_____ (1989), *The Economic Consequences of Immigration*, Cambridge, Mass: Basil Blackwell in association with The Cato Institute.

Organization for Economic Co-operation and Development (1990), *SOPEMI 1989*, Paris: OECD.

Thomas, Derrick and Strategic Planning & Research, Immigration Policy (1990), *Immigrant Integration and the Canadian Identity*, Ottawa: Employment and Immigration Canada, Immigration, November.

Usher, Dan (1977), "Public Property and Effects of Migration upon Other Residents of the Migrants' Countries of Origin and Destination," *Journal of Political Economy*, 85, 5.

Yeager, Leland B. (1958), "Immigration, Trade and Factor-Price Equalization." *Current Economic Content*, August.

Chapter 6

The Economic Effects of Immigration: Theory and Evidence

Julian L. Simon

Introduction

IN CHAPTER 5, HERBERT GRUBEL DOES A fine job of setting forth the standard theoretical considerations pertaining to the economic consequences of immigration. I associate myself with his general approach and conclusions (though my agreement does not necessarily extend to his non-economic considerations). My own statement of these theoretical issues, at greater length and in more detail than most readers will desire unless they are serious students of the subject, may be found in my recent book (1989), from which this article is largely drawn.

Because Professor Grubel states the main theoretical issues so well, Section II shall simply elucidate and reinforce them by presenting much the same ideas in very different form: as what economists call a "parable."

There are some additional theoretical matters that ought to be considered here also. In particular, one new theoretical matter seems paradoxical at first: The theory of migration has nothing whatsoever to do with the theory of trade. Section III briefly sets forth these theoretical matters.

Professor Grubel correctly asserts that whether the externality effects of immigrants are on balance positive or negative is an empirical question. The most important externalities concern welfare services received and taxes paid. And there are excellent data for both Canada and the United States which show—almost identically—that on balance these effects are positive. I shall discuss these data briefly in Section IV.

Section V describes an overall assessment of the effects of immigrants upon the incomes of natives. And Section VI discusses the most powerful traditional charge against immigrants, that they displace natives from jobs.

Though many of the data available are for the United States rather than Canada, the results are equally applicable to both countries. We can rely on this because of the astonishing similarity for all available comparable data series and analyses for Canada, Australia, and the United States (See Simon, 1989, Chapters 3 and 4).

The parable

Consider an idealized farming "nation" composed of a hundred identical farmers, each with the same amount and quality of farmland, each working the same hours and producing the same output. Along comes a foreigner who offers himself as a hired laborer to the first farmer he meets. (For now this is entirely a male community, with no other family members.) The "rational" farmer is willing to hire the foreigner as long as the wage will be even a bit less than the value of the increase in output that the foreigner produces. A shrewd bargainer, however, the farmer offers the foreigner a wage considerably less than the amount the foreigner asks. Not less shrewd, the foreigner proceeds to offer his labor to all hundred farmers, going back and forth until he can strike the best deal. He eventually settles for just a tiny bit less than the value of the additional output if the "market" works well. This is his "market wage."

Let us assess the economic impact of the entry of this immigrant into the community. The farmer who employs the immigrant increases his own income by just a tiny bit, but that tiny bit is preferable to no increase at all. The "nation's" citizens as a whole are better off, because 99 farmers have their incomes unchanged whereas one has his income increased slightly, and hence the average income goes up just a tiny bit. If we include the immigrant "laborer" in the calculation, computed mean income goes down, however, because the immigrant laborer's income is lower than the average farmer's; in the very short run, and assuming the number of hours worked per person stays the same, the incremental output of the second person working on the farm is not as great as that of the first worker—the famous "law" of diminishing returns. But that decline in the average masks the fact that each person's income has gone up—including the immigrant's, because we assume he would not immigrate here unless his income is higher than in the country which he left.

A word about the impact during the first moments that the immigrant is in the hypothetical society: Any simpleton can—and a great many do—show conclusively that a new immigrant or a new baby has an immediate negative effect upon the country's standard of living. Before the new person begins to work, s/he reduces per person income purely by arithmetic. (To paraphrase Peter Bauer, when a new calf arrives, per person income automatically increases, but when a new person [baby or immigrant] arrives, per person income automatically decreases.) Of course the changed statistical measure does not necessarily hurt the rest of us, but it surely sounds bad. And if the new entrant gets any help from the society before he or she goes to work, then there is a real negative effect upon the rest of us, as well as the apparent effect.

Now let us change the story by moving ahead to a moment after considerable immigration has occurred, when there is one immigrant laborer working for wages on each farm, a hundred in all. The wage of each will be just about the same as the market wage that the first immigrant got. And let's say that each immigrant now has been made a new citizen. But the new citizens have not yet had time to buy any land, so the old citizens still have higher incomes than the new citizens.

Now along comes still another foreigner looking for a job. He goes back and forth until he strikes the best deal, which will be for a wage just a tiny bit below the value of the increase in output his employer will obtain from the third person working on his farm. And then another 99 more foreigners follow, so on each farm we now have one native-citizen owner (who also does farm work), one naturalized-citizen laborer, and one new-immigrant laborer.

But now something else happens, too: The wage of the naturalized-citizen laborers falls to the level of the new-immigrant laborers. The reason is that all 200 of the landless laborers are now competing for the same jobs, and no owner needs to pay more than the incremental output of a second laborer on the farm in order to hire two laborers, because the amount of work done by all the laborers is the same. And the farm owners are now making a bigger profit than before, because they only have to pay the "first" laborer the value of the "second" laborer's output; the fact that some laborers are citizens while others are not does not affect their wages.

The overall results of the second wave of immigration may now be seen as follows: The native owners are better off than before. The new-immigrant laborers are better off than in the country from which they came. The naturalized-citizen laborers are better off than in the old country, but worse off than before the second wave of new-immigrant laborers came. And therefore, the naturalized-citizen laborers will (in advance of the event) surely make a political protest against letting the second wave enter the country, although some of them will, for sentimental reasons, wish to have more of their compatriots enter the country even though the wage does fall.

Let us again change the facts. Assume that the one hundred naturalized-citizen laborers have been in the country long enough to buy half-ownership in each farm from the native-citizen original owners. The total yearly proceeds from each farm are now split between the native citizen and the naturalized citizen. Along come the hundred new-immigrant laborers. Assume that all three workers on each farm receive as wages only the value of the incremental output of the third worker. The native-citizen and naturalized-citizen owners are no worse off, however, because the drop in their "wages" is equal to their gain in "returns to capital." If this is so, the naturalized citizens are not injured by the entry of the second wave of immigrant laborers.

It seems, then, that whether the existing stock of workers is or is not injured by the new wave of immigrants depends upon who gets the returns to the capital with which the workers work. And here we may refer back to the realistic world of Canada and the United States in 1991. The "workers"—that is, people who earn wages and salaries—own a very sizable portion of the productive capital of the country, to a considerable extent through pension funds. This means that the situation is not simply one in which "labor" loses and "owners" gain by immigration. The extent to which a working person gains or loses by immigration depends upon the actual facts about the extent to which that working person has an ownership stake in the capital of the country.

Now let us complicate the situation just one bit more before we leave this analysis of the effect of immigrants through the labor market. There is also some additional benefit to natives from immigrants because the immigrants do not arrive in such neat one-to-a-farm waves as assumed above. If a given farm successively employs two new immigrant laborers at a wage equal to the incremental output of the "last" of the two (the "marginal" worker), then the citizen owner(s) of the land will obtain the difference between the wage of the next-to-last immigrant—which now equals the incremental output of the last immigrant—and the incremental output of the next-to-last immigrant. But this quantity is not of much practical importance and therefore can be disregarded, though it is very neat theoretically.

The main conclusion to be drawn from the model so far is that in the short run, additional immigrant workers do not damage the welfare of citizens taken altogether by diluting the capital stock, but may damage "workers" if as a class the workers do not get most of the returns to capital. This effect is transitory, however, and in the long run it is likely to be dominated by many other dynamic effects—especially the effect of immigration upon productivity, and the effect through welfare transfer from and to, and tax transfers to, the public coffers—even for classes of people who might be hit hard by this particular effect.

This model (as is the propensity of such models) has operated frictionlessly and instantly. But real markets do not operate so perfectly, and this leads us to the question of unemployment. Instead of assuming all the original hundred citizens to be farmers producing the same output, let us assume that they constitute a self-contained community producing a variety of goods and services which they then consume—grain, laundry service, transportation, religious services, meat, and the like. Each business is composed of one citizen owner and one citizen laborer.

Along comes an immigrant looking for a job. But there are no laborer's jobs open. So the immigrant goes to one of the farmers whose barn obviously needs painting, and says, "I'll paint your barn for a cheap price, and do a good job." The farmer thinks about it for a few minutes, and decides that at the price the immigrant has set, the farmer's own time is more valuable—either for other work or for recreation—than that amount, and he therefore tells the immigrant to go ahead. So unemployment is not increased by the immigrant's arrival.

The immigrant spends her resulting income for goods and services in the community, while the farmer spends an equal amount less because he has that much less to spend. So total income to businesses remains the same, though some businesses will lose as others gain if the immigrant buys different goods than would the farmer. If the farmer uses the time to paint a picture instead of the barn, average income of the community (including the new immigrant who is now included in the calculation) goes down because total income remains the same, and now is divided among more persons. But everyone is better off, or at least no worse off, than before the immigrant came. (The reader will note that the pictures the farmer paints are not counted as income even though the farmer is getting benefit from them.) If instead of painting the barn the farmer uses the time to paint pictures that he sells to others, total income goes up, and average income might either go down or go up.

But perhaps one of the citizen laborers is out sick, or meditating in the woods on unpaid leave, at the moment the immigrant arrives. The immigrant latches onto that citizen's job. When the previous occupant of the job gets back, he cannot immediately find another job and classifies himself as unemployed. Another possibility: The immigrant arrives, goes to the nearest business, and says: "I'll work harder and cheaper than the laborer you now employ." And the owner promptly fires the citizen and hires the immigrant. These are the cases that the labor unions worry about most, and which constitute the strongest political objection to immigration now and always. And it undoubtedly does happen this way sometimes.

Another possibility: After she finishes the farmer's barn, the immigrant goes around to all the other farmers, points to the fine job that she did, and makes deals to paint four other buildings. She realizes that she cannot do all the work by herself, so she hires three footloose citizens, and brings over her cousin from the old country as well. Presto, a new business, and increased total employment; unemployment might then be either less or more than before.

As noted above, some "displacement" of particular natives from jobs by immigrants takes place, just as some new creation of jobs by immigrants and on account of immigrants, surely takes place. But the job-creating forces must typically operate at least as strongly as displacement, because on balance immigrants do not cause much if any native unemployment. (See below.) The newest immigrants themselves do at first suffer from relatively high unemployment when times are bad, but that suffering by immigrants provides something of a buffer for natives.

Now let us add to the original farmer model that each farmer has a wife, two aged retired parents, and two dependent children. Each farm family pays (say) 20 percent of its income in taxes to provide stipends for the aged and schooling for the children, along with standard family welfare services. The immigrant laborers come without aged parents, though wives, single women, and some children do come with them. The immigrants also pay 20 percent of their income as taxes at first. But it is soon found that there is a surplus in the public coffers because most of the taxes go to support aged people, the cohort of which remained the same while tax collections rose as the immigrants arrived. So the tax rate to natives (and to immigrants) would thereby be reduced below 20 percent. Hence the tax-and-transfer mechanism results in benefits to natives because, as the data show (and contrary to popular belief) immigrants use less rather than more of the standard family welfare services than do native families.

Some other theoretical matters

Natural resources

What about the supply of farmland and other natural resources as immigrants swell the population? Will that phenomenon not eventually cause income to be lower than otherwise? The answer is clear cut, though difficult to explain. The short answer is that the element of land and other capital in the production process benefits the owners of capital when more immigrants arrive because the value of their capital goes up. And natives benefit even if they sell some of their land to new immigrants because the sale price is higher than it would otherwise be; that higher sale price reflects the expected higher demand for food and fiber in future years due to the presence of the immigrants. The land sales give the natives wealth in other forms from which they benefit later on. And the new immigrants who buy a share of the land are better off than in the old country.

But will not average income fall over the years due to the restricted supply of land and other capital, if immigrants swell the population larger than it would otherwise be? This is the heart of the Malthusian nightmare. And the nightmare will become reality, at least in part, if the society does not quickly expand the supply of capital. But countries do expand the capital base, as even did China throughout much of her millenia (Perkins, 1969; Jones, 1981).

Throughout earlier history, communities have responded to tightness of the land supply mainly by reclaiming wasteland through a variety of techniques (Simon, 1977; 1981). And the new land has not been poorer land than the old land, on balance, just as Ontario after it had been developed was not poorer land than was Quebec. Of course there were heavy costs to be paid in building the land. But the "new people" paid the price while their descendants reaped the benefits, and eventually all persons were better off because the price was paid by the early comers and a bigger and better supply of capital was built. This resource-creating mechanism is a central element in the history of humanity. It is part of the story of problems being caused by additional demand flowing from more people and higher income, and the solutions leaving us better off than if the problems had not arisen.

The story is different—and less problematic—in modern economies such as Canada and the United States, where land and other natural resources are relatively unimportant. (Consider the small share of agriculture and other natural resources in total national output, even though the U.S. is the greatest agricultural producer in the world; the incredulous may consult Simon, 1981, Chapter 6; or Simon, 1988.) Even more astonishing to some—but an indubitable economic fact—natural resources are increasingly less important with each passing decade. The crucial capital nowadays is "human capital"—people's skills plus the stock of knowledge—and migrants bring this human capital with them. Furthermore, nowadays much physical capital is created sufficiently quickly so that, even considering only the effect through the supply of such capital (apart from the beneficial aspects of immigration), an immigrant with average skills and earnings probably has a negative (partial) effect on natives' computed per-person income for only a short time. Additionally, the longer-run dynamics of the creation and replacement of physical capital are such that the whole community is eventually caused to be better off by additional capital being needed, and the newest existing capital therefore being bought and inventions made; this process causes the stock of capital to be more up-to-date than it otherwise would be.

In short, whatever the relevance of the Malthusian production-capital nightmare in earlier times and other places, in a modern country the concern lacks reality and should not disquiet natives. Human capital is the main element of production in a modern country, and the supply of physical capital is normally expanded relatively easily and quickly.

The availability of wilderness is not essentially different than the supply of productive capital and natural resources; in the short run more immigrants mean more people visiting existing parks, but in the long run more people create more wilderness areas and greater access to them, as the history of the U.S. throughout this century illustrates.

Are there increasing problems as the flow of immigrants increases?

If some immigrants are, on balance, a benefit, then why should not even more immigrants—or a completely open door —be even better? There are two possible negative effects of immigrants that could come more strongly into play with much higher immigrant levels: congestion, and negative educational externalities.

It is reasonable that in Canada ten million or even one million immigrants in a year would on average be absorbed more slowly than 200,000 or 100,000 immigrants, simply because at any given moment there are a fixed number of potential employers looking for workers, a fixed number of empty stores looking for new shopowners, and a fixed amount of housing. During the period that capital and organizational structure are relatively fixed—that is, before they have a chance to adjust—more people working with the same capital leads to less output per person. Additionally, there is congestion. Additional people make it more difficult for the original persons to do the work they were doing before, just as a great many additional trucks in a market place may prevent all of them from moving except with extreme difficulty. This gridlock congestion effect is different than Malthusian capital dilution, which does not operate more strongly at higher levels of immigration than at lower levels.

A second possibly important drawback to very large-scale immigration—which has not appeared in previous technical discussions of immigration—is a force which we may call "human capital externalities." A person's output depends not only on the person's own skills and the quality of the machines one works with, but also on the quality of the skills of the people one works with. Immigrants from poor countries possess poorer productive skills than do people with the same amount of formal education in richer countries; this is almost definitionally true, and the effect can be seen in the lower incomes of those immigrants in the countries from which they have come than in the incomes they expect in the U.S. (which is exactly why they come). So until they improve their informally learned skills—handling modern communications systems, for example, or getting used to doing things by telephone and computer rather than in person and with pencil and paper—they represent lower-quality human capital for Canadian workers to cooperate with. And this would reduce the productivity (and growth of productivity) of Canadian workers until the immigrants—in perhaps 2 or 5 years—pick up the informal learning, after which time they likely forge ahead of natives.

(There also is a linked positive effect, the beneficial impact of working with someone from a different culture. Immigrants cause new ideas to arise, even when higher-skilled persons are exposed to more "primitive" ways of doing a job.)

The size of the negative human-capital externality effect must depend upon the proportion of immigrants that natives work with. If your work companions are one percent new immigrants, the negative effect surely is small, and outweighed by the positive effect. But if you work with immigrants 50 percent or 90 percent of the time, the outcome might be quite different. But such scenarios are wholly unlikely in the Canadian context.

Immigrants and productivity

The most important effect of immigrants almost surely is their impact upon productivity. This occurs partly through increased demand, which leads to learning-by-doing productivity increases. Even more important is the gain in productivity through the immigrants' new ideas which enlarge technology and thence improve production technique. This productivity effect cannot be captured in simple theory. But we should not allow difficulty of description to cause us to slight the phenomenon. It is this phenomenon that literally makes our world go round, and advances our civilization.

Immigration theory and trade theory

The common view is that international trade and international migration are similar phenomena, to be analyzed with the same general theory. But the analogy is not sound. International trade and international migration are theoretically different phenomena rather than similar. The gains from trade are quite unlike the gains from migration. Consumers do not obtain the same sort of gains from the international movement of people as they do from international exchange of goods, though there are important gains from immigration to the countries of destination through mechanisms other than trade-like effects. And the "explanation" of why people move is different from the explanation of why goods move.

A numerical example helps illuminate the issue. Consider first the more difficult case of an "occupationally unbalanced" migration, that is, the immigrants are not in the same proportion as the workforce in the country of destination. Let just a single male barber move between countries ("U.S." and "India") which have only barber and chicken-farming sectors. The analysis proceeds in two stages, the first stage before the destination economy fully adjusts, and the second stage after it reaches its new equilibrium.[1]

Assume that initially the "U.S." and "India" each have 400 man-hours per week available to the economy and that they produce chickens and haircuts as in Table 6–1.

Table 6–1: Prior to migration

	U.S.	India	Total
Haircuts	200	200	400
Chickens	600	400	1000

One man-hour produces 1 haircut in both countries, but produces 3 chickens in the U.S. and 2 chickens in India. One haircut is worth 3 chickens in the U.S. and 2 chickens in India. Now let one barber migrate, shifting 40 man-hours per week of barbering.

In the first adjustment stage, the migrant barber forces U.S. haircut prices down enough to create demand for his services, but as yet no native barbers have left the trade. The opposite happens in India. Production in the two countries is as shown in Table 6–2.

Table 6–2: After migration but before adjustment

	U.S.	India	Total
Haircuts	240	160	400
Chickens	600	400	1000

---

1   The numbers and some of the language in this example are adapted from a letter by Ivy Papps, who kindly granted me permission to do so, though his argument was different than mine.

Total world production is the same as prior to migration, so there clearly is no total gain in consumer welfare. The barber is better off, however, because he/she is paid at a higher price than before—more than 80 chickens-worth though less than 120 chickens-worth—which explains why the migration takes place.

After some time, the shift in prices leads to occupational adjustments. That is, some individuals in the U.S. will move from cutting hair to raising chickens, with the reverse being true in India. There is no reason to expect the fully-adjusted occupational proportions to be different than before the migration. Hence the structure of production will be as shown in Table 6–3, and prices should therefore return to what they were prior to the migration. Now there is an increase of 20 chickens in total world production, but all the increase goes to the migrant barber, in connection with the higher price of haircuts that he gives in the U.S., and represents the increase in his/her standard of living. But everyone else's standard of living is as before, ignoring costs associated with occupational adjustments. So we distingish three groups—the natives of the origin country who do not move, the natives of the destination country, and the immigrant. The first two groups do not benefit from the move, whereas the immigrant does.

Table 6–3: After adjustment to the immigration

	U.S.	India	Total
Haircuts	202	180	400
Chickens	660	360	1000

To repeat, trade-induced shifts in prices and production benefit consumers in both countries, whereas the shifts due to international migration benefit only the migrant. And after full adjustment, international migration leaves prices as before, whereas trade in goods alters the price structure. Capital has been omitted from the model for simplicity.

If migrants come to the destination country in the same proportion as the existing labor force—not wildly different from reality in the U.S.—the entire process can be seen as a single stage. Prices then simply remain unchanged, the total economy expands in proportion to the migrants, natives' incomes are unchanged, and immigrants obtain a higher standard of living. This discussion does not answer the question of why production of the tradeable good is higher in the destination country. There are many possible explanations, just as in trade theory. But this question is not part of the matter at issue here.

Trade theory refers to goods—oranges, chickens, autos, computer programs—which can be sold separately from the services of the persons who own the means of production of these goods. In contrast, the benefit which the migrant confers upon the person or organization that pays the migrant for her/his services cannot be delivered at a distance. That is, trade theory deals by definition with internationally traded goods, while international (economic) migration is a response to the fact that that person's output cannot be directly sold at a distance. It should not be surprising, then, for trade theory to be silent about the immigration that takes place.[2]

---

2   Standard trade theory does explain why migration need not take place under certain conditions. But it does not explain why the migration that does take place should occur. To put the point differently, people either migrate internationally or they do not. One class of people who (in trade theory) do not immigrate are those engaged in the production of internationally traded goods, whose wages are thereby equalized in all relevant countries (at least the wages are equalized in principle, though by another principle the equality of wages is not testable empirically); they therefore have no motive to move. Another group of people choose not to migrate because their earnings are greater in the country of origin than in the country of destination. But some people do migrate internationally, even some whose skill in their professions is average. Factor-price-equalization theory provides no motive for these people to migrate. And most important, there is no gain to non-moving natives similar to the Ricardian wine-and-cloth increase in total production whose benefit is realized by native consumers in both countries.

The effects of immigrants through the public coffers

Transfers and taxes

A recent Canadian study by Akbari (1989) and an earlier study of mine reach almost identical results about the effects of immigrants through the public coffers. Hence, I will present my own data.

My analysis of a large Census Bureau survey shows that, contrary to common belief, immigrants do not use more transfer payments and public services than do natives; rather, they use much smaller amounts in total.

The services that catch the public eye are welfare and (as they are labeled in the U.S.) Supplemental Security, unemployment compensation, Aid to Families with Dependent Children, and food stamps. Comparing immigrant and native families of similar education and age, there is almost no difference in usage levels. The costs of schooling are somewhat higher for immigrants after the first few years in the U.S., because their families are younger than native families, on average. But when we include public retirement programs—Social Security, Medicare, and the like—immigrant families on average are seen to receive much less total welfare payments and public services than do average native families.

Summing the categories we find that the average immigrant family received $1,404 (in 1975 dollars) in welfare services in years 1-5, $1,941 in years 6-10, $2,247 in years 11-15, and $2,279 in years 16-25. In comparison, natives' receipts averaged $2,279, considerably more than the immigrants got during their early years in the U.S. Furthermore, these early years are especially relevant because rational policy decisions weigh the distant future less heavily than the near future.

The costs of Social Security dominate the entire system of transfers and taxes. Natives get a windfall from immigrants through the Social Security mechanism. By the time the immigrant couple retires and collects, the couple typically has raised children who are then contributing Social Security taxes and thereby balance out the parents' receipts, just as is the case with typical native families. In this way, there is a one-time benefit to natives because the immigrants normally do not arrive accompanied by a generation of elderly parents who might receive Social Security. Admitting additional immigrants may be the only painless way for the U.S. to ease the trade-off between Social Security benefits and taxes that now cramps the nation's economic policies.

If immigrants paid relatively little in taxes, they might still burden natives by way of the public coffers, even with less use of welfare services by immigrants than by natives. We lack direct information on taxes paid, but from data on family earnings we can estimate taxes tolerably well. Within three to five years after entry, immigrant family earnings reach and pass those of the average native family, due mainly to the favorable age composition of immigrant families. The average native family paid $3,008 in taxes in 1975. In comparison, immigrant families in the U.S. 6 to 10 years paid $3,359, those in the U.S. 11 to 15 years paid $3,564, and those in the U.S. 16 to 25 years paid $3,592. These are substantial differences which benefit natives.

Taken together, the data on services used and taxes paid show substantial differences in favor of natives. If we assume that 20 percent of taxes finance activities that are little affected by population size—for example, maintaining the armed forces and the Statue of Liberty—the difference is an average of $1,354 yearly for the years 1-5 in the U.S., and $1,329, $1,535 and $1,353 for years 6-10, 11-15 and 16-25 respectively, in 1975 dollars. These are the amounts that natives are enriched each year through the public coffers for each additional immigrant family. Evaluating the future stream of differences as one would when evaluating a prospective dam or harbor, the present value of a newly-arrived immigrant family discounted at 3 percent (inflation adjusted) was $20,600 in 1975 dollars, almost two years' average earnings of a native family; at 6 percent the present value was $15,800, and $12,400 at 9 percent.

An integrated model of the aggregate economic effects

Using a simple macro-model and what seem to be reasonable parameters, I estimated the difference between natives' incomes with or without immigrants. When looked at by natives as an investment, similar to such social capital as dams and roads, an immigrant family is an excellent investment worth somewhere between $15,000 and $20,000 to natives, even calculated with relatively high rates for the social cost of capital. (This is in 1975 U.S. dollars, to be compared with mean yearly native family earnings of about $11,000 in that year.)

Labour-market effects of immigrants

The most powerful political argument against admitting immigrants always has been that they take jobs held by natives and thereby increase native unemployment. The logic is simple: If the number of jobs is fixed, and immigrants occupy some jobs, then there are fewer jobs available for natives.

In the immediate present, the demand for any particular sort of worker is indeed inflexible. In theory, therefore, additional immigrants in a given occupation must have some negative impact on wages and/or employment among people in that occupation. There must even be some additional general unemployment while the economy adjusts to additional workers. But this effect could be insignificantly small. A line of reasoning based on queuing theory suggests that, all else equal, an additional immigrant is likely to cause well less than two months of additional unemployment of natives. Moreover, to the extent that immigrants consume and purchase even before they go to work, they decrease native unemployment, even if immigrant unemployment is observed to be much higher than native unemployment.

Several recent studies have tackled the matter of "displacement" empirically using a variety of approaches. No study has found across-the-board unemployment caused by immigrants, either in the U.S. as a whole or in particular areas of relatively high immigration. And effects on particular groups are surprisingly small or non-existent, even groups such as blacks and women in California seemingly at special risk from Mexican immigrants.

In short, immigrants not only take jobs, they make jobs. They create new jobs indirectly with their spending. They also create new jobs directly with the businesses which they are more likely than natives to start.

Concerning wages now: Additional persons outside of native Alpha's occupation—especially persons with different levels of education—improve Alpha's earning situation because they are complements to her; if, for example, Alpha is a person with much education and skill, she can therefore be better off if there are additional immigrant people of low skill available, as a trained surgical nurse may be more productive if there are additional less-skilled helpers available. Similarly, if Alpha has few skills, Alpha benefits from having additional immigrants of high skill enter the country. Additional persons in Alpha's own occupation, however, drive down Alpha's earnings due simply to additional competition. Evidence concerning both the competitive and complementary effects on wages suggests that the effects are small, at least in the U.S., but competitive effects are observed to drive down some natives wages—as immigrant physicians worsen the economic position of native physicians (though other persons benefit from lower prices).

Conclusion

Additional immigrants raise the standard of living of native-born persons in Canada and the United States, and have little or no negative effect upon any occupation or income class. The economic objections to immigration asserted by the opponents of immigration have all been falsified in the past decade or so. More specifically: Immigrants pay much more in taxes than the cost of the welfare services and schooling that they use. Immigrants do not displace natives from jobs. Immigrants raise productivity and make the countries more competitive internationally. And in the long run immigrants make natural resources more available rather than more scarce. All this is true at levels of immigration at least as large as at present.

References

Akbari, Ather H., "The Benefits of Immigrants to Canada: Evidence on Tax and Public Services," *Canadian Public Policy*, December, 1989, pp. 424-435.

Jones, Eric L., *The European Miracle*, (Cambridge: Cambridge University Press, 1981).

Perkins, Dwight, *Agricultural Development in China*, 1368-1968, (Chicago: Aldine, 1969.

Simon, Julian L., *The Economics of Population Growth*, (Princeton: Princeton University Press, 1977).

Simon, Julian L., *The Ultimate Resource*, (Princeton: Princeton University Press, 1981).

Simon, Julian L., "Trade Theory Throws No Light on Migration," xerox, 1988.

Simon, Julian L., *The Economic Consequences of Immigration*, (Oxford: Basil Blackwell Ltd, 1989).

Chapter 7

Macroeconomic Impacts of Immigration

Alice Nakamura, Masao Nakamura, and Michael B. Percy

This study was supported in part by a grant to Alice Nakamura and Masao Nakamura from the Social Sciences and Humanities Research Council of Canada.

Introduction

IMMIGRATION HAS MOLDED THE DEMOGRAPHIC composition of the Canadian population, and current and projected immigration levels are high enough so that immigrants will continue to alter the structure of the population of Canada. There is agreement on this. Most also agree that immigration policies and demographic change affect the economy. In fact, Canadian immigration policy is treated in large measure as part of Canadian economic policy. However, the economic implications of the demography of Canada are not well understood. This paper explores some of the reasons for this lack of understanding, and offers suggestions in this context for policy formation and for future research on the macroeconomic effects of immigration.

For purposes of analysis we find it useful to consider the following decomposition of immigration-related economic effects:

(1) *General responses* to the individual attributes of immigrants such as years of schooling and skill types and levels, ignoring possible immigrant-native differences in economic behaviour.

(2) *Immigrant-specific effects* due to behavioural differences between immigrants and the native born, controlling for general responses.

Most studies of the economic effects of immigration fall into one or the other of these two categories. Moreover, large bodies of more general research on economic behaviour are relevant for understanding the first category of immigration effects on the economy.

The problems of gauging the effects of demographic changes that affect multiple aspects of the Canadian economy are briefly discussed in Section II. In order to illustrate the need for, and the problems with, using macroeconometric models to explore the net effects of immigration, an analysis of these effects using the RDX2 model is presented in Section III. The results of this exercise are used to introduce, and as a basis of comparison with, other published studies of the effects of immigration based on macroeconometric models. These other studies are reviewed in Section IV. Section V considers three dimensions in which macroeconometric models might be improved. Concluding remarks are presented in Section VI.

Assessing overall macroeconomic effects

Will the average Canadian be better or worse off as a result of the interrelated macroeconomic changes due to increased immigration? Single sector studies (of, say, consumer demand or labour supply) cannot provide empirical linkages between demographic changes and changes in overall economic performance. These linkages can only be established within a multisector framework such as a macroeconometric model. Macroeconometric models are simplified equation representations of how economists envision the sectors of the economy as functioning and interacting. If a macroeconometric model perfectly captured the functioning of the economy, then experimentally altering immigration flows in such a model would allow us to say a great deal about the economic consequences of changes in actual immigration flows.

Macroeconometric models have been used to examine the potential impacts of alternative immigration policies. A macroeconometric model is first run over a historical period with the values of all variables that are inputs to the model set at the observed values over this period. Operationally, the equations of the model are solved quarter after quarter using computer simulation methods for the values of the various variables and economic indicators determined by the model. In the *baseline forecast* with all input variables set at their historical values, the forecasted values of the variables and economic indicators determined by the model should closely track the actual movements of these indicators. This simulation exercise can then be repeated with experimental variations from the historical immigration flows. The forecasted values of the economic indicators for the experimental simulations can be contrasted with the values of these indicators for the baseline case.

The validity of macroeconometric analyses of immigration effects rests heavily, of course, on the extent to which the models used actually capture the functioning of the economy. A second qualification to be borne in mind has to do with the interpretation of commonly used indicators of economic performance. An example can be used to make this point. Suppose immigrants to Canada take low wage jobs throughout the economy that those already in Canada are unwilling to fill. Suppose this enhances the productivity of the economy, allowing the earnings of all those who were already living in Canada to rise a little. The immigrants would have lower earnings, but would presumably be better off in some sense than in their countries of origin or else they would not have migrated. In fact, it would be possible for all of the original residents and all of the immigrants to be economically better off as a consequence of immigration even with a fall in per capita income or expenditure due to the low earnings of the immigrants. Economists such as Usher (1977) and Marr and Percy (1985) discuss a host of interpretive problems of this sort. Nevertheless, politicians and the public are interested in and continue to base policy decisions on their perceptions of how immigration affects key measures of economic performance.

The macroeconometric models that have been most widely used in studies of Canadian immigration policies fall into three distinct families: the large models developed by the Bank of Canada, including RDX2; the huge CANDIDE models developed through inter-departmental support by the Government of Canada and managed in recent years by the Economic Council of Canada; and the even larger TIM models developed by Informetrica. Bodkin and Marwah (1987) provide a helpful summary of the various ways in which demographic factors are treated in these three families of macroeconometric models. They also discuss the use of these models for assessing the economic effects of immigration. Relevant points emerging from their discussion include the following:

1. Only general demographic effects of immigration, such as the effects of changes in the sizes of various age groups, are allowed for in most macroeconometric models. No allowances are made for labour supply, consumption, fertility, savings, investment, or other possible immigrant-native behavioural differences.

2. There are substantial differences among the various existing macroeconometric models for Canada in how demographic factors are accounted for.

3. In numerical terms, emigration has been as important as immigration in shaping the demography of Canada. However, emigration levels are difficult to explain empirically. Part of the problem may be the fact that Canada does not collect and maintain data about those moving out of the country as is done for immigrants. Rather, Canadian emigration figures must be built up from the immigration records of other countries. Poor emigration forecasts may distort forecasts for net migration (immigration minus emigration), and may distort macroeconometric analyses of the impacts of immigration policies.

4. Different studies using different macroeconometric models and exploring different sorts of immigration scenarios arrive at different conclusions.

Examining the effects of immigration using RDX2

The following analysis of alternative immigration scenarios using RDX2 illustrates some of the advantages, and also some of the difficulties, of using macroeconometric models to predict overall economic effects. Key features of the model are outlined first. The design of our illustrative simulation experiments is explained in a second subsection. Simulation results are presented next. Observations concerning the basic approach are outlined in a fourth subsection. This material provides the basis for a discussion in Section IV of ways in which empirical research on particular aspects of economic behaviour could improve the quality of future macroeconometric analyses of the effects of immigration.

Key features of RDX2

RDX2 has far fewer equations and a much simpler treatment of demographic factors than the CANDIDE and TIM models. However, the complexity of the model still necessitates that we narrowly confine our discussion of it. We will explore how demographic variables enter into the determination of gross national expenditures; wage income in the RDX2 industry category of mining, manufacturing and other business; and the quarterly baseline levels of immigration and emigration.

Gross national expenditures

In RDX2, gross national expenditures (GNE) is computed as the sum of more than 35 distinct variables. These include consumer expenditures on various categories of goods and services, business investment of several types, government purchases and payments, and exports and imports. Only the determination of consumer expenditures and of municipal government education expenditures will be discussed, focusing on the role of demographic factors.

Per capita consumer expenditures on durables (excluding motor vehicles and parts), on non-durables and semi-durables, and on services, as well as per family expenditures on shelter (actual or imputed rent) are determined by five equations and four identities. It is reasonable to think that the per capita specification of the expenditure relationships would make total consumer expenditure quite sensitive to changes in population size. In addition, the specified proportion of the population living in urban centres plays a role in the determination of consumer expenditures on housing via the choice between single and multiple dwelling units.

Employment in elementary and secondary schools under municipal control is determined on a per student basis. It is modeled as a function of real personal income per capita which, of course, depends definitionally on the size of the total population. School construction expenditures are determined by a relationship incorporating an 11 quarter distributed lag for the size of the student population. Hence municipal expenditures for personnel and for construction of elementary and secondary schools are expected to be sensitive to demographic influences.

Mining, manufacturing and other business wage income
The mining, manufacturing and other business industry group used in RDX2 accounts for over 80 percent of total business employment. Three equations combine to determine wage income for this segment of the labour force: an equation for the number of persons employed, an equation for hours of work per person, and a wage rate equation.

The number of paid employees in mining, manufacturing and other business is determined by seasonal factors and by the desired number of employees which is determined by another equation. To the extent that the required labour exceeds the supply with the projected labour force working regular hours, a portion of this gap is closed by an adjustment in the number of hours worked per week. Any additional adjustment in short-term output is assumed to be accomplished through changes in productivity. Real wages in mining, manufacturing and other business are determined by an equation in which the quarterly percentage change in wages is given as a function of seasonal factors, productivity changes, real wages in previous quarters, hours worked, and unemployment.

Immigration and emigration
Emigration is treated as a function of the recent levels of emigration and unemployment in Canada and the recent unemployment in the United States. Of these latter two influences, the pull from the U.S. is found to be somewhat stronger than the push from Canada.

Immigration into Canada is determined as a function of past immigration, unemployment in Canada, and the ratio of real wages in Canada to a weighted average of real wages in three European countries (Great Britain, Italy, Germany) and the United States. The unemployment rate plays an important role in the RDX2 immigration equation. This is not surprising since unemployment conditions have been an important factor historically in debates over, and the administration of, Canadian immigration policies.

The simulation experiments

Historically, even if it had been decided to admit more immigrants, year-to-year admissions would presumably have fluctuated with variations in Canadian labour market conditions. Hence in using macroeconometric models to explore the effects of higher (or lower) immigration flows, it may not be realistic to increase the historical figures by some fixed constant. Percentage adjustments in the historical (or forecasted historical) figures might be better from the perspective of mimicking the observed cyclical variation in immigration flows. This is the approach adopted in our simulation exercises.

A control simulation and five experimental simulations were performed over the time period of the first quarter of 1961 (1961-1) through the fourth quarter of 1970 (1970-4). There are two key reasons for the choice of the 1961-1970 period as the context for our simulation experiments: the magnitudes of the immigration flows, and published evidence concerning the forecasting performance of RDX2 over this historical period.

As is documented in the *Historical Statistics of Canada* (2nd edition, 1983, series A1 and A350, Statistics Canada), the immigration flows into Canada over the 1961-1970 period were large. In 1967, for example, the flow of immigrants as a percentage of the population stock reached a peak of approximately 1.09 percent. Even during the early 1960s this share was never lower than 0.4 percent and it remained above 0.69 percent until 1970. The numerical importance of immigration in this period becomes even clearer when we shift from comparing a flow (immigration) to a stock (population) to focusing on the contribution of immigration to the change in population. In 1967, for example, immigration contributed almost 60 percent of that year's population growth.

Over the 1961-71 decade, net migration contributed 27.7 percent of Canada's population change.

Without large immigration flows for the baseline case (the case with the actual—or predictions of the actual—immigration figures), it would not be possible to examine experimental scenarios in which immigration flows were substantially reduced. There is interest in comparing predictions for reductions as well as for increases in immigration flows relative to the baseline case.

The version of RDX2 used in this study is the one documented in Helliwell and Maxwell (1974). Helliwell and Maxwell provide documentation of many aspects of the performance of this version of the model over the 1961-1970 period.

One further advantage to the 1961-1970 period as a "natural labouratory" for studying changes in immigration levels is that there was an important change in Canadian immigration policy in 1967. Seward summarizes the nature of this change:

> The open policy of the 1960s was expressed in the expansionist 1966 White Paper, which assumed that immigration plays a critical role in population and economic growth, particularly by permitting realization of economies of scale and thereby lowering prices of goods and services. The 1967 Regulations established a "points system" for selection of independent immigrants that placed priority on education, skills and occupational background of immigrants and which corresponded to current labour market needs.[1]

This focuses attention on the importance of the decomposition of immigration-related economic effects presented in the Introduction, and on the extent to which the macroeconometric models used for examining immigration effects capture at least the general responses to population attributes such as education, skills and occupation that are altered by immigration (the first of the two categories specified in the Introduction).

The RDX2 behavioural relationship used in our baseline case to generate the number of immigrants predicted to enter each period

---

1   Seward, 1987, p. 1.

(denoted by NIMS) was estimated using quarterly data for 1958-1 through 1970-4. Actual immigration figures for our 1961-1970 forecast period are tracked quite closely in the baseline simulation.

In the experimental simulations, the quarter-by-quarter baseline immigration figures were altered on five successive simulation runs by +60 percent, +40 percent, +20 percent, -20 percent, and -40 percent, respectively. Also, in the experimental simulations, we have altered a number of other exogenous population variables in accord with the experimental immigration flows. These variables are listed below, along with the RDX2 mnemonics that will be used in referring to these variables:

NBIRTHS — births
NDEATHS — deaths
NHH — number of families in Canada
NPOP0-19 — population aged zero to 19 years
NPOPS — students enrolled in elementary and secondary schools
NPOPSS — total population 14 years of age and over attending school

The immigrants simulated to be admitted in each quarter were assumed to have the actual immigrant age distribution for 1970, and the same family-to-person ratio as the actual 1970 immigrants. These assumptions allow calculation of the experimental values for NPOP0-19 and NHH. The values of NBIRTHS and NDEATHS were altered by applying the age-specific fertility and death rates for Canada as a whole in 1970. The historical baseline values of NPOPS were altered in each of the experimental simulations by assuming that all immigrants 6 to 14 years of age are enrolled in school. In our experimental simulations the values of NPOPSS were altered by assuming that all immigrant teenagers between 14 and 19 years of age are enrolled in school, but no immigrants over 19 years of age attend school.

The values for NIMS, NBIRTHS, and NDEATHS (that are determined as stated above) and the model-generated emigration figures determine the values for NPOPT, the total population at the beginning of each quarter. The variable NPOPT enters into all of the equations in RDX2 that are specified in per capita form. Also the labour force population, NPOP, defined as the noninstitutional population 14 years of age and over, is computed in RDX2 as a given fraction, EPOP, times NPOPT.

The labour force, NL, is determined as a first-difference function of the gross private business product which is a function of NPOP and also of the gross national expenditure, the desired output, and the variable NPOPSS.

Total employed persons, denoted by NE, is computed by summing the specified employment variables, such as paid workers in non-commercial institutions (excluding schools) and paid farm workers, and also the model determined employment variables. Many of the relationships for employment variables involve demographic variables such as NPOPS and NPOP.

Total unemployed persons, denoted by NU, is specified as NL minus NE. The unemployment rate is then computed as 100 times the ratio of NU to NL.

Simulation results

Each simulation run consists of 40 consecutive quarters (from 1961-1 through 1970-4). In Table 1, the figures for several economic indicators are shown for our baseline simulation and for each of our experimental simulations for two selected quarters over the simulation period. The selected quarters are the 20th and the 40th: 1965-4 and 1970-4. The top figure in each pair in Table 1 is for 1965-4 and the bottom one is for 1970-4.

Figures for five of the 35 variables that make up gross national expenditures (GNE) are shown in the bottom five pairs of rows of Table 1.

Expenditures on these five components of GNE increase, in total, as immigration flows are increased from 40 percent below the control figures to 60 percent above. However, this increase is small in percentage terms. Moreover, looking at the figures for the individual expenditure categories, it can be seen that only the consumer expenditures on non-durables and semi-durables in 1970, and the municipal investment expenditures on school construction in both 1965 and 1970, rise consistently with increases in immigration.

The total GNE figures rise slightly with increases in immigration. However, there is no apparent immigration-related pattern in the per capita GNE figures.

Table 7-1: Selected RDX2 simulation results for the fourth quarter of 1965 and 1970

Economic indicators	Forecast year	Percentage age deviation from control immigration flows					
		+60	+40	+20	Base-line Case	-20	-40
GNE ($ millions)	1965	14,488	14,482	14,476	14,457	14,464	14,458
	1970	22,207	22,190	22,166	22,165	22,125	22,105
Per capita GNE ($)	1965	726	726	726	725	726	726
	1970	1033	1034	1033	1034	1033	1032
Unemployment rate	1965	5.10	5.14	5.19	5.19	5.27	5.32
	1970	4.47	4.56	4.57	4.57	4.66	4.71
Consumer price index	1965	1.084	1.083	1.083	1.082	1.083	1.082
	1970	1.301	1.300	1.299	1.299	1.298	1.297
Consumer expenditure on durables, excluding motor vehicles and parts ($ millions)	1965	695	695	695	695	696	695
	1970	976	976	976	977	976	976

Table 7-1: *Continued*

Economic indicators	Forecast year	Percentage age deviation from control immigration flows					
		+60	+40	+20	Base-line Case	-20	-40
Consumer expenditure on motor vehicles and parts ($ millions)	1965	683	683	683	684	683	683
	1970	898	899	899	900	899	899
Consumer expenditure on non-durables and semi-durables ($ millions)	1965	4411	4410	4410	4408	4410	4410
	1970	5338	5337	5334	5333	5330	5329
Consumer expenditure on services ($ millions)	1965	2967	2967	2967	2967	2968	2968
	1970	3729	3730	3730	3730	3730	3731
Municipal investment in school construction ($ millions)	1965	73	72	72	70	70	69
	1970	104	102	101	99	98	96

From the third and fourth pairs of rows in Table 1, it can be seen that the predicted unemployment rate figures fall slightly and the values for the Consumer Price Index rise a bit as the immigration flows are increased from -40 percent to +60 percent of the control figures.

Comparisons with other studies

The RDX2 immigration simulation exercise presented in the previous section is highly simplified. Before using this as a context for more general observations, it is important to assess how our methodology and results compare with other macroeconomic simulation analyses of immigration effects.

Apparent similarities

Davies (1977) conducted a comparative study of the predicted effects of immigration using RDX2, CANDIDE, and a much smaller macroeconometric model called TRACE that was developed at the Institute for Policy Analysis of the University of Toronto. Davies fixed the level of emigration at 60,000, and then conducted simulation experiments over the period of 1961-1974 with each of the models using annual net immigration levels of 0, 100,000, and 200,000 (corresponding to annual immigration levels of -60,000, 40,000, and 140,000). For all three models, Davies found that increased immigration increased predicted GNE and employment, and slightly reduced the predicted rate of inflation, but also lowered per capita GNE and raised the unemployment rate.

Davies carefully qualifies his comparative results. The caveats he offers relate almost exclusively to the second of the two components of immigration-related economic effects designated in the Introduction of this paper: effects due to *behavioural* differences between immigrants and the native born. For example, he calls attention to the fact that, in all three of the macroeconometric models he used, immigrants are treated as having the same consumption propensities, the same labour force behaviour, and as being geographically distributed in the same way as native born residents. Davies also notes that the models he used take no account of the capital funds immigrants bring with them.

Rao and Kapsalis (1982) investigated the macroeconomic effects of increased levels of immigration using version 2.0 of the CANDIDE 'model family (Davies used version 1.0). In their baseline case, annual net immigration (that is, immigration minus emigration) was fixed at 50,000 per year. They show the differences in results between this case and an experimental simulation in which net immigration was raised 50,000 per year over the baseline case for the forecast period of 1980-1990. Like Davies, they report modest increases in the unemployment rate and reductions in inflation with increased immigration. However, Rao and Kapsalis also report a drop in per capita GNP which they term "staggering."

Sonnen and McLaren (1978) studied the macroeconomic effects of immigration using the TIM model. In their baseline case, net immigration was fixed at 25,000 in 1978 and in 1979, and then increased by another 10,000 per year for 1980 through 1985. Hence, in their baseline case, net immigration was 85,000 in 1985. In three of their five experimental simulations, annual net immigration levels were altered from the baseline levels by a constant minus 50,000, plus 50,000, and plus 100,000, respectively, over the simulation period of 1978-1985. In their other two simulations, annual net immigration levels were altered by minus 50,000 and by plus 100,000, respectively, and also fiscal and monetary policies represented in the government sector of the TIM model were adjusted so as to hold the predicted unemployment rate at the values for the baseline case. Sonnen and McLaren (1979, Executive Summary) conclude "that increases in immigration lead to a larger economy, probably some slight increases in the unemployment rate, negligible effects on prices, and some likely deterioration in government and current account balances." They go on to argue "that the unfavourable effects are small; that governments could act to offset wholly or partially many of these unfavourable effects; and that the administration of immigration may itself lead to quite different results."

The relationship between the results of these studies and our own results could be summarized as follows. In all cases, increased levels of immigration were found to raise the predicted values of real GNE and of aggregate consumption expenditure. Barring offsetting government policies, all the studies except ours also predict that increased immigration will raise the unemployment rate and reduce the rate of inflation.

In our study, the directions of the unemployment and inflation effects are reversed. The main result, however, is that in all of the studies except the Rao and Kapsalis analysis, the predicted effects of immigration on key economic indicators are *modest* despite large experimental variations in immigration flows. Except for the Rao and Kapsalis study, the overall conclusions of Sonnen and McLaren (1979, p. 58) appear to hold:

> ... reasonable, alternative levels of immigration are not likely to cause major instabilities to the Canadian economy or to lead to the forfeitures of major opportunities. The choice of whether more or fewer persons are permitted to immigrate must rest on grounds other than those of macroeconomic effects.[2]

Policy lessons

Despite broad similarities in the findings of macroeconometric simulation studies of immigration, both critics and supporters of the approach draw attention to problems that should be borne in mind in using these results as a basis for policy formulation. For example, commenting on the Rao and Kapsalis study, Robertson and Roy write:

> It is stated in the paper that "the key assumption underlying the simulation is that—except for age/sex differences—the additional immigrants would have job characteristics similar to those of Canadians." The available evidence on comparative occupational distributions would strongly suggest the contrary. In addition, the paper also ignores significant differences with regard to some of the other characteristics of immigrants and Canadian residents. Such differences could considerably alter the results in either direction. In particular, we would like to mention considerable differences that exist between immigrants and Canadian residents with regard to labour force participation, level of education, and the unemployment experience.[3]

In fact, Robertson and Roy present simulation evidence suggesting that, for the CANDIDE model, there may be problems with the predicted responses to population change of any sort. Setting immigration

---

2   Sonnen and McLaren, 1979, p. 58.

3   Robertson and Roy, 1982, p. 386.

to *zero* and allowing only for emigration, they obtain the following implausible results:

> an emigration of 50,000 per year (that is, a net immigration of -50,000) from Canada would increase *per capita* real income and reduce the unemployment rate substantially as compared with the base case scenario.... If the results of the CANDIDE simulations are correct, it logically follows that financial incentives should be provided to Canadians to leave the country![4]

Supporters of the macroeconometric simulation approach concede most of the problems cited in the Robertson-Roy article, but do not agree with the Robertson-Roy conclusion on the value and policy relevance of the approach. For instance, Bodkin and Marwah assert:

> the CANDIDE, TIM, and RDX2 results should probably be interpreted as "lower bound" results, as the compensated TIM solutions bring out clearly. In our view, these simulations are quite useful as "ball park figures," and the fact that their application to concrete problems of policy must be tempered with other evidence and (especially) with good judgment does not vitiate their usefulness.[5]

In fact, some supporters of the macroeconometric simulation approach go to the extreme of claiming that some of the acknowledged limitations are really disguised advantages. Commenting on their CANDIDE simulation experiments Rao and Kapsalis write:

> The key assumption underlying the simulation is that—except for age/sex differences—the additional immigrants would have job characteristics similar to those of Canadians. As a result, there would be direct competition for jobs between Canadians and immigrants. This assumption becomes quite realistic once a minimum level of immigration—selected to meet the most needed skills—has been exceeded.[6]

---

4   Robertson and Roy, 1982, p. 385.

5   Bodkin and Marwah, 1987, p. 24.

6   Rao and Kapsalis, 1982, p. 381.

Who is right?

The simulation studies reviewed in this paper are a fertile ground for learning how macroeconometric models could be transformed into more valuable experimental tools for examining the effects of demographic change, including the effects of increased immigration. Some of these possibilities are outlined in the following section.

Toward improved models for exploring immigration effects

Single sector studies cannot reveal the net impacts on the macro economy of changes or policies that affect multiple sectors. We see no feasible alternative to the use of macroeconometric simulation models for exploring the overall economic effects of immigration. Yet there are three areas of inadequacy of available macroeconometric models that undermine confidence in any conclusions that might be drawn from immigration studies based on these models. These areas of weakness are discussed in this final section, and suggestions for improvement are put forward.

Demographic impacts on exogenous factors

In summarizing the Sonnen and McLaren (1978) study of the macroeconomic effects of immigration, Bodkin and Marwah write:

> There were two mechanisms through which alternative assumptions about future immigration were made to influence the calculations: (a) the population module, and (b) the set of exogenous variables. . . . These exogenous variables were deemed to be related directly to the number of immigrants and the subsequent demographic changes, or indirectly to those economic factors, such as the size of real GNP and the level of prices, that the number of immigrants are most likely to affect. Forty-two such exogenous variables of TIM were adjusted in total.[7]

---

7   Bodkin and Marwah, 1987, p. 22.

All of the macroeconometric models have large numbers of exogenous factors that must be specified by the analyst. In this context, an exogenous factor is simply any factor for which the value or values are determined entirely apart from the functioning of the simulation model. Some variables are treated as exogenous because they are determined by policy makers in such a way that it is felt the past cannot provide a guide to future values. Bodkin and Marwah explain the exogenous treatment of net immigration (immigration minus emigration) in TIM from this perspective:

> TIM abandoned the endogenous mechanism for explaining net immigration, developed in Model 1.1 and succeeding versions of CANDIDE. This was done with the view that immigration is critically a policy variable, so that it makes little sense to project it on the basis of a regression based on past sample data, when a change in policy regime is almost certain to produce a critical break in structure.[8]

Some variables are treated as exogenous because data for them, or an understanding of how these variables relate to other observable factors, are not readily available. Perhaps this is the case for exogenous variables in RDX2 such as average gasoline consumption per registered non-commercial motor vehicle, current expenditure on goods and services by hospitals, direct NHA loans approved by CMHC for single-detached dwellings, unpaid and paid farm workers, and paid workers in non-commercial institutions (excluding schools). In experimental simulations or in forecasting over some future period, variables like these are often fixed at values observed for some base period.

However, in reality many of the variables treated as exogenous are strongly affected by immigration. Relationships could be added that would capture these demographic effects. Variables of this sort in RDX2 include births (NBIRTHS), deaths (NDEATHS), number of families (NHH), population aged zero to 19 years (NPOPS0-19), and total population 14 years of age and over attending school (NPOPSS). These are the "exogenous" variables that were adjusted in our simulation experiments described in Section III. Many researchers who are intent on

---

8   Bodkin and Marwah, 1987, p. 15.

using a macroeconometric model to study the effects of immigration may not be prepared to invest the effort to carefully adjust large numbers of exogenous factors.

The CANDIDE and TIM models have demographic sectors containing equations that adjust a substantial number of population-related variables in response to changes in population size and composition. However, even in these models the population is distinguished only by factors such as age and sex. The importance of this simplified treatment of population is underlined by the objections that Robertson and Roy (1982, p. 385) raise to the use in CANDIDE of a net immigration variable, rather than separate variables for immigration and emigration. They draw attention to some pertinent facts about Canadian immigrants and emigrants:

> The use of the *net* immigration (immigration minus emigration) variable as the basis of the simulation assumes that immigrants and emigrants are identical. This assumption is questionable and could lead to misleading conclusions. . . . The occupational distribution of emigrants from Canada to the US is dominated by managerial, professional, and technical workers. The data indicate that in recent years about 60-70 percent of emigrants to the US belong to the managerial, professional and technical occupational category while only 25-30 percent of immigrants to Canada belong to this occupational group . . . *per capita* income could be reduced even if an immigration flow of, say, 100,000 is offset by an emigration flow of the same magnitude, that is, net immigration of zero. This simply reflects the fact that persons in the managerial, professional and technical occupational group (who dominate outmigration from Canada) tend to have a higher earnings level than other groups.[9]

Note that there would not necessarily be a problem with treating population flows into and out of Canada using a net immigration variable if the population were categorized by all economically important characteristics including, for example, educational level and occupational specialization. The sizes of these population groups could then be adjusted to reflect net immigration effects.

---

9   Robertson and Roy, 1982, p. 385.

Census data could be used to determine the initial numbers of individuals of different types. If individuals are to be differentiated by a large number of characteristics (such as sex, five or more age groups, marital status, child status, educational level, and so on), it may prove operationally difficult to update or forecast the numbers of individuals of the different types over a simulation period. These problems might be dealt with by substituting a simple microsimulation model for the demographic sector in a macroeconometric model (see, for example, Nakamura and Nakamura, 1978, 1987, and 1990). The microsimulation model could probably be treated as exogenous, in a current sense, from the rest of the macroeconometric model and run first in each quarterly or annual simulation period. This would be far simpler than a fully interactive solution of the combined system. (The demographic sector of CANDIDE is solved interactively along with the rest of the model.)

Macroeconometric models that carry economically relevant information about the Canadian population, and that appropriately update and adjust this population information over time in a simulation run, should yield more realistic predictions of the macroeconomic responses to demographic changes, such as immigration, than currently available models such as RDX2, CANDIDE and TIM. A macroeconometric model enhanced in this way would potentially be a more accurate and convenient tool for examining the effects of alternative levels of immigration. Surely this would be an improvement over the current practice of different researchers making different ad hoc (and often poorly documented) adjustments in "exogenous" factors deemed to be affected by immigration.

Incorporating demographic variables in behavioural relationships.

More demographic information should also be incorporated directly into the economic behavioural relationships of macroeconometric simulation models. Data availability and econometric problems on the one hand, and the traditions and objectives of economic analysis on the other, have interacted to inhibit progress in this regard. An additional inhibiting factor is that macroeconomic effects are, by definition, aggregate effects while demographic attributes such as sex, age, marital status, and number of children are, in the first instance, characteristics of individuals and families. The choice of the level of aggregation for empirical investigations of the macroeconomic effects of demographic change thus necessarily involves trade-offs. Consideration of these issues in the context of three alternative bodies of literature on household demand behaviour may help to clarify their relevance.

The first of these bodies of literature consists of micro data studies on the demand for specific types of goods and services like baby clothes, day care, selected foods, dental services, airline travel, and so on. Many of these studies were undertaken to meet the planning needs of providers or regulators of these goods and services, and are published in trade-related journals and collections of readings. In many studies of this sort, demographic effects are found to be very important.

Equations for individual buying behaviour can be evaluated for "representative individuals" by fixing the explanatory variables at the mean values for specified types of individuals. Aggregate purchase predictions could then be computed by adding up the values for different types of individuals, using the numbers of individuals of each of the types as weights. To explore the effects of demographic change, the population figures for the various groups could be changed in accord with the hypothesized scenarios.

However, no one has estimated a system of demand equations for individual products and services covering all, or even most, consumer expenditures. Therefore, it would not be possible to "add up" the implications for aggregate *total* household demand of the predictions of the demographic effects on the demand for specific products and services.

A second relevant body of literature is based on empirical studies at the other extreme of aggregation: studies of aggregate consumption expenditure. In these studies, the dependent variable is aggregate total household expenditures (that is, aggregate total household demand) in each quarter or year, or aggregate total expenditures divided by population size. Consumption expenditure is related to aggregate or per capita personal income and other control variables. Sometimes variables for various aspects of population structure, such as the proportions of the population in specified age groups, are included as control variables.

Macroeconomic effects of any included demographic variables are easily derived from estimated aggregate consumption functions. However, in a macro time series environment, there are data problems that complicate estimation of economic relationships. Also the relatively small number of available observations in macro time series make it harder to find suitable variables to represent the relevant demographic changes.

A more fundamental problem is that different categories of household consumption expenditure are probably affected differently by demographic factors, with the nature of these differences depending on the level of household income. The relationship between aggregate total household expenditure and the explanatory variables of interest may be complex, or even unstable.

Certainly, intuition and economic theory are more helpful for relating specific goods and services—or, at least, specific categories of consumer demand, such as shelter or food expenditures—to demographic factors and household sector income variables. These considerations point in the direction of a third body of literature based on demand equations for broad expenditure categories. Demand equations of this sort have been estimated using both macro time series data and micro data for individuals and families. In many studies, the specified expenditure categories add up to a large share of total household consumption expenditures.

When expenditure category equations are estimated using aggregate time series data, the problems of obtaining good estimates of the responses to demographic factors are much the same as in studies of aggregate consumption expenditure. Statistical problems may be less severe when these systems of expenditure category equations are estimated using cross-sectional or pooled micro data for individuals or families.

Yet even those systems of expenditure category equations that have been estimated using micro data typically incorporate very little demographic information. This shortcoming may be due, in part, to traditions of analysis arising from the aggregate time series history of empirical demand analysis research. In this literature, a great deal of attention has been devoted to trying to determine the effects of family size on household expenditure patterns (see, for example, Pollak and Wales 1978 and

1981) but other attributes of households have been largely ignored. It seems unlikely that family size is the only, or even the most, important demographic attribute affecting individual or family expenditure behaviour. Recognizing this possibility, some researchers have tried to incorporate at least some information about the ages as well as the numbers of children in families.

In a study of the macroeconomic effects of demographic change, it is desirable to use a macroeconometric model that incorporates information about important demographic factors. Immigrants are known to differ from native born residents in terms of their distributions for age, family characteristics, education, work experience, place of residence, recent migration experience, and so on (see, for instance, DeVoretz 1989, and Seward and Tremblay 1989). Differences in these characteristics are known to be associated with differences in economic behaviour, even for native born residents. For instance, housing expenditures appear to be affected by whether a person or family has recently moved from another country or province, whether the place of residence is urban or rural, and the presence and ages of children. Likewise the current labour supply of women has been shown to depend on previous work experience, education, family characteristics, and age. Macroeconometric or integrated macroeconometric-microanalytic simulation systems incorporating demographic effects such as these in housing expenditure, labour supply, and other behavioural equations have the potential to more fully and accurately reflect the macroeconomic effects of immigration.

Immigrant-native behavioural differences

There is fragmentary evidence that immigrants differ from native born residents in terms of their expenditure patterns, their labour supply behaviour, their propensity to import (and export) financial capital, their utilization rates for certain public services, their migration behaviour within Canada, and their family formation choices (see, for example, Johnson 1980, DeVoretz 1989, Marr and McCready 1989, Seward and Tremblay 1989, and McLaughlin 1981). Many of these apparent differences may become minimal or even vanish, however, if important individual and family characteristics other than immigration status are properly controlled for. Marr and McCready find this to be the case for certain immigrant-native differences in expenditure patterns:

> The findings for arrival year combined with those for birthplace indicate that existing differences in allocation among expenditure categories are due to influences such as age, education, and income to a large extent and not to birthplace or time spent in Canada *per se*.[10]

Concluding observations

We began this paper by stating that we find it useful to consider a two-part breakdown of immigration-related economic effects:

(1) *General responses* to the individual attributes of immigrants such as years of schooling and skill types and levels, ignoring possible immigrant-native differences in economic behaviour.

(2) *Immigrant-specific effects* due to behavioural differences between immigrants and the native born, controlling for general responses.

Our main conclusion is that research attention should be focused on taking fuller account of the first of these two components of immigration effects. This can be accomplished by incorporating more demographic information into macroeconometric models to be used in examining immigration effects, and by adding relationships that will make appropriate adjustments in other variables in a macroeconometric model that, in reality, would be affected by immigration. Large bodies of more general literature on demographic effects on economic behaviour may be useful in accomplishing these tasks.

If the effects of demographic characteristics such as family size, ages of children, marital status, education, place of residence (urban or rural), and recent migration status (whether a person or family recently moved from another province or country) are accounted for, it may be that the remaining immigrant-native differences in economic behaviour are relatively minor. This is an assertion that could, and should, be explored empirically. It would be helpful if this were true, since research on immigrant-native behavioural differences is hampered by the difficulty

---

10   Marr and McCready, 1989, p. 29.

of modelling, and estimating or controlling for, the effects of country-of-origin and length-of-stay in Canada. At any rate, macroeconometric simulation models will be better tools for exploring immigration (and other demographic) effects if demographic factors are more fully taken account of in the equations of these models.

References

Bodkin, R.G. and K. Marwah, "Some Observations on Demography in Selected Macroeconometric Models of Canada," Discussion Paper 87.A.1, The Institute for Research on Public Policy, 1987.

Davies, G.W., "Macroeconomic Effects of Immigration: Evidence from CANDIDE, TRACE, and RDX2," *Canadian Public Policy/Analyse de politiques* III: 3, 1977, 299-306.

DeVoretz, D.J., "Immigration and Employment Effects," Discussion Paper 89.B.3, The Institute for Research on Public Policy, Ottawa, 1989.

Helliwell, J. and T. Maxwell, *The Equations of RDX2 Revised and Estimated to 4Q 1970*, Bank of Canada, Ottawa, 1974.

Johnson, G.E., "The Labour Market Effects of Immigration," *Industrial and Labour Relations Review*, 1980.

Marr, W.L. and D.J. McCready, "The Effects of Demographic Structure on Expenditure Patterns in Canada," Discussion Paper 89.A.1, *Studies in Social Policy*, The Institute for Research on Public Policy and Employment and Immigration Canada, 1989.

Marr, W.L. and M.B. Percy, "Immigration Policy and Canadian Economic Growth," in J. Whalley (ed.), *Domestic Policies and the International Economic Environment*, Volume 12, Royal Commission on the Economic Union and Development Prospects for Canada, University of Toronto Press, Toronto, 1985.

McLaughin, N., "The Labour Force Participation of Canada's Immigrants," *The Labour Force*, Catalogue No. 71-001, Supply and Services, 1981.

Nakamura, A. and M. Nakamura, "On Microanalytic Simulation and Its Application in Population Projection," *Journal of the Operational Research Society* 29: 4, 1978, 349-360.

Nakamura, A. and M. Nakamura, "Forecasting the Family Life Cycle," in C.S. Yadav (ed.), *Perspectives in Urban Geography* 29: 4, 1987, 349-360.

Nakamura, A. and M. Nakamura, "Modelling Direct and Indirect Impacts of Tax and Transfer Programs on Household Behavior," in J.K. Brunner and H.G. Peterson (eds.), *Prospects and Limits of Simulation in Tax and Transfer Policy*, Campus Verlag, 1990, 461-478.

Pollak, R.A. and T.J. Wales, "Estimation of Complete Demand Systems from Household Budget Data," *American Economic Review* 68, 1978, 348-359.

Pollak, R.A. and T.J. Wales, "Demographic Variables in Demand Analysis," *Econometrica* 49: 6, 1981, 1533-1551.

Rao, S. and C. Kapsalis, "Labour Shortages and Immigration Policy," *Canadian Public Policy/Analyse de politiques* VIII: 3, 1982, 379-383.

Robertson, M. and A.S. Roy, "Reply," *Canadian Public Policy/Analyse de politiques* VIII (3), 1982, 383-387.

Seward, S.B., "The Relationship Between Immigration and the Canadian Economy," Discussion Paper 87.A.10, The Institute for Research on Public Policy, Ottawa, 1987.

Seward, S.B. and M. Tremblay, "Immigrants in the Canadian Labour Force: Their Role in Structural Change," Discussion Paper 89.B.2, The Institute for Research on Public Policy, Ottawa, 1989.

Sonnen, C.A. and M.L. McLaren, "Macroeconomic Effects of Immigration," Employment and Immigration Canada, 1978.

Usher, D., "Public Property and the Effects of Migration upon Other Residents of the Migrants' Countries of Origin and Destination," *Journal of Political Economy* 85: 5, 1977, 1001-1020.

Chapter 8

Immigration and the Canadian Labour Market

Don J. DeVoretz

The critical comments of S. Fagnan, R. Coulson and R. Simmons are noted with appreciation.

Introduction

EDITORIALS AND NEWS ITEMS IN the popular press set the background for this essay. A sample of the recent press themes relevant to this paper include a view of the benefits of immigrants:

> "Immigrants a Winning Bet" Immigrants pay more into the tax kitty than they take out. (*The Province*, January 4, 1990, p. 7.)

or a critical accounting of the technical workings of the system:

> "Overhaul of Immigrant Point System Proposed" Job quotas for selecting immigrant workers are continually over- or under-filled, a confidential federal government document says. (*Globe and Mail*, Sept. 19, 1988, p. 1.)

and finally an admonishment to the misinformed:

> The reality (of immigration) is that the vast majority of immigrants are a good investment, becoming highly motivated ... as well as above average taxpayers and job generators. (Editorial, *Times Colonist*, Sept. 22, 1990)

It is a rare intellectual event when popular debate, contemporary policy issues and the professional economic literature all focus on a common economic issue. In the Canadian context just such a set of issues exist with respect to Canada's immigration policy. In short, a series of reoccurring questions are posed whenever immigration levels rise: Do immigrants displace native born workers and lower wage levels?; Do immigrant earnings exceed or fall short of previous immigrants or Canadian born workers' earnings?; Do immigrants earn enough to keep them off the dole?; Has the quality of immigrants changed over time? The aim of this essay is to report the results of recent empirical work which attempt to carefully assess these questions. The essay is divided into four parts. First, the historical background and relevant Canadian immigration policies will be reviewed. Second, standard models and associated empirical studies are presented to discuss the labour market impact of immigrants. Finally, an analysis of the policy implications of these reported findings will be made.

Historical context

Dales (1966) summarizes Canada's turn of the century "National Economic Policy" as higher tariffs, railroad investment and increased immigration. The efficacy of these policies have all been questioned and in particular the wage and employment effects of this early burst in immigration are critically assessed by Dales. The problems, arising from immigration according to Dales, were twofold. First, immigration became increasingly urbanized resulting in lower Canadian urban wages. The effect of this wage decline was allegedly to displace or force native-born Canadian workers to the United States in search of higher wages. Thus, although Canadian G.N.P. grew via immigration, Dales argued that Canadian per capita income was retarded, especially relative to the growth in U.S. per capita income.[1] In addition, the immigration flow at

---

1   Dales and others have analyzed this period's immigration flow with a

the turn of the century was very inefficient; inefficient in the sense that net immigration was much smaller than the gross flows due to job displacement.[2] The modern legacy of this historical period is the continued preoccupation by modern policy makers of the effect of immigration on job displacement and earnings of immigrants in the Canadian economy.

Canadian immigration policy: circa 1951-1987

The examination of the impact of immigration in the Canadian labour market requires a basic knowledge of recent Canadian immigration policy. Throughout the 1950s economic forces were present to remove the continuing country preference clause of the 1953 Act. For example, Green (1976) argues that the post-war boom and resulting demand for skilled workers required a more liberal immigration policy. In 1967, a point system was adopted to allow immigrants to Canada to be chosen on the basis of suitability to Canada and the Canadian labour market needs and to mitigate any discrimination owing to religion, race or country of origin. This policy has been termed an "open policy" since the country of origin was not a criterion.[3] The unit assessment or point system was formally introduced into immigration regulations in 1967 as a means of ensuring that the immigrant selection process would be non-discriminatory with respect to sex, colour, race, nationality, and religion and yet still link the admission decision to domestic labour

---

neo-classical three factor growth model. Thus, with this well behaved production function an increase in labour via immigration in the absence of a corresponding increase in physical and human capital increased G.D.P. but per capita income declined.

2 Net immigration is defined as the difference in the total inflow into Canada minus the movement out, basically to the United States during this period.

3 It must be remembered that immigration policy during this period (and later policy revisions) were implemented in a wider context to reflect Canada's general foreign policy objectives. Nonetheless, it is still proper to assess the economic impacts of the resulting immigration policy.

market requirements (Marr and Percy, p. 62). The open policy of 1967 with its point system resulted in a substantial change in the composition of immigrants with a rise in the flow from less developed countries. In 1978 a new immigration act was implemented. In comparison to the 1967 Immigration Act, the 1978 Act could be termed a "restrictive policy." The restrictions inherent in the 1978 Act included specific yearly immigrant target levels tabled in the House of Commons coupled with a closer scrutiny of the immigrant's potential labour market impact. This latter policy had three major goals: Canadian demographic needs; family reunification and finally, tying immigration to the Canadian labour market requirements.

Entry under the 1978 Act could occur via three main avenues; family reunification, refugee class or as a selected worker (See Marr's Table 6). Assessment for each entry class reflected varying degrees of scrutiny for possible labour market impacts (See Marr, p. 14). In particular, the 1978 policy linked entry into Canada under the independent class almost solely to labour market requirements. During the recession years 1982 through 1985, immigration to Canada under the selected worker category was prohibited, except in the event of arranged employment. Arranged employment required certification from a Canada Employment Centre, which required the employer to demonstrate that he had been unable to engage a Canadian citizen. The emphasis therefore moved from educational qualifications to explicit employment. This restriction was lifted in 1986 (see Howith, pp. 16-27).

The 1978 policy clearly cannot be termed an open one. Rather, the policy reflected the view that scrutiny was required to insure that immigration costs did not exceed benefits (Marr and Percy, p. 58). Thus, two contradictory forces appear to change the potential labour market impact of the post-1978 immigrant flow. First, the emphasis on job certification potentially reduced the possibility of short-term unemployment for the independent class of immigrants. In addition, the acceleration of the family re-unification class partially circumvented the job certification criterion for entry and opened the possibility of substantial negative impacts on wages and jobs.

In short, these major changes from a closed (prior to 1967) to open (post-1967) and then, restrictive policy (after 1978) are strong *a priori* reasons to expect changes in the labour market impacts from recent Canadian immigrant inflows.

Trends in immigration

The successive policy changes are reflected in the recent trends in the size and composition of immigrants. The initiation of the 1967 open policy resulted in Third World immigrants to Canada increasing as a proportion of total Canadian immigration.[4] This trend continued even after the restrictive policy of 1978. In 1967 total Third World immigration represented 23.0 percent of total immigration. By 1986 this proportion had risen to 71 percent of the total.

As Canada moved from the open policy of 1967 to the more restrictive 1978 policy, total immigration began to decline. until a recent resurgence in the latter part of the 1980s. Clearly, total immigration flows are responsive to the business cycle in Canada. For example, between 1982 and 1985 immigration levels were one-third of the boom period level of 1967. Second, Third World immigration became an increasing percentage of the immigration total, regardless of the business cycle. For example, of the immigrants in the labour force, those originating from the Third World accounted for 67.9 percent in 1986, a substantial increase over 16.6 percent in 1967.

The post-1978 policy also had an effect on the labour force participation of all immigrants as well as those from the Third World. Between 1967 and 1974 approximately 50 percent of all immigrants were destined for the labour force. After 1977 a substantial decline in labour force participation for all immigrants occurred with a resulting average participation rate of 42.4 percent. The participation rates for Third World immigrants were generally lower throughout the post-1967 period (i.e. 42 percent) with the post 1977 period exhibiting a 40 percent average labour force participation rate. In short, as Third World immigrants became the predominate source of immigrants, the total labour force participation rate tended to equalize that of Third World immigrants.

---

4   For the purposes of this essay Third World is defined as those sending regions whose G.D.P. per person was less than $2,000 (U.S.) circa 1986.

A model of immigrant impact in the labour market

Before we analyze the literature pertaining to actual immigrant impacts in the labour market a theoretical exposition of the displacement and wage effects will be outlined. The displacement effect has been defined earlier. The wage effect is simply a recognition that the increased supply of labour (via immigration) could reduce the prevailing wage.

Consider an immigrant receiving country that produces a single, non-exported output by means of two inputs, capital and homogeneous labour. The left panel of Figure 1 presents a situation in which the world supply of labour is perfectly elastic at wage rate (We). Thus, at the

Figure 8–1: Immigration and Labour Displacement

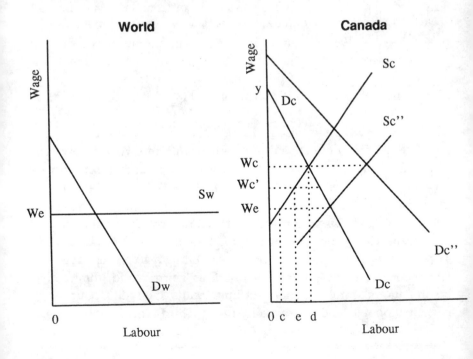

prevailing wage rate Canada could receive an unlimited amount of immigrants. The right panel shows the labour market in the immigrant receiving country, i.e., Canada. If labour were to seek its maximum earnings with negligible transportation and other costs and with no institutional impediments then (cd) workers would migrate to Canada. Thus, the Canadian labour supply would increase from (Sc) to (Sc") and its wage rate would fall to the world equilibrium level or (We). On the other hand, if Canada closed its borders, the wage rate in Canada would be (Wc).

In addition, if independent events occur such as a rise in product price or increased capital brought in by immigrants then these supply shifts induced by immigration could be offset by labour demand shifts. For example, even with large scale but, controlled immigration (i.e. supply shifts to Sc") the original equilibrium wage of Wc could be maintained by a shift in the demand curve equal to Dc". This of course would result in no domestic displacement and a constant wage rate. The actual wage and employment changes resulting from any immigration flow depend upon the slope of the labour demand and supply curves, the magnitude of the quota, and other assumptions implicitly embedded in Figure 8–1.[5] However, it must be remembered that Figure 8–1 represents a static world. If immigrants enter Canada with human or financial capital then both greater employment of native and foreign labour could result with a higher wage rate as the demand curve for labour shifts to the right.[6]

Literature review

There exist several Canadian studies which test several formal hypotheses concerning job displacement. In short, they ask: Do old or new

---

5   In general, the more inelastic the demand and supply relationships, *ceteris paribus*, the greater will be the reduction of domestic wages due to any given amount of immigration. Moreover, the displacement effect will be greater the more elastic the labour supply and the less elastic the labour demand.

6   The outward shift in the labour demand curve results from complementary capital raising the marginal product of labour at any wage rate.

immigrants displace themselves or the native born worker? If displacement occurs, is the effect isolated to certain industries or occupations? In addition, immigrants' relative earnings performance is a central concern in the literature. Important hypotheses put forward in the literature include the alleged declining income performance of immigrants and the associated delay in achieving the "catch up" point *vis à vis* the native born. Finally, the most recent literature tests quality degradation of the immigrants in terms of their human capital content and educational attainment. The central point to emphasize in this literature review is how this review will aid our assessment of recent immigration policy. Since immigrant policy specifically awards points for age, language, education, etc. the resulting immigrant earnings, occupational mobility and geographical location depend to a large degree on these selection criteria. Much of the econometric literature cited below will quantify the effects of these selection criteria and allow us ultimately to assess the merits of recent Canadian immigration policy.

The displacement literature

Akbari and DeVoretz (1992), DeVoretz (1989), Clark and Thompson (1986) and Roy (1987) provide modern econometric estimates of the displacement effect in Canada.

Table 8–1 reports the Akbari and DeVoretz's (1992) economy wide estimates of substitution elasticities (circa 1980) between pre-and post-1971 immigrants and native born labour and capital.[7] The substitution elasticities measure the percentage change or displacement of one type of input used when an alternative input is introduced into the industry. When these values are negative then displacement occurs since the introduced input causes a decline in the use of the alternative input (i.e. a loss of jobs equal to a-e in Fig. 8–1). Akbari and DeVoretz report

---

7   This distinction between immigrant vintage is an attempt to explicitly recognize the hypothesis that the two immigrant pools are drawn from different populations. Post-1971 immigrants are obviously younger, have a higher amount of human capital and differ in ethnicity when compared to the earlier immigrant flow.

insignificant economy wide elasticities of substitution between native-born workers and earlier immigrants (pre-1971) as well as between native-born workers and recent (post-1971) immigrants (see Table 8–1). Hence, according to Akbari and DeVoretz the hypothesis that there is no displacement of native-born workers by immigrants can be accepted for both the earlier and recent immigrant flows. This finding can be rationalized in Fig. 1 as a result of an upward shift of the labour demand curve from Dc to Dc''. Moreover, older and newer immigrants do not displace one another.

Table 8-1: Akbari and Devoretz
Elasticities of factor complementarities: 1981
125 Industries

Elasticity	Value	Std. Error	t-value
Between native born and –0.41 earlier immigrants (Cn b)	-0.41	1.10	-0.37
Between native born and recent immigrants (Cn d)	-0.41	2.46	-0.17
Between native born and capital (Cn k)	0.98	0.43	2.28*
Between recent immigrants and capital (Cd k)	0.99	0.88	1.12
Between earlier and recent immigrants (Cb d)	1.45	9.39	0.15

* A single asterisk indicates significance at the .05 level of significance.

Source: Akbari and DeVoretz (1992, Table 3).

Akbari and DeVoretz do find an important exception to their overall findings. When they sub-divide the Canadian economy into the foreign-born labour intensive sector, significant displacement occurs between any vintage of immigrants and the native-born labour force (or a movement from e to a in Fig. 8–1). This foreign-born labour intensive sector consists of 59 industry groupings which are mostly labour intensive in nature. Moreover, in the foreign labour intensive sector immigrants require significant amounts of domestic complementary capital. Thus, they conclude that the negative impact of immigrants in the Canadian economy is limited to a well defined foreign sector.[8]

In light of the major policy issue of job displacement, Akbari and DeVoretz findings indicate that in general Canada's point system and the later more restrictive policy (i.e. post-1978) coupled with increased capital inflows were successful in mitigating job loss economy wide. However, this general conclusion masked the significant job displacement in a labour intensive subsector of the economy.

Roy (1987) partially confirms the Akbari and DeVoretz findings when he concludes that all native-born and all foreign workers are neither substitutes or complements in the aggregate. Furthermore, when Roy disaggregates his study by area of origin for immigrants he finds significant displacement between Third World immigrants and the native-born labour force.

The key analytical point is to tie, if possible, this discovery of limited job displacement to particular immigration policies. In our concluding section we will attempt to analyze the particular aspects of immigration policy which made job displacement minimal economy wide but significant in some subsectors.

---

8   The foreign intensive sector included 59 industries out of the 125 covered in their study. These industries covered a wide range including the meat and poultry, clothing (combined) and university sectors. In general, across the pre-selected 59 industries, a one percent rise in foreign-born labour was calculated to reduce native-born employment by 2543 workers. Foreign labour intensive was defined as any 3 digit SIC industry which had twice the standard deviation above the mean number of foreign-born workers economy wide.

Figure 8–2: Age earnings profile

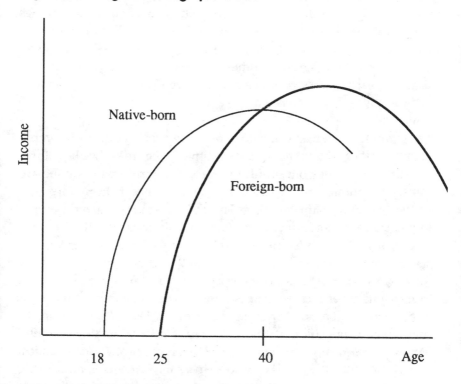

Earnings of Canadian and foreign born

The second obvious manifestation of the effect of the foreign born in the labour market is on earnings. Several questions emerge in both the professional literature and the general debate. These questions illustrate the confusion in the debate. For example, Do immigrants represent a very abundant supply (i.e. elastic supply) of labour which continually undercuts the prevailing wage for the Canadian born? or Do immigrants "catch up" and eventually outperform Canadian born earners due to an immigrant screening process which insures marketable skills and a greater willingness to work? Finally, does this immigrant earnings performance significantly affect net contributions to the treasury? The professional literature addresses these various possibilities by introducing the analytical concept of a life cycle earnings profile (Figure 8–2).

The aging process increases the human capital investment of the employed and their earnings grow accordingly. Under the life cycle view (i.e. Figure 8–2) the foreign born initially experience an earnings disadvantage relative to the native born. Then after a period of relative earnings growth the foreign-born catch up and surpass their native-born cohort. This diagram assumes a constant skill or quality mix over time with each successive vintage of immigrants such that a continuous age-earnings profile is traced out over the elapsed 15 year period (i.e. 40 minus 25).

It would seem reasonable to expect however that the skill composition of immigrants is changing over time. In Figure 8–3 we have three age earnings profiles: one profile for the native-born and two for the two vintages of immigrants. Note the distinct difference in the performance of the two immigrant vintages. The old-foreign-born arrives with a higher skill level and experiences a rapid assimilation in the Canadian labour market. The old vintage surpasses the earnings power (at b) of the native-born. The more recent foreign-born cohort enters the labour force at the same age as the earlier group but, this newer vintage of immigrants never surpasses the earnings of the native-born. The crucial policy related question for these diagrams is: Did the change in the immigrant composition that partially resulted from the 1967 and 1978 Immigration Acts produce Figure 8–2 or Figure 8–3? In other words, will immigrants ever catch up and surpass the Canadian born (Figure 8–2) or will the newer immigrants remain below (Figure 8–3) the earnings levels of their Canadian cohorts?

Moreover, since much of the reported literature will analyze earnings in terms of the immigrant's occupation, age, schooling, country of origin, language, marital status, years in residence and provincial residence a precise assessment of policy criteria can be made.

The key question to first answer is: Do immigrants actually "catch up" to the native born in terms of earning power? The available literature gives us a mixed picture. Under an older methodology the standard answer was that after 10 to 15 years the average immigrant overtook his Canadian cohort and thereafter earned more (Akbari, 1987; Chiswick and Miller, 1988 and Meng, 1987) and paid more in taxes than the native born cohort. The newest econometric estimates of the age earnings profiles dissent from this view. Borjas (1989) in a recent book argues that a quality decline has appeared in the newer vintages of Canadian immigrants which is due to unobserved variables. Thus, as time passes in Canada the immigrant's earnings falls relative to his Canadian cohort and given the initial earnings disadvantage of most immigrants they never catch up. DeVoretz and Fagnan (1990) employing the Borjas methodology with 1986 Canadian data conclude:

> The data indicates that the quality of Canadian immigrants in general has experienced a secular decline circa 1971-1986. There exists some evidence that the general decline however, may

Figure 8-3: Composite earnings profile

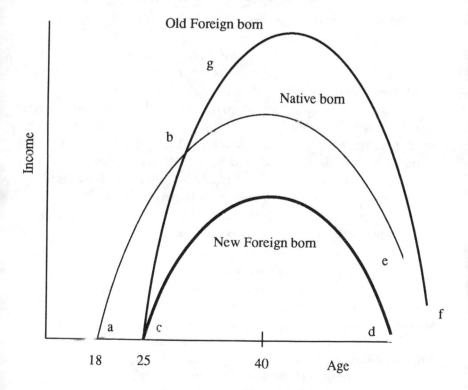

have halted by 1986. The conclusion can be drawn that assimilation during 1971-1986 into the Canadian labour market did not afford ever increasing returns to immigrants. Moreover, tests by skill level reveal that unskilled immigrants have experienced the largest decline in quality as measured by the years in residence variable. In addition, this effect on unskilled workers is growing over census periods and did not halt by 1986. (DeVoretz and Fagnan, 1990 p. 23)

Borjas also disaggregates his earnings profiles to detect if this decline in earnings is specific to a country or area of origin. Borjas states his views quite clearly:

The decline in Canada is mostly due to the fact that more immigrants are coming from countries that tend to perform worse in the labour market. (Borjas, 1988, p. 61)

More specifically Borjas finds that Canadian immigrant earnings are gaining slowly on the native-born at only four-tenths of one percent per annum. Thus, given the standard initial earnings disadvantage of 25 percent for immigrants it is unlikely that an average immigrant would live long enough to surpass his Canadian cohort.

Other modern studies are more optimistic about the assimilation process. Chiswick and Miller (1988) and Bloom and Gunderson (1989) argue that the catch up process occurs and does so in a reasonable time frame. In particular, Chiswick and Miller (1988) find that each year's duration in Canada adds approximately 1.5 percent to their earnings regardless of other socioeconomic characteristics.

Bloom and Gunderson (1989, p. 20) state that their cross-sectional findings imply that immigrants circa 1971 would surpass natives' earnings after 12.8 years and that correctly employing the recent techniques of Borjas does not alter this conclusion.

At this point the available literature yields a mixed view of the relative success of immigrants *vis à vis* their ability to catch up and surpass the native born earnings functions. An equally important analytical point focuses on the determinants of immigrant earnings since this will ultimately reflect on immigrant selection criteria.

Table 8–2 reports a typical set of arguments which affect immigrant earnings from DeVoretz and Fagnan (1990) for two periods of entry from two areas of origin. The variable I or foreign birth status reflects

Table 8-2: DeVoretz and Fagnan
Earnings differential parameter estimates by area:
1981 - 1986

Independent Variables	Asia		United Kingdom	
	1981	**1986**	**1981**	**1986**
I	0.3044** (-8.298)	-.3957** (-3.324)	.06529** ((3.258)	-.2808** (-1.69)
Age	.06499** (12.543)	.1003** (11.11)	.7229** (24.43)	.08103** (15.02)
Educ.	.043803** (24.10)	.03650** (6.653)	.04742** (42.42)	.0510** (16.9)
Mar.	.15734** (7.417)	.03650** (6.653)	.1270** (10.5)	.1153** (3.84)

Notes:
t-values are given in brackets.
* Coefficients significant at the 1 percent level
** Coefficients significant at the 5 percent level

the earnings penalty or premium resulting from foreign birth.[9] Table 8–2 row 1 indicates that Asian immigrants suffer an earnings penalty from place of birth of 3 to 4 percent respectively in 1981 and 1986. In contrast, U.K. immigrants had a slight (i.e. six tenths of one percent) premium in their earnings due to place of origin in 1981.[10] The specific point to note

9   In each year after their date of arrival this premium or penalty persists throughout the foreign-born working life.. Thus, it is possible to apply a discounting technique to calculate the lifetime effect on earnings of this foreign-born effect.

10   The country of origin variable has no significant effect for U.K. immigrants in 1986.

is that holding all other major factors constant country of origin independently affects the foreign-born workers earning power upon entry. The next three rows in Table 8–2 reflect the efficacy of Canadian policy makers attempts to choose young, educated and married workers. The aging process adds from six to ten percent per annum to the earnings of immigrants (row 2) from either area of origin with the largest effect of age occurring for the most recent Asian immigrants (i.e. ten percent). Education (EDUC) yields a 3 to 5 percent increase in earnings for each additional year of schooling with a lower rate accruing to recent Asian immigrants.[11] Finally, marital status has a once and for all large positive effect on earnings (i.e. 12 to 16 percent), except for the most recent Asian immigrants (i.e. only a 4 percent increase). Other (unreported) factors (province of residence, gender and part-time versus full-time status) influence earnings. In sum, living in Ontario or British Columbia, being male and working full time has a significant positive impact on earnings.

In short, most of the immigration policy criteria employed had a positive effect on earnings. The exception was the shift away from educational criteria to job certification. Both Coulson and DeVoretz (1989) and Seward (1989) have noted the decline in recent educational attainment of immigrants. This has had a profound effect on earnings. Also, DeVoretz and Fagnan report age earning profiles by skill level and note:

> For unskilled and skilled immigrants, quality as captured by years in residence variable declined. On the other hand, for immigrants in the professionally trained occupations their associated earnings functions did not reveal any quality decline. (Devoretz and Fagnan, 1990, p. 24)

---

11 This later point is also reflected in Chiswick and Miller's research which indicates that the return from education depends on whether English is the mother tongue. They found that the return to schooling for the foreign born from non English speaking underdeveloped countries is one half the rate of the immigrant from English speaking developed countries (Chiswick and Miller 1988, Table 2, p. 200).

Figure 8-4: 1986 age earning profiles for professionals

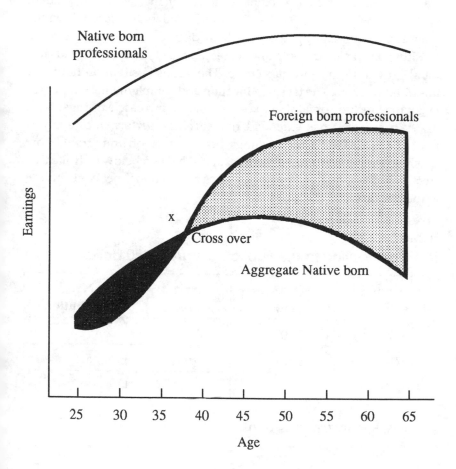

Figure 8–4 illustrates DeVoretz' and Fagnan's findings. After only ten years in residence the earnings of foreign-born professionally trained workers exceed the average native born Canadian.[12] On the other hand, the unskilled foreign-born immigrant circa 1986 does not

---

12 Years of residence is defined as age minus date of arrival.

catch up to the average Canadian until retirement age. Hence, as the composition of the foreign born becomes less skilled, on average, their elapsed time to catch up to the earnings of the average Canadian becomes longer. Figure 8–4 can be interpreted as the case where the foreign born are equipped with a high degree of education and the resulting on-the-job training and increased facility in English leads to a rapid growth in the earnings curve. The opposite situation holds for unskilled workers. The lack of education and complementary inputs of language preclude obtaining the experience to increase earnings.

Akbari (1989) has extended this earnings performance analysis when he asks; Given the earnings performance of immigrants how much do they contribute to the treasury? The data below indicate that circa 1980 the foreign-born stock makes a substantial net contribution to the treasury.

Table 8–3:
Net Contribution to the Public Treasury (1980 dollars)

Year of entry	Taxes paid	Services used	Net contribution
1979	2,107	1,980	127
1971-75	3,527	3,008	519
1966-1970	4,879	3,506	1,373

Source: Akbari, 1987, Table 15, p. 81.

Akbari concludes from the above computations that "An immigrant household entering Canada in 1980 when evaluated at a real discount rate of 2 percent was worth $19,630" to the federal treasury (Akbari, 1987, p. 80). Moreover, these large positive values imply a subsidy to the Canadian resident born taxpayer. Akbari is careful to point out that these findings are primarily a consequence of the relatively higher earnings of immigrants which simultaneously raise immigrant taxes and reduce their need for social services.

Human capital flows

The above review of the two major labour market impacts on labour displacement and earnings have in general shown that the negative impacts are minimal in the Canadian context. However, two disquieting trends emerged from this review. First, there exists labour displacement in subsectors of the economy. Second, earnings for unskilled immigrants and those moving from certain areas are falling behind the native-born cohorts. This section addresses one possible source of these disturbing trends. The 1978 Immigration Act shifted the emphasis from formal education to job certification and de facto after 1980 the family re-unification class (which is less subject to strict economic criteria) became the dominate flow.[13] Coulson and DeVoretz (1989) have estimated the decline in the educational content of immigrants after the implementation of the 1978 Immigration Act. They conclude:

> We have found that the more restrictive post-1978 policy substantially reduced total human capital flows. Since the policy resulted in fewer highly skilled immigrants entering the country, presumably the emphasis upon job certification has substantial implications from a domestic standpoint. (1989, p. 10)

The decline in human capital inflows estimated for the post 1978 period is large. For the 1979-1987 period the replacement value of the education content of immigrants fell to 30 percent of the amount estimated by DeVoretz and Maki (1980) for the 1967-1973 period. For the 1966-1973 period the yearly average value of human capital inflow was over $300 million (1968) dollars while for the 1979-1987 period this average yearly value had declined to $ 100 million (1968) dollars (Coulson and DeVoretz, 1989, p. 10).

We have already observed from the literature review that the foreign labour intensive sector experience and Third World immigrants caused significant labour displacement. The common factor in both the recent Third World inflow and the 59 industries in the foreign labour intensive sector is low educational content. Couple this decline in formal

---

13 See Coulson (1989), for a more complete description of the immigration policy changes which affected the flow of human capital.

training with the lack of language facility of more recent immigrants (see Chiswick and Miller, 1989) and a two tier labour market emerges. In short, the unskilled portion of the labour market with newer immigrants with less education and language facility experience declining earnings relative to their native-born cohort. Moreover, the less educated immigrants caused job displacement in the foreign labour intensive sector of the market. The question is whether formal or on-the-job training in Canada can reverse these trends in the labour market. This strategy is possible, but to replicate the human capital content of the pre 1978 immigration inflow according to the Coulson-DeVoretz estimates would cost $3.1 billion (1986) dollars.

Policy conclusions

Before any assessment of the success or failure of recent Canadian immigration policy can be made vis a vis the labour market one important caveat must be noted. The supply of immigrants available to Canada is ultimately based upon a self-selection process. Potential immigrants to Canada experience a process of self-selection in which they compare the benefits of moving to the economic prospects of remaining in their country of origin. Hence, the source country and characteristics of the available immigrant pool is changing over time. Thus, for example, the decline in skilled western European immigrants after 1970 has little to do with Canadian policy, but is an outgrowth of rising economic prosperity in Europe. In a similar fashion, the rise in the supply of economically qualified immigrants from the Third World again was a byproduct of immigrant self-selection. The key policy question is Did Canada alter its policies to attract the most qualified immigrants in light of the changing supply patterns? Moreover, did Canada's immigrant policy allow Canada to successfully compete for highly trained immigrants vis à vis other destination regions?

Immigration policy between 1967 to 1978 must be judged a success in terms of labour market adjustment. Highly qualified immigrants were available and the existing policy favoured their admission. Armed with high educational attainment these immigrants' earnings grew quickly with little associated job displacement and made immigrants net contributors to the treasury. After 1978, the economic consequences of Canada's immigrant flows changed. The value of the transferred human capital stock declined, earnings of certain skill groups now fell below the average Canadian and some research (Roy, 1987) detected job displacement by the largest fraction of movers (i.e from the Third World) during this period. How much of this reduced assimilation in the labour market is due to self-selection and how much can be attributed to the post 1978 policy? Clearly self-selection limited Canada's supply to predominantly Third World movers during this period since this was a world-wide phenomenon. Nonetheless, the shift in admissions classes with the growth of the family reunification class and the decline in the independent class resulted in a less stringent application of economic criteria to the post 1978 immigrant flow. This less stringent policy was partially offset in the post 1978 period with the growth in importance of the job certification criterion. Nonetheless, this latter criterion applied to a smaller fraction of post 1978 movers and denied the possibility that highly trained immigrants could create jobs for themselves or others. In addition, the shift in policy away from formal educational qualifications meant that the long run occupational mobility of immigrants and the associated rise in earnings was thwarted.

On balance, immigration policy circa 1967-1990 followed by several governments under widely varying economic conditions must be judged successful in terms of the labour market performance of the resulting immigrant flow. However, recent disquieting trends in the labour market performance of immigrants imply that a return to a policy which emphasizes the independent or economic immigrant class with high formal educational standards would insure continued success in the future.

References

Akbari, A. "Some Economic Impacts of the Immigrant Population in Canada" Ph.D. dissertation, Dept. of Economics, Simon Fraser University, Nov, 1987.

_____, "The Benefits of Immigrants to Canada: Evidence on Tax and Public Services," *Canadian Public Policy*, Vol. XV, No. 4, pp. 424-435.

Akbari, A. and D.J. DeVoretz, "The Substitutability of Foreign Born Labour in Canadian Production circa 1980," *Canadian Journal of Economics*, August, 1992.

Bloom, D.E. and M. Gunderson, "An Analysis of the Earnings of Canadian Immigrants," Unpublished manuscript, July, 1989, p. 24.

Borjas, G.J., *International Differences in the Labour Market Performance of Immigrants*, W.E. Upjohn Institute for Employment Research, 1988, p. 106.

Coulson, R.G., "The Change in Human Capital Transfers to Canada from Less Developed Countries: 1967-86." M.A. thesis, Simon Fraser University, 1989.

Coulson, R.G. and D.J. DeVoretz, "Human Capital Content of Canadian Immigration 1966-1987," presented at the 16th Conference on the Use of Quantitative Methods in Canadian Economic History, March, 1989.

Chiswick, B.R. and P.W. Miller, "Earnings in Canada: The Role of Immigrant Generation, French Ethnicity, and Language," *Research in Population Economics*, VI (JAI Press, Inc., 1988), pp. 183-228.

Clark, D.P. and H. Thompson, "Immigration, International Capital Flows and Long Run Income Distribution in Canada," *Atlantic Economic Journal*, XIV: 4, Dec. 1986, pp. 24-29.

Dales, J.H., *The Protective Tariff in Canada's Development*, University of Toronto Press, 1966.

_____, "The Cost of Protectionism with High International Mobility of Factors," *Canadian Journal of Economics and Political Science*, 30, Nov. 1964, pp. 512-524.

DeVoretz, D.J. and S. Fagnan, "Some Evidence on Canadian Immigrant Quality Decline: Foreign Born versus Resident Born Earnings Function for 1971-1986," Presented at the Canadian Economic Association Meetings, Victoria, B.C. June, 1990.

DeVoretz, D.J. and D. Maki, "The Size and Distribution of Human Capital Transfers from LDC's to Canada 1966-73," *Economic Development and Cultural Change*, XXVIII: 4, July, 1980, pp. 779-800.

_____, "The Immigration of Third World Professionals to Canada," *World Development*, II: 1 (1983), pp. 55-64.

_____, "The Brain Drain and Income Taxation," *World Development*, III: 10, (1975), pp. 705-716.

Green, Alan G., *Immigration and the Post-War Canadian Economy*, Macmillan of Canada, 1976.

Howith, H.G. "Immigration Levels Planning: The First Decade," Ottawa: Employment and Immigration Canada, March, 1988.

Marr W. and M. Percy, "Immigration Policy and Canadian Economic Growth," in J. Whalley, *Domestic Policy and the International Environment*, (University of Toronto Press, 1985), Ch. 3., pp. 57-109.

Rao, S. and C. Kasalis, "Labour Shortages and Immigration Policy," *Canadian Public Policy*, July, 1982.

Roy, A.S. "An Analysis of Substitutability and Complementarity of Immigrants and Canadian-born Work Force," *Labour Market Bulletin* IV: 9, Oct. 1987, pp. 5-11.

Seward, S. "Immigrants in the Canadian Labour Force: Their Role in Structural Change," paper presented at the Canadian Population Society Annual Meeting, Learned Society Meetings, Universite Laval, Quebec, June 5-7, 1989, p. 42.

Chapter 9

Immigration and the Housing Market

J.F. Miyake

Introduction

VARIOUS GOVERNMENT OFFICIALS AND INDUSTRY representatives have indicated that the expected increase in immigration over the next several years will be "good" for housing in Canada. The popular press and books such as *The New Landlords* suggest that increases in the demand for housing are a direct function of immigration. The notion that immigration increases the demand for housing is accepted as a truism, although there is very little quantitative evidence on the strength and durability of this relationship. This chapter offers a preliminary examination of the relationship between immigration and housing prices. The first section synthesizes census demographic data to provide a broad overview of the linkage between immigration and housing demand. The second section examines available time series data, to determine the extent to which immigration among other variables has contributed to changes in the price of housing.

I have chosen to focus on Greater Vancouver as a representative housing market, primarily for empirical convenience. Greater Vancouver is similar to other large Canadian cities, primarily Toronto, in the proportion of immigrants received each year. However, Greater Vancouver is different from other large Canadian cities in its geography. Development in the Greater Vancouver area is restricted by mountains and sea on one side and an agricultural land reserve on the other. Therefore, if immigration does have a significant impact on the housing market, there is a greater likelihood of identifying this link in Vancouver than in other cities where supply may be more expandable. In this respect, findings for Vancouver may not necessarily be generalizable to the rest of Canada.

A background model of housing demand

Demand for urban housing is in large part a function of a city's changing demographic structure. This structure is, in turn, a function of natural population growth, of immigration and emigration.

The demanders of housing in the Lower Mainland fall mainly into three categories: 1) residents of the Vancouver area who are separating from established households to set up households on their own; 2) residents of other regions of British Columbia or Canada who are migrating to Greater Vancouver to establish households; 3) residents of other countries who are settling in the Lower Mainland. Together, these three types of demanders constitute the demand for housing. It is generally agreed that the quantity of housing demanded is in inverse relation to its price. That is, lower housing prices stimulate a greater quantity demand of housing.

The supply of housing is composed at any point in time of a stock of residences which have been vacated (or will soon be vacated) by their previous occupants, and a stock of new housing which has become available for occupancy. At any point, this stock is fixed, although it can expand or diminish over time. Where demand and supply intersect is an equilibrium point. Figure 9–1 portrays a hypothetical housing market for one city at three different dates.

Figure 9–1: A hypothetical housing market for one city at three different dates

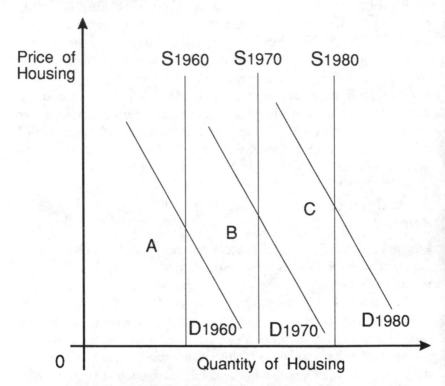

Demand has increased from 1960 to 1970, and from 1970 to 1980. So has supply. The points A, B and C are equilibrium points. The distance from A to B, and from B to C, represents growth in housing over the ten-year periods. It is this growth in Greater Vancouver's housing and the price movements which accompanied it over the last twenty years that we seek to explain.

Ignoring the question of price for the time being we turn our attention to the demand pressures that caused this increase in the supply of housing. David Baxter of the Laurier Institute has written a landmark report, *Population and Housing in Vancouver: Changing Patterns of Demographics and Demand,* on this subject. His report uses census data to examine demographic changes that have increased the demand for housing. He is able to suggest the proportion of increased housing supply that can be attributed to each demographic change. To understand how he reached the conclusions he does, a cursory understanding of the demographic tools used is necessary.

A household is a group of people who live in one residence. The group can consist of one, or two, or many people. The household formation rate (HFR) is the ratio of households to the population of a given region:

$$HFR = \frac{\text{number of households in a region}}{\text{total population in that region}}$$

The HFR, when inverted, yields the average number of people per household. It is the form given above, however, which will allow us to partition the demand for housing into its various components.

Growth in housing is measured by subtracting the number of households existing at any given time, for example 1966, from the number existing at a later date, say 1971. Growth in population is measured in the same way. Indices of housing and population growth can be constructed by dividing the number of households or the population in any time period by the number that existed at some arbitrary year, and then multiplying by 100.

$$\text{Housing Index} = \frac{\text{number of households in year t}}{\text{number of households in base year}} \times 100$$

These indices yield percentage increases in households and population over their levels at the base year. The year 1951 has been used as the base year. It is interesting to note that the number of households has grown faster than the population. This implies that the average size of household has been falling since about 1961.

An age cohort is an age category, for example 15-24 years, or 65+ years. An age cohort is measured by the number of people who fall into that category at a particular date. Over time a person passes through many age cohorts: a person born in 1950 will fall into the 0-14 age cohort until 1964, then into the 15-24 cohort from 1965 through 1974, and so on. The post-war baby boom (1946-62), for example, can be tracked through time by the unusual increases in the relative sizes of the appropriate age cohorts from census to census. A census period is the five-year period between regular Canadian censuses, i.e. 1966-71, 1971-76 and so on. With these demographic tools in hand, we can now analyze the nature of demand for Vancouver's housing since 1966.

Baxter partitioned the demand for housing in Vancouver into three categories: natural population increase, net migration, and changes in the household formation rate. For the purposes of this chapter, net migration was further divided into net domestic migration and net international migration.

The contribution of natural population increase is the change in demand that would be caused by population growth if the average number of people per household were held constant. This contribution is found first by adjusting the previous census period's population for births, and for changes due to aging and deaths in each age cohort. Column three of table 9–1 provides an example of this methodology. The household formation rate derived for each age cohort from the last census is then multiplied by the new cohort estimates to determine the expected change in the number of households in each age category. (See Column three in table 9–2). The expected changes (column 4, table 9–2) are then summed and divided by total growth in housing to yield the percentage contribution of natural population increase to housing demand.

The contribution of net migration is calculated, again holding the average household size constant. Net domestic migration since the last census is broken into age cohorts, multiplied by the age-specific household formation rate (column 5, table 9–2), summed, and divided by total growth in housing.

Net migration was divided into net domestic migration and net international migration using ratios estimated for the same census periods used by Baxter. These ratios were taken from another Laurier Institute report by Gregory Schwann, *When Did You Move to Vancouver?: An Analysis of Migration and Migrants into Metropolitan Vancouver*.

For example, using Schwann's finding that 29.3 percent of net migrants in 1971 were international migrants, it can be approximately estimated that 29.3 percent of the changes in housing supply resulting from changes in net migration can be attributed to international migration. These approximations may in fact be generous as Schwann notes that international immigrant households tend to be larger than average, thus their specific household formation ratio should be lower.

The contribution to the demand for housing due to changes in the household formation rate is calculated as a residual. Since the effects of natural population increase and net migration are estimated holding the household formation rate constant, any remaining unexplained demand is attributed to changes in this rate.

Table 9-1: Components of increases in housing demand, 1961 to 1966
Population

Age Group	1961 Actual	1966 No Migration	Natural Increase	Net In Migration	1966 Total
0-14	238,957	243,727	4,770	18,305	262,032
15-24	100,968	125,188	24,220	16,838	142,026
25-34	111,007	98,733	–12,274	16,548	115,281
35-44	119,477	119,466	–11	6,394	125,860
45-54	98,789	109,359	10,570	3,358	112,717
55-64	65,867	75,918	10,051	2,202	78,120
≥ 65	91,732	93,018	1,286	4,847	97,865
Total	826,798	865,409	38,611	68,492	933,901
Growth			36.1%	63.9%	107,103

Source: David Baxter (1990), *Population and Housing in Vancouver, Changing Patterns of Demographics and Demand*, The Laurier Institute, p. 52.

Table 9-2: Components of increases in housing demand, 1961 to 1966
Households

Age Group	1961 Actual	1966 No Migration	Natural Increase	Net In Migration	Changes in HFR
15-24	8,048	9,979	1,931	1,342	4,468
24-34	44,577	39,648	-4,929	6,645	4,569
35-44	54,393	54,388	-5	2,911	4,228
45-54	49,896	55,235	5,339	1,696	829
55-64	34,166	39,380	5,214	1,142	2,214
≥ 65	48,069	48,743	674	2,540	3,684
Total	239,149	247,372	8,223	16,276	19,992
Growth			18.5%	36.6%	44.9%

Table 9-3: Contribution of demographic variables to the demand for housing

Census Period	Natural Migration (%)	Domestic Migration (%)	International Migration (%)	Changes in Household Formation (%)
1966-71	23.9%	38.2%	15.8%	22.1%
1971-76	43.7	18.6	11.3	26.4
1976-81	45.5	24.9	10.5	19.2
1981-86	63.4	31.4	11.7	−6.5

Source: David Baxter (1990), *Population and Housing in Vancouver, Changing Patterns of Demographics and Demand*, The Laurier Institute, p. 52.

From Table 9–3 we note that international migration has accounted for about 10 percent to 16 percent of the demand for housing over the past twenty years. However the largest single factor accounting for demand is natural population increase. The increasing importance of this category is due in large part to the maturing of the post-war baby boomers. At the last census, the youngest members of the baby boom would have been 24 years old, while the majority would have been in their mid-30s. Given typical household formation rates which are very high in the 25-34 age cohort, it is not unreasonable to suspect that the 1991 census will reflect the fact that the majority of the baby boomers have already been absorbed into the housing market.

Baxter and Schwann both draw the conclusion from the census data that immigration seems to have played a moderate role in the demand for housing in Greater Vancouver over the last twenty years. Their findings indicate that changes in the natural population and interprovincial migration have played a more important role in the demand equation.

The census methodology used in these studies effectively assumes that supply changes in direct proportion to changes in demand. However, short term supply, as can be seen in figure 9–1, is assumed fixed. Thus any shifts in short term demand will be reflected as price increases. Over the long-run, shifts in demand will increase housing prices if the average cost of houses increases with increased scale of construction; that is, if the long-run supply curve for housing is upward sloping.

Immigration and housing prices

The impact of changes in demand on average housing prices may not be the same for all groups. For example, one group of "demanders" may favour higher priced housing. Consequently, growth in the demand of this group will have a proportionally greater impact on average housing prices than will growth in the demand of other groups.

For an intuitive examination of the relationship between the price of housing and the demographic variables specified in Baxter's study, we will use simple correlation and partial correlation analysis. A regression analysis is presented in Appendix A, which examines the model in greater depth.

The demographic variables of interest have been defined by variables that are available on an annual basis. We examined annual data from 1962 to 1990. The average housing price for greater Vancouver was supplied by the Multiple Listing Service of Greater Vancouver. It covers only residential house prices. This price has been deflated to 1981 levels using the Canadian CPI (this variable is the designated real housing price or RHsPR). Immigration (Imm) is the number of immigrants who come to Canada who indicate they are destined for B.C. at the time of immigration. The assumption is that most will settle in the Lower Mainland. Interprovincial migration (Inter) was also defined on a provincial basis. This figure represents the net of incoming and outgoing interprovincial migration. In some years this figure is negative.

Natural population (Npop) change was the hardest of the demographic variables to translate into annual form. The census measured changes in housing demand caused by changes in the size of age cohort groups. Given the time span examined, the most important demographic change tracked by the "natural population" variable was the entry of the baby boom generation into the housing market. The annual proxy used to approximate the number of potential house buyers coming of age each year was the crude birth rate (the crude birth rate is the number of births per 1000 people in a given year) twenty-eight years ago in Canada. Twenty-eight years was chosen through trial and error and seems to correspond to the average age at which most individuals would be making a first house purchase. The birth rate of Canada, not B.C., was used as it was the most readily available. It is assumed that the B.C. birth rate would reflect similar figures. As our data set begins in 1962 and ends in 1990 the birth rate of interest starts in 1934 and ends in 1962.

The household formation ratio (HFR) was the only datum taken from the census, or in this case taken second hand from the report. Due to the lack of observations in years between censuses, this variable is recorded in a stepwise fashion, i.e. it is the same for the first five years and then shifts with the data found in the next census.

Table 9–4 presents a correlation matrix of the above variables. The first column describes the correlation between the variables of interest i.e. real housing price and the designated demographic variables. A simple correlation describes the extent to which changes in one variable are similar to changes in another variable. It is a description of similarity as opposed to a causal relationship.

Table 9-4: Simple correlation matrix

	RHsPR	Imm	Inter	Npop	HFR
RHsPR	1.00				
Imm	0.26	1.00			
Inter	0.24	0.66	1.00		
Npop	0.78	-0.15	-0.25	1.00	
HFR	0.81	0.001	-0.08	0.91	1.00

Changes in the natural population (Npop) and the effects of the baby boomers contributing to the household formation ratio (HFR) appear to have higher correlations with real housing prices (RHsPR) than do immigration or interprovincial migration. The simple correlation figures support the results of the report. However, the observed simple correlation between two variables can be the result of the effects of other variables, with which they are both correlated. For instance, the HFR is highly correlated with Npop which in turn is also correlated with RHsPR. Therefore, part of the correlation found between RHsPR and HFR may be indirectly attributed to the relationship between HFR and Npop.

The partial correlation matrix (table 9–5) avoids the above problems. The correlations between real housing prices and the demographic variables or independent variables have been purified by using statistical methods to remove the effects of any correlation between independent variables. A partial correlation matrix is equivalent to holding all other independent variables constant when finding the correlation between a given independent variable and the dependent variable. Therefore, it can be said that r=0.58 is the correlation between immigration and real housing prices, holding all other tested variables constant. It should be noted that these correlations can not be regarded as denoting a causal relationship between real housing prices and the demographic variables.

Table 9-5: Partial correlation matrix

	Imm	Inter	HFR	Npop
RHsPR	0.58	0.4	0.12	0.62

The partial correlation analysis suggests that immigration plays a more important role in influencing the price of housing, than the report, as summarized in the preceding section, suggests. The partial regression analysis suggests that the effect of immigration on housing prices is almost equivalent to that caused by changes in the natural population. Moreover, the partial correlation associated with immigration flows is higher than that associated with household formation rates and inter-provincial migration. These findings suggest that demand associated with international immigration may be skewed above-average housing (in terms of price), in that their impact on average price seems disproportionate to their numbers.

Summary and conclusion

The Baxter report concludes that "If we seek someone to blame for this increase in demand, we find that the enemy is us, not some unusual or exotic group of residents or migrants. In fact there is no one to blame: the future growth in housing demand is a logical and normal extension of trends in the nation's population, trends that have their roots in the baby boom of 1946 to 1961 period, and the historical desirability of metropolitan Vancouver as a place of residence" (Baxter, p. 79).

I feel that our results are strong enough (see Appendix A) to disagree with this statement. The time series analysis suggests that there is a significant link between immigration flows into B.C. and the price of housing in greater Vancouver. Though natural trends in the population absorb most of the increased supply of housing the price of housing is a direct function in part of immigration flows.

Appendix A

Using the demographic variables defined in the body of the text, as independent variables, we estimated an ordinary least squares equation with real housing prices as the dependent variable. The results are summarized below:

Table 9A-1: OLS: 1962-1990
Dependent variable: real housing price (RHsPR)

Variable	Estimated Coefficient	t-Ratio
Immigration	1.69	3.5
Interprov.	0.49	2.14
Npop.	7794.5	3.9
HFR	115280	0.62
Constant	-190920	-7.4

Though the R squared associated with this regression is high (R=0.87), there are several potentially important statistical problems. In particular, the simple correlation matrix contained in the body of the text indicates a significant multicollinearity problem. The high correlation between household formation ratios (HFR) and natural population (Npop) indicates the presence of multicollinarity in the sample. This condition suggests that the coefficient for the NPOP and the HFR are unreliable; however, the coefficient for the immigration variable is not necessarily biased.

The estimated equation also apparently suffers from autocorrelation. We corrected for the autocorrelation using a Cochran-Orcut procedure (rho=0.27). This correction seemed to correct the autocorrelation problem. The new estimated results are as follows:

Table 9A-2: Auto: 1963-1990
Dependent variable: real price of housing

Variable	Estimated Coefficient	t-Ratio
Immigration	1.48	2.58
Intprov.	0.52	1.97
Npop	6126.9	2.59
HFR	268430	1.23
Constant	-197160	–6.1

The R squared is still high (R = 0.88) and all variables except the HFR are statistically significant. However, just to check the robustness of this model, which was not after all designed for time series data, the possibility of misspecification or missing variables was explored.

The real price of housing has been on an overall increase over the last twenty-eight years. Many of the independent variables such as immigration, natural population and household formation ratios have also been increasing over the last twenty-seven years. A trend was thus introduced to the regression in an attempt to capture this general upward movement. Another variable that was found to be highly negatively correlated with the real price of housing was the vacancy rate (r = -0.71). As renting is a direct substitute for buying we would expect that the vacancy rate would figure prominently in a consumer's buying decision and should be considered in this model. The vacancy rate is taken from the Canadian Mortgage and Housing Corporation's Rental Survey for the Greater Vancouver region. This survey is done twice a year. The vacancy rate for the fall/winter survey was used in this study as it was available for the greatest number of years. The ordinary least squares regression is reported below.

Table 9A–3: OLS: 1963-1990
Dependent variable: real housing prices (RHsPR)

Variable	Estimated Coefficient	t-Ratio
Immigration	1.19	1.67
Inter	0.52	2.26
Npop	5769.5	2.70
HFR	-128310	-0.35
Trend	1426.5	1.07
Vac	-4932.6	-1.75
Constant	-79746	-0.81

The R squared is 0.89 and the Durbin-Watson statistic is 1.95 signalling that no autocorrelation is detected. All coefficients are significant, except HFR and the trend. A simple correlation matrix reveals high correlation between HFR and Npop, and between Trend and HFR. The presence of multicollinearity between theses variables is depressing the t-ratios, which means the trend estimated coefficient is probably significant.

A problem with this model is the negative coefficient in front of the HFR, although the coefficient is statistically insignificant. As the household formation ratio is the inverse of the average number of people per house, the demand for housing should be increasing with the decrease in the number of people per house or increasing with HFR. Thus the coefficient should be positive.

However, a non-nested test comparing the R squares between the expanded model and the basic demographic model suggests no improvements in predictive power is made by adding vacancy rate and trend (F=1.8). Therefore, the robustness of the original model is proven.

References

Baxter, David (1990) *Population and Housing in Vancouver, Changing Patterns of Demographics and Demand.* The Laurier Institute: Vancouver, B.C.

Goldberg, Michael (1985) *The Chinese Connection: Getting Plugged into Pacific Real Estate, Trade and Capital Markets.* University of British Columbia Press: Vancouver, B.C.

Gutstein, D. (1990) *The New Landlords: Asian Investment in Canadian Real Estate.* Porcepic Books: Victoria, B.C.

Schwaan, G.M. (1990) *When Did You Move to Vancouver? An Analysis of Migration and Migrants into Metropolitan Vancouver.* The Laurier Institute: Vancouver, B.C.

Data References

Canadian Mortgage and Housing Corp. *Rental Market Report—Vancouver.* Vancouver, B.C.

Multiple Listing Services, Average Price of Housing in Greater Vancouver. Courtesy of Ann Broadfoot.

Statistics Canada (1989/91) *Canadian Economic Observer-Historical Statistical Supplement.* Cat. 11-210.

Statistics Canada *Post Censal Annual Estimates of Population by Marital Status, Sex and Components of Growth for Canada, Provinces and Territories.* Cat. 91-210.

Chapter 10

The Social Integration of Immigrants in Canada

Derrick Thomas[1]

Introduction

The issues

THE NATURE AND EXTENT OF the social and cultural changes wrought by immigration is a question of new urgency in Canada. Following nation-wide consultations, the federal government has recently announced increases in planned immigration levels. Although the new levels are still well within historically observed bounds, they do mean that issues surrounding the social adaptation and integration of new-

---

1   The opinions expressed in this chapter are the author's own and do not reflect immigration policy or the opinions of Employment and Immigration Canada.

comers will be more important. Over the longer term gradual changes in the source countries of immigration have also affected this debate. As noted in William Marr's chapter and elsewhere in this volume, the racial, ethnic and cultural character of Canada's immigrants has changed radically since the 1960s. The new ethnic and cultural composition of immigration clearly has implications both for the integration of newcomers and for the Canadian identity. Many Third World immigrants diverge more radically from historic Canadian norms in terms of their economic, social and cultural experience than do immigrants from the traditional source areas. Many Third World immigrants also differ racially from the host population. No amount of adjustment or acculturation can remove these visible differences. Clearly, Canadians will be called upon to make some accommodations. Canada's image of itself, its culture and perhaps its social structures will probably have to undergo some changes. The challenge will be to ensure that these changes occur smoothly and in a way that involves everyone, immigrants and Canadian born.

Immigration affects social structures, institutions and the rules which govern inter-personal and inter-group relations in Canada. Our national languages, values, morals, beliefs, knowledge, art, symbols and ideals are all affected in some degree by immigration. Our culture is the mechanism through which we communicate our values and transmit our patterns of social behaviour to each other and to succeeding generations. Immigration is not unique among social forces or policy areas in its capacity to affect these things but it does have undeniable consequences for how we relate to each other and even for who we are as a people.

The social and cultural benefits of immigration are especially difficult to gauge and may even go largely unattributed. They are nonetheless authentic and important. They include a culturally more diverse, richer, more interesting and vibrant society. Immigration can generate a broader base of ideas and models on which a community can draw as it evolves. An immigrant-receiving country will be more flexible and capable of adapting to changing situations. There may also be an optimum level of social tension that can lead to greater creativity. Basically an ethnically diverse society will be one in which a wider range of ideas and solutions is available to each individual. Such a society quite simply offers more personal freedom.

Most of these benefits are of a relatively long-term nature. They are also predicated on the successful integration of immigrants into mainstream society. The social and cultural benefits of immigration may well outweigh the social and cultural costs. As a practical matter, this is an impossible proposition to prove. Benefits are especially hard to quantify and most research has focused on the downside. The real constraint to increased immigration policy is its short- and longer-term costs. This paper will deal with the nature of the social and cultural costs of imigration and how they can be minimised.

Many of the social and cultural problems associated with immigration are ultimately traceable to a failure in the integration process. They emerge when immigrants fail to or are not allowed to play a fair role in the larger society. In segregated societies established groups tend to monopolize institutional power and to claim a disproportionate share of the economic and other rewards. Immigrants can be forced into an underclass. The economic, social and cultural opportunities of individuals are circumscribed in an ethnically segregated society. Several kinds of problems can emerge:

1. Alienated individuals experience social and psychological problems and become a burden to society. At the extreme they are institutionalized for incapacity or criminality.
2. Racial and ethnic conflict could spill over into violent incidents or full blown race riots as have occurred in the U.S. and more recently the U.K.
3. The potential for a socio-political paralysis brought about by racial and ethnic squabbling exists. Canada could disintegrate into a country of contending ethnic enclaves in which no common rules or values are recognized.

In short the society could lose its capacity to function as such if immigrant or ethnic groups are isolated or are ineffectual parties to an evolving social contract. The basis of our governments in individual suffrage and their ability to protect the rights of individuals could be eroded.

This paper will explore the tendency, if any, toward ethnic segregation and stratification in Canadian society. It will attempt to identify problems of the type outlined and to examine the ways in which they are influenced or addressed by immigration policy.

Historical context

Canada's immigration law and its policy toward newcomers is to a great degree conditioned by the society's particular history. These constraints will continue to operate in the future.

Canada, more than most countries, has experience in making the compromises and accommodations required of ethnically diverse societies. As we are now keenly aware, the dangers of intractable conflict, paralysis and disintegration have always been present in Canadian society. They will remain serious even without immigration.

In an often quoted phrase, Lord Durham described Canada as "two nations warring in the bosom of a single state." His important pre-confederation report focused on the struggle between French and English Canadians. He noted "that dissensions which appear to have another origin, are but forms of this constant and all-pervading quarrel: every contest is one of French and English in the outset, or becomes so ere it has run its course." In his opinion this quarrel had produced a political paralysis. "It would be idle," suggested Durham, "to attempt any amelioration of laws or institutions until we could first succeed in terminating the deadly animosity." He saw a resolution in British immigration and complete anglo ascendency. This of course proved impossible. By the turn of the century it was observed that "The dominant race suffers the presence of the French because it cannot do other-wise."[2]

Canada thus rests on a necessary, sometimes delicate and always evolving compromise.[3] Attempts to adjust the agreement persist. No final resolution has been achieved. Unlike, for example, the U.S., Canada was not the product of a national revolution and thankfully, our values

---

2 Andre Siegfried, *The Race Question in Canada*, MacMillan, 1978, p. 15.

3 Note that the groups which lacked the number and political power of the French Canadians did not fare so well. Canada's native people, for example, were segregated on reserves and their children were removed for education and assimilation in white run boarding schools.

and symbols were not forged in a decisive civil war. A history of peaceful accommodation does mean, however, that the country today has no clear homogenous ethnic self-image or single culture. Canada is cursed, or blessed, with a week national identity.

The French and English conflict is also at the basis of our social system. This duality largely dictated the federal institutional form of the country. The balance between French and English necessitated the enshrinement of official languages. It also had profound implications for immigration policy and the integration of immigrants from other than French or English speaking countries. An official policy of complete assimilation was not possible in the context of this truce. To which of the "two solitudes" would the newcomers assimilate? The Canadian "mosaic" was thus juxtaposed to the American "melting pot."

Immigrant and smaller ethnic groups are naturally envious of the position of the two charter groups and would like the same sort of status. They are able to appeal to precedent and principle. The product has been our current policy of multiculturalism and the celebration of our diversity. The existence of official languages and an official policy of multiculturalism affects the integration of immigrants in all parts of the country.

Models of integration and segregation

Defining integration and segregation

The integration of immigrants is a key concern of policy makers and observers. Integration deals with the fitting together of different subgroups or parts of a social system to constitute a whole. Integrated societies are characterized by the acceptance of common cultural values and wide adherence to these values in behaviour. Integration also implies the use of common communication networks and functional interdependence or a division of labour among parts of the social system.[4]

---

4   Werner S. Landecker, "Types of Integration and Their Measurement,"

Immigrants can be integrated into the host society in a number of ways. Assimilation implies the absorption of the migrant minority into the dominant culture or society. Completely assimilated immigrants are indistinguishable in an unchanged host culture. The partly mythical American "melting pot" is a model based on assimilation.[5] Some writers distinguish between different gradations and types of assimilation. Behavioural assimilation occurs when all groups adhere to the values of the majority and behave accordingly. Structural assimilation implies that all groups have access to and utilize the same institutions and social structures. Although they are interdependent and share in the division of labour, structurally assimilated groups need not behave or believe alike. They may retain some of the values and behaviours of their own group, at least for a time. Pluralism denotes a somehow integrated system wherein group identities are maintained indefinitely.

Complete assimilation is at one end of a continuum. Complete segregation is the other extreme. Segregation implies barriers between ethnic groups. Immigrants remain separate or are not allowed to become real members of the mainstream culture. Segregation is indicative of a failure to integrate, although some elements of integration such as, for example, economic interdependence may be present. Initially at least many groups might be more comfortable in a segregated society. Immigrants could retain their values unchanged and would have to make only a minimal adjustment to the host country. Similarly, the Canadian majority could retain its position of economic and social privilege largely unchallenged by newcomers. It is difficult, however, to see how such an apartheid-like system would not eventually produce problems. As we have mentioned segregation or ghettoization is often associated with ethnic conflict, minority group criminality and race riots.

As noted, the ongoing French/English conflict and Canada's allegedly weak national identity render any explicit attempt at the complete

---

American Journal of Sociology, 56, 1951, pp. 322-340.

5   Frank G. Vallee, Mildred Schwartz and Frank Darknell, "Ethnic Assimilation and Differentiation in Canada," *The Canadian Journal of Economics and Political Science*, Nov. 1957. See also Milton Gordon, *Assimilation in American Life*, Oxford University Press, 1964.

assimilation of immigrants problematical. No agreed upon norm exists to which they could conform. The balance between the charter groups could, moreover, easily be disturbed if immigrants disproportionately assimilated to one group over the other. Complete assimilation, because it involves a total surrender of their ethnic identity, also imposes a sometimes painful sacrifice on immigrants. It is therefore likely to be resisted by some immigrant groups.

Paradoxically segregation is the only sanction really available to enforce assimilation. The selective exclusion from the country of groups who resist assimilation on an ethnic or racial basis would constitute a departure from the policy of non-discriminatory immigration annunciated since the 1960s.[6] It would also be a reduction in the rights of certain groups already represented in the country and as such an institutional segmentation of our society. Laws which differentiate reinforce segregation.

Canada has been officially committed for some time to a model of integration which allows immigrant groups to maintain at least a portion of their ethnic identities.[7] Academics have also long advocated a recognition of immigrant integration "as a process in which a number of ethnic groups become increasingly similar to one another in particular respects."[8] In conjunction with its recent levels announcement, the federal government has stipulated that it views integration as a bidirectional process involving accommodation and adjustment on the part of both migrants and the host society. The Federal Integration Strategy emphasises the removal of barriers to the participation of minorities in the common culture.[9] Other initiatives such as the Federal Employment

---

6 Manpower and Immigration Canada, *Canadian Immigration Policy: the White Paper on Immigration*, October, 1966, p. 6.

7 *Report of the Royal Commission on Bilingualism and Biculturalism*, vol. 4, Ottawa, October 23, 1969, p. 5.

8 Vallee, Schwartz and Darknell, *op. cit.*

9 Employment and Immigration Canada, *Annual Report to Parliament: Immigration Plan for 1991-1995*, Minister of Supply and Services Canada, October 1990, pp. 13-15.

Equity Program and similar provincial efforts buttress this strategy. The effort is to find some ideal medium between assimilation and segregation. Integrated individuals, it is hoped, will be able to participate fully in all aspects of their society while retaining some portion of their original identity. The participation of immigrants and all Canadians will hopefully ensure that this society is to the greatest degree possible an integrated one characterized by a set of agreed upon values and consequently able to function and evolve as a complete system.

While forced assimilation and complete segregation are not viable options, the precise form which the accommodation between immigrants and the host society will ultimately take is perhaps not predictable. The situation will be fluid. The common values of the society will continue to be debated. Discussion will centre around what level of ethnic independence will be tolerated in various areas. Segregated groups will be those who do not take part in this discussion. There are many views of segregation and its implications.

Before we attempt to measure the extent of ethnic or immigrant group segregation in Canada we must make a distinction between cultural retention and segregation. As Wserolod Isajiw points out "Canadian identity is not necessarily gained to the extent that ethnic identity is lost and, vice versa, ethnic identity is not necessarily retained to the extent that Canadian identity is not acquired."[10] Immigrants have the right, in so far as they respect the similar rights of others, to celebrate and practice their cultural traditions. This right and a host of others is conferred by virtue of an evolving social contract and protected by a hopefully impartial and democratically elected government. Segregation exists when groups refuse to or are not permitted to take part in this social contract.

The ethnic enclave as a problem

One measure of segregation or ghettoization is the degree to which the groups in question have evolved parallel structures and institutions to

---

10   Wserolod W. Isajiw, "Ethnic-Identity Retention," in Breton, Isajiw, Kalbach and Reitz, *Ethnic Identity and Equality: Varieties of Experience in a Canadian City*, University of Toronto Press, 1990, p. 34.

perform economic, social, cultural and political functions necessary for the maintenance of the community.[11] The more functions that an ethnic group is able to perform within itself through the replication of institutions, the less contact its members will need to have with the larger society and the more enclosed the community will be. Ethnic enclosure is indicated by the existence of such boundaries and mechanisms for their maintenance between the group in question and the larger society. Many groups, for example, have their own school systems.[12] The Doukhobors of British Colombia represent an extreme case. They have historically avoided participation in the larger economy and the general society. Certain sects also eschew any involvement in the wider political process. "A Doukhobour declaration says that 'They have never given, nor will they ever give their votes during elections, thereby are free from any responsibility before God or man for the acts of any government established by men.'"[13]

To the degree that ethnic communities are enclosed and have their own parallel institutions, individual members are limited in their access to other institutions and markets.[14] In order to expand personal markets and opportunities, individuals in segregated societies must work for the expansion of their own ethnic institutions and structures.[15] Economic, social and political struggles thus become struggles between ethnic

---

11 R. Breton, "Institutional Completeness of Ethnic Communities and the Personal Relations of Immigrants," *American Journal of Sociology*, 70:2, September, 1964, pp. 193-205.

12 Lynn Moore, "Immigrants Transforming French Schools," *The Gazette*, Montreal, Saturday, March 3, 1990.

13 Hugh Herbiron, "Doukhobor Religion," in H.B. Hawthorn (ed.), *The Doukhobours of British Columbia*, University of British Columbia and J M. Dent and Sons Ltd., Canada, 1955.

14 Raymond Breton, "Stratification and Conflict between Ethnolinguistic Communities with Different Social Structures," in Bienvenue and Goldstein (eds.), *Ethnicity and Ethnic Relations in Canada*, 2nd ed., Butterworths, 1985, pp. 45-59.

15 Ibid., p. 48.

groups rather than between individuals or issue oriented interest groups.[16] Frequently, victory goes to the best organized group and this further reinforces oligarchic structures within the ethnic communities. In short, individual freedoms and rights are sacrificed in the interests of group power both within and outside the ethnic enclosure.[17] It has also been suggested that ethnic segregation leads, inevitably, to ethnic stratification.[18]

Ethnic elites may benefit economically and politically from the segregation of their group. Recent immigrants are especially vulnerable to exploitation by their community and its leaders. Evidence from the U.S. suggests that some subgroups including immigrant women have been disadvantaged in ethnic economic enclaves while others have benefited.[19] Organized criminal elements may also pray upon ethnic enclaves. Independent social structures which seek to enforce the differing moral values, collective decisions or internal hierarchies of an ethnic enclave are likely to be perceived as illegitimate and perhaps even criminalized by the larger society.

A potential threat to democracy even arises through the exploitation in the political process of individuals who have little knowledge of the languages or relevant traditions of the larger community. These people are open to manipulation by unscrupulous elites or ethnic "godfathers." The problem is amplified if the group is a cohesive and enclosed one in competition with others. Ethnicity may come to dominate the political agenda and voting pattern of the group to the exclusion of all other issues and interests. The stage is thus set for a kind of brokered politics in which the elites bargain and are accommodated. "The emergence of 'power brokers' and 'gate keepers' presents a barrier

16   Ibid., p. 48.

17   Ibid., p. 50.

18   R.A. Schermerhorn, *Comparative Ethnic Relations: A Framework for Theory and Research*, The University of Chicago Press, 1987, p. 68.

19   Min Zhou and John R. Logan, "Returns on Human Capital in Ethnic Enclaves: New York City's Chinatown," *American Sociological Review*, October 1989.

to the [meaningful] civic participation of ethnic and racial communities."[20]

At the same time, debates and political decisions in the larger community can disintegrate into conflict and bargaining between cohesive and internally oligarchic groups. Intergroup jealousies become paramount.[21] The capacity of overarching social institutions to serve individuals or to protect their rights is thus impaired and common resources are monopolized by the most powerful ethnic groups. As a consequence, the status of individuals is determined ascriptively by their ethnicity.

The ethnic enclave as a resource in integration

One of the key determinants of ethnic segregation is, of course, discrimination. Negative attitudes in the larger society tend to reinforce, if not precipitate, a group's enclosure.[22] Ethnic solidarity is one means to mobilize groups against discrimination.

According to one commentator "The greater the opposition-economic, political, social, religious or some combination thereof—perceived by an ethnic group, the greater the degree to which its historical sense of distinctiveness will be aroused, and hence the greater its solidarity."[23] Some attitudinal research does suggest "community for-

20 George W. Bancroft, Dorothy A. Wills and Cecille M. Depass, "The Civic Participation of Visible Minorities in Canadian Society: Framework and Issues for Research and Analysis," prepared for Policy and Research, Multiculturalism Sector, Multiculturalism and Citizenship Canada, April 1990.

21 Gilles Paquet, "Multiculturalism as National Policy," *Journal of Cultural Economics*, 13:1, p. 28.

22 John W. Friesen, *When Cultures Clash: Case Studies in Multiculturalism*, Calgary: Detselig, 1985, p. 137.

23 George M. Scott, Jr., "A Resynthesis of the Primordial and Circumstantial Approaches to Ethnic Group Solidarity: Towards an Explanatory Model," *Ethnic and Racial Studies*, 13:2, April 1990, p. 164.

mation for protective or defensive purposes rather than for cultural retention as such."[24]

Many commentators take a more positive view of ethnic segregation. They see ethnic enclaves as temporary and necessary for new immigrant groups.

Existing ethnic enclaves help recent immigrants to adjust. The shock of migration can be eased and spread over a greater time frame in an ethnic enclosure. The immigrant can draw on the experiences of those who have preceded him/her and can access information about the new society in his/her own language. Established ethnic groups provide many of the services offered by mainstream settlement and social service agencies, perhaps even more effectively. In many cases, "ethnics" run or staff the settlement servicing agencies and often they act as mediators and translators between new arrivals and the wider public.

The model suggested by the optimists is one in which immigrants move through the ethnic enclave using its resources in order to enter the mainstream society. In this view, ethnic enclaves consist of individuals linked by common interests in removing barriers against their participation in the broader community. Ethnic groups may continue to exist but individuals fall away as they adjust to the host society.

The question of the persistence of ethnic ties over time for individuals and across generations is thus an important one. Are immigrants and their descendants permanently ghettoized in ethnic enclaves? Or do ethnic groups facilitate and promote integration?

Another question concerns the existence of an ethnically based social stratification over time.

---

24 Raymond Breton, "The Ethnic Group as a Political Resource in Relation to the Problems of Incorporation: Perceptions and Attitudes," *Ethnic Identity and Equality: Varieties of Experience in a Canadian City*, University of Toronto Press, 1990, p. 249.

Official languages and the integration of immigrants

Canada's official languages

The ability to speak English or French is the leading determinant of immigrant integration in other spheres of Canadian life. For example we know that immigrants unable to speak either language have lower rates of labour force participation, higher unemployment rates and lower incomes.[25] The inability to speak one of Canada's chief languages also renders participation in the culture and politics of the larger society impossible. It may even have the effect of limiting access to basic human rights.[26] Immigrants without official language skills are almost certainly destined for segregation and isolation.

Owing to the balance of forces in play at Confederation, and still in play, language rights in Canada are formally recognized in the Constitution for both charter groups. At the federal level French and English have the status of official languages. Conformity in this respect is demanded. The ability to speak an official language is a requirement for Canadian Citizenship.

The position of the official languages in the Constitution has had many implications for immigrants in Canada. In the U.S. where, by way of contrast, there has traditionally been no official language legislation, electoral ballots are printed, and mainstream services are offered in minority languages according to demand. It has been largely due to market forces that the U.S. has remained an English speaking country. In Canada the approach has been more proactive. The position of the official languages in the political process, courts and—in some cases—the workplace is protected and more emphasis is placed on the provi-

---

25 Ravi Pendahur and Michel Ledoux, *Immigrants Unable to Speak English or French: A Graphic Overview*, Multiculturalism and Citizenship Canada, 1991, pp. 35-39.

26 Brad Munro, "Literacy: A Citizenship Participation Issue," *ESL and Citizenship*, 19:1, 1989, pp. 80-85.

sion of official language training than on the provision of mainstream services in minority languages.

Official language ability at arrival

Throughout the 1980s between 40 percent and 50 percent of immigrants arriving in Canada could not speak either official language. Independent immigrants to Canada are selected on labour market criteria which include official language ability. Refugees and immigrants sponsored by family members in Canada, on the other hand, are not assessed on these skills and more often don't speak English or French.

As we can see from figure 10–1, the proportion of immigrants unable to speak an official language has grown over the past decade. This is not due to the change in source areas which has proceeded steadily since the 1960s, but to the expansion of the Family and Refugee Classes after 1978. In fact, official language skills among immigrants were probably at their highest between 1966 and 1978 when more immigrants were selected as independents and source area preferences had just been eliminated.

Figure 10-1: Proportion of immigrants with no official language ability at landing versus proportion selected as independents, 1968 - 1990

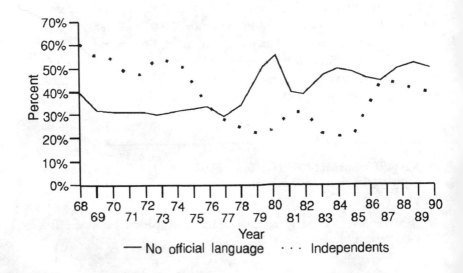

The present situation is not an unprecedented one. The level of language ability among immigrants in the 1940s and 50s compares with the situation of the 1980s. At the time of the 1951 census over 21 percent of immigrants who had arrived in the past two and one half years[27] were unable to speak either official language. In 1986 about 17 percent of those who had arrived in the previous two and one half years could not speak an official language.

The acquisition of an official language

While most foreign-born persons eventually acquire an official language, there are variables which condition the speed at which this happens. Data from the 1986 Census indicates that language learning occurs fairly quickly for over one half of those immigrants initially unable to speak English or French. Nevertheless, a significant group is still unable to speak an official language after 3 or even 8 years in the country.

Research indicates "that immigrants and refugees from Third World countries, who have limited formal education and/or whose mother tongue is not a Western language, experience greater difficulties in achieving fluency in one of the official languages."[28] Indeed, as of the 1981 Census, 94 percent of those who did not speak either official language had secondary level education or less. Almost 80 percent had less than a grade 9 education.[29]

---

27 Owing to the classification of immigrants by period of arrival on Statistics Canada's Public Use Microdata File for the 1986 census and in the published cross-classification tables from the 1951 Census, two and a half years is the shortest period after arrival for which a comparison was possible.

28 Gertrud Neuwirth, "Immigrant Settlement Indicators: A Conceptual Framework," *EIC*, March 1987, p. 11.

29 Teega Research Consultants Inc., "Profile of Canadians Who Speak Neither French or English," paper prepared for Multiculturalism, Secretary of State, 1987, p. 27.

As might be expected, immigrants who arrive when they are older also seem to experience more difficulty in acquiring an official language.[30]

Differential access to language training also plays an important role in language acquisition. In the past, language training programs in Canada emphasised training for those who were labour market bound and required it to perform the job for which they were qualified. Living allowances were provided in conjunction with the language courses. Other types of training were made available for those who were not labour market bound. In general, however, there was a shortage of all types of language training and waiting lists for courses were long.[31]

Groups not well served by the old language training programs included: those who were not fluently literate in their first language; those who lived in areas where there was no large concentration of recent immigrants; and immigrant women.[32]

Immigrant women, more often than men, are sponsored into the country by family members. As such they are not considered labour market bound and may not in the past have enjoyed equal access to language training. They may also be isolated at home or encumbered by family responsibilities.[33] Over 20 percent of females who arrived between January 1, 1983 and the 1986 Census reference week were unable to speak either official language at the time of the census. This was true for only 15 percent of males who arrived in the same period despite the fact that they enjoyed only a slight advantage in official

---

30   Pendakur and Ledoux, *op. cit.*, p. 24.

31   Peter A. Cumming, Chair, *Access!*, Task Force on Access to Professions and Trades in Ontario, Ontario Ministry of Citizenship, 1989, p. xv.

32   Mary Ellen Belfiore, Jill Bell, Marjatta Holt and Barbara Burnaby, "A Framework for Assessing Immigrant Integration to Canada, Phase II: Final Report," study prepared for the Department of the Secretary of State, March 1985, p. 17.

33   Monica Boyd, *Migrant Women in Canada: Profiles and Policies*, (Ottawa, Employment and Immigration Canada and The Status of Women, Canada, March 1987), p. 21.

Figure 10-2: Foreign born who cannot speak either French or English

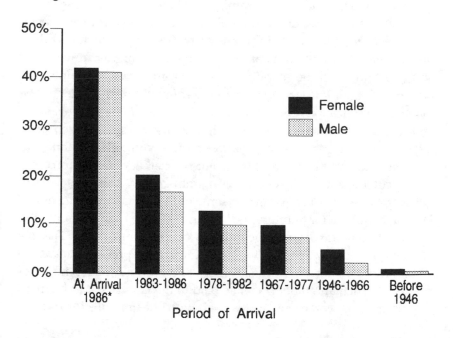

Source: From Statistics Canada "Profile of the Immigrant Population in Canada," *Dimensions*, Census Canada #93-155.
* Immigration Statistics, 1986.

language competency at landing.[34] Language skills improve for both sexes with time in the country, but the rate of improvement is slower for females and, after some time has elapsed, they are twice as likely to speak neither official language.

For immigrant women and all immigrants, failure to acquire an official language is a significant barrier to participation in almost all facets of Canadian society. In fact, the National Organization of Immigr-

---

34 Employment and Immigration Canada, Tabulations from the Landed Immigrant Data System, 1980-98.

ant and Visible Minority Women of Canada views language training as the "single most important issue for immigrant women."[35]

The language training of immigrant children and the Canadian-born children of recent immigrants takes place in mainstream provincial school systems. Although immigrant children are known to adapt quickly, high concentrations of immigrants and refugees arguably result in a burden to the school systems in some areas. Certainly, the Canadian School Trustees Association has argued that this is so.[36] "The long-term implications for Canada of not funding the language-training and related settlement needs of immigrant and refugee children [they argue] will be a generation of young people who lack the ability to integrate successfully into and contribute to their adopted country."

In conjunction with its five year immigration plan, the federal government has moved to correct some of the deficiencies in existing language training for immigrants. More funds have been committed to expand the amount of language training for adult immigrants. The role of official language ability in the general integration process is acknowledged and training programs are now aimed at a broader range of clients. "Particular attention will be paid to the language and learning requirements of women and individuals with little formal education."[37]

Acquisition of English versus French

It keeps things in perspective to note that, according to the 1986 Census, over 98 percent of Canadian residents speak one or both official languages. About two-thirds of the population speaks only English, just under 16 percent speak only French and a little over 16 percent speak

---

35   NOIVMWC "Status Report on Recommendations and Action Plan," 1989, p. 3.

36   CSTA, "Report on the Scholastic Adaptation and Cost Effectiveness of Programs for Immigrant/Refugee Children in Canadian Schools," May 1989.

37   Employment and Immigration Canada, *Annual Report to Parliament: Immigration Plan for 1991-1995*, Supply and Services Canada, October 1990, p. 14.

Table 10-1: The ability to speak Canada's official languages among Canadian residents born in various countries

Country	English & French (%)	English only (%)	French only (%)	Neither (%)
Canada	18.6	63.7	17.6	0.1
U.S.A.	16.7	80.2	2.9	0.1
Belgium/ Luxembourg	45.1	37.8	17.1	0.0
France	59.4	9.7	30.9	0.0
Germany	11.1	87.6	0.6	0.8
Netherlands	7.3	92.3	0.0	0.3
Austria	9.5	89.9	0.0	0.7
Ireland	8.1	91.1	0.8	0.0
U.K.	8.3	91.7	0.0	0.0
Yugoslavia	6.7	89.3	0.6	3.5
Greece	11.0	76.9	0.5	11.5
Italy	16.3	63.3	6.9	13.5
Portugal	12.0	62.5	5.9	19.6
Hungary	10.3	85.9	0.8	3.0
Poland	8.5	86.5	0.9	4.1
U.S.S.R.	6.7	88.8	0.5	4.0
Czechoslovakia	12.7	83.8	0.4	3.1
Other Europe	18.0	76.0	3.9	2.1
Eastern Asia	3.1	74.9	0.4	21.6

Table 10-1: *continued*

Country	English & French (%)	English only (%)	French only (%)	Neither (%)
South East Asia	8.9	75.3	6.9	8.9
Southern Asia	6.6	85.9	0.1	7.3
Western Asia	31.7	57.6	4.9	5.7
Northern Africa	66.8	14.9	16.3	1.9
Southern Africa	19.0	91.3	0.0	0.0
Other Africa	8.7	91.3	0.0	0.0
S. & C. America	11.6	76.8	5.9	5.7
Caribbean	11.0	77.1	11.4	0.6
Other	7.9	89.5	0.6	1.9

Source: Special tabulation from Public Use Sample Tape, 1986 Census of Canada.

both languages. Only about 1.2 percent of those who reside in Canada do not speak an official language.

As we can see, however, the two languages are not equally secure. Although almost all immigrants eventually learn an official language, there has been a tendency to learn English as opposed to French.

It has always been a concern that additional immigration might upset the linguistic balance. A large proportion of immigrants lack any facility in French at arrival. Over 93 percent of those who landed in Canada in 1988, for example, had no ability to speak French on arrival. For those destined to Quebec the proportion was still 70 percent. Nor has the rate of French language acquisition been high. Nationally, about 84 percent of those identified as immigrants in the 1986 Census could not speak French. Over 30 percent of the one-half million foreign born people living in Quebec could not speak French. For those who had been in the country less than 3.5 years, the proportion was about 40 percent.

In part, the explanation for the paucity of French language ability is to be found in the attitudes of the migrants themselves. Faced with an investment in terms of learning one of the official languages, many apparently choose English as likely to produce the best return in the North American market. Some immigrants and refugees may also feel that in learning French rather than English, they are cut off from a broader community, the power and importance of which they are keenly aware. Central Americans, for example, actually feel a closer affinity to the English culture of the U.S. than to the supposedly related Latin culture of Quebec.[38]

French Canadians and Quebecers have been understandably apprehensive about the provisions in the Multiculturalism Act that provide for the "enhanced use of languages other than English and French" and about multiculturalism in general. Immigrants have learned English and multiculturalism has in practice meant Anglo-conformity, at least for the purposes of interaction in the larger community. French Canadians see the danger that their language could become only one of a number of languages spoken in enclaves while English assumes a hegemonic role as the *lingua franca*.[39] They also perceive the possibility that their progress could be slowed if their language and group rights were to become bundled with those of other smaller groups. These apprehensions probably account for the stipulations in the 1988 Act that multiculturalism should be advanced "in harmony with the national commitment to the official languages of Canada." A hierarchy between Canada's official languages and its other languages seems to be intended. Although some concessions have been made, certainly the "minimal" right to communicate with their government in their own

---

38 Cecilia Taiana, "Cultural Interaction between Canadians and Salvadorean Newcomers in Quebec and Canada," forthcoming paper for Strategic Planning, Immigration Policy Branch, Employment and Immigration Canada.

39 Guy Rocher, "Les ambiguites d'un Canada bilingue et multiculturel," *Quebec en Mutation*, (Montreal: Hurtibise, 1973), pp. 117-126.

language and the right to a publicly funded education in their own language[40] has never been conceded to immigrant groups.

In order to address some of the concerns of Quebecers, the province has been given a greater role in the selection of immigrants and more authority over their settlement and integration under a succession of federal/provincial agreements.

Other evidence of ethnic segregation and its persistence

Indicators of segregation

In their 1963 examination of ethnic and racial minorities in New York City, Glazer and Moynihan noted a disturbing pattern of persistent and highly segregated groups.[41] Although racial segregation is now disappearing in most of the American South it continues and may even be intensifying in cities such as New York. Glazer and Moynihan saw the distinct possibility of increased ethnic conflict and ultimately violent confrontation.

Most of Canada's immigrants do concentrate in a few cities. These cities are becoming less and less typical of the rest of the country in terms of their ethnic composition. Perhaps Toronto, with almost 40 percent of its population foreign born, is only two or three decades behind cities which have experienced race riots.[42]

This section will examine the evidence of ethnic segregation, its strength and persistence.

---

40   C. Michael MacMillan, "Language Rights, Human Rights and Bill 101," *Queens Quarterly*, 90 (1983), p. 357.

41   Nathan Glazer and Daniel P. Moynihan, *Beyond the Melting Pot: The Negroes, Puerto Ricans, Jews, Italians and Irish of New York City*, (Cambridge: M.I.T. Press, 1970).

42   Jeffrey G. Reitz, "Less Racial Discrimination in Canada or Simply Less Racial Conflict?: Implications of Comparisons with Britain," Centre for Industrial Relations and Department of Sociology, University of Toronto, November, 1987.

Immigrants in Canada might segregate themselves or might be segregated according, for example, to their area of origin, religion, language, race, or culture. While differences on these dimensions do not in and of themselves constitute evidence of it, persistent dissimilarity in one or more of them is probably a necessary condition for segregation. As discussed in the last section, the inability to communicate in one of Canada's official languages, in particular, can insure that a group remains isolated from the mainstream society. Segregation might also be evidenced by the strength—especially over time—of ethnic identity, the perception of social distance, the propensity for mixing or intermarriage, the tendency toward geographic separation, and independent group institutions. Problems like open intergroup conflict or violence and high crime rates among group members are ultimate products of segregation.

Ethnic identity

Many of the dimensions upon which immigrant groups differ can be subsumed under the rubric of ethnicity.[43] It is instructive, however, to note how multifaceted the concept of ethnicity is.

Black ethnicity, for example, is primarily a racial category and those who identify themselves as Black can differ widely as to their geographic origin, language, culture and religion. Jewish ethnicity is primarily a religious category and similarly Jews can differ on one or many of the other dimensions of ethnicity. Nor are the categories mutually exclusive. It is possible, for example, to be both Black and Jewish.

Canadians are encouraged to identify themselves as belonging to one or more ethnic groups on the national Census. In 1986, over 8.5 million Canadians or about 34 percent of the population claimed some element of non-charter group and non-aboriginal heritage. Of these about 5 million or over 20 percent of Canadians identified themselves exclusively with one non-charter/non-aboriginal ethnic group.

Out of the total population, 25.3 percent of Census respondents identified themselves solely as part of the British charter group. About

---

43 Wsevolod W. Isajiw, "Definitions of Ethnicity," *Ethnicity* 1:1, 1974.

24.4 percent said they were exclusively French. A further 15.6 percent identified with a group of European extraction. Germans were the largest single group at 3.5 percent followed by Italians, Ukrainians and Dutch.

Table 10-2: How Canadians identified themselves on the 1986 census with respect to ethnic origin

Origin	Single Responses	Percentage (%)
British	6,332,730	25.31
French	6,093,165	24.35
European	3,913,225	15.64
Arab	72,315	0.29
West Asian	41,305	0.17
South Asian	266,780	1.07
East and South East Asian	600,535	2.40
Pacific Island	6,625	0.03
African	4,980	0.02
Latin, Central & South American	32,235	2.40
Caribbean	48,480	0.19
Black Origins	174,970	0.70
Aboriginal	373,265	1.49
Other	75,045	0.30
Multiple Responses	6,986,345	27.92

Source: Special tabulation from 1986 census data, Multiculturalism Branch, Secretary of State for Canada.

Table 10-3: Home use of mother tongue in 1986

| Mother Tongue | Canadian born (%) | Immigrants Arrived | | | | TOTAL |
		1945 & before	1946-67 (%)	1968-77 (%)	1978-86 (%)	
English	98.5	98.6	97.6	94.0	90.5	98.2
French	92.1	74.9	73.6	72.0	69.8	91.7
Chinese	56.7	—	81.1	86.2	89.8	83.3
Portuguese	66.4	—	68.3	82.2	89.1	76.5
Aboriginal	76.8	—	—	—	—	76.8
Greek	68.1	—	75.7	82.1	81.7	74.6
Spanish	61.5	—	51.3	74.9	82.8	74.2
Iranian	69.6	—	51.9	71.6	81.1	73.3
Italian	47.1	40.1	75.0	78.4	80.9	65.9
Polish	22.9	35.8	50.6	68.4	82.8	49.5
German	27.9	29.9	40.3	47.7	74.0	35.9
Ukranian	20.8	52.6	63.8	62.8	56.7	29.6

Source: Special Tabulations from Public Use Sample Tape, 1986 Census of Canada.

As mentioned above, the Third World and particularly Asia has been supplanting Europe as the source area of Canada's immigrants. As of 1986 about 1.4 percent of Canadians identified themselves as Chinese and 0.88 percent identified as East Indian.

While large proportions of the Canadian population identify themselves with a non-charter group, they are diverse in terms of origin, language, culture and religion. No other single culture or language truly contends with the two major ones. Census responses, moreover, are not a good indicator of the strength of ethnic feeling. Indeed for many people, identifying themselves on the Census may be the only time they think of themselves as a member of an ethnic community.

Retention of mother tongue

Ethnic language retention is not by itself a measure of segregation. However, a common and unique language is naturally an aid to ethnic solidarity and to the extent that original language retention and use declines it may be fair to assume that ethnic enclosure is also declining.

As of the 1986 Census, over 13 percent of Canadians had a mother tongue other than English, French or an Aboriginal language. Among the foreign-born population 42 percent had a non-official language as their mother tongue. Over two thirds of those who arrived between 1978 and the 1986 Census had a non-official mother tongue. Yet, in 1986 fewer than 10 percent of Canadian residents spoke a non-official language at home. As we can see from table 10–3, home use of the mother tongue clearly declines with time in the country. Moreover, those groups with the highest rates of retention have more recent arrivals among them.

Religion

Ethnic groups which are unified by a single strong religion exhibit the greatest capacity to resist assimilation.[44] Religious taboos and sanctions are available to keep group members in line. The Hutterites and Doukhabours, for example, are highly enclosed rural communities held

---

44 Edward N. Herberg, *Ethnic Groups in Canada: Adaptations and Transitions,* Nelson Canada, 1989, p. 222.

together largely by "deeply internalized religious values and beliefs."[45] The strength of religion, and thus the importance of religious monopoly, has long been declining in almost all ethnic groups, however.[46]

Social distance

A clue as to the strength of cleavages in Canadian society can be obtained from an examination of the attitudes and feelings of Canadians concerning the various ethnic groups. One attitudinal measure of ethnic cleavages is the "social distance" scale as pioneered by Bogardus (1925). This much used indicator rests on the stated willingness of individual respondents to interact on a number of levels with members of various ethnic groups. How willing are they, for example, to have a member of group X as a citizen of their country, a co-worker, a neighbour or a spouse? It is hypothesized, and has been empirically demonstrated, that the closer the suggested interaction the lower the tolerance (i.e respondents are normally less willing to tolerate members of different groups as marriage partners and relatives than as co-workers or citizens of their country). The closeness of the proposed relationship thus constitutes a scale.

In 1981 a large sample of Winnipeg high school students indicated a higher level of tolerance for groups with European origins than for non-European groups.[47] American and British groups were the most desirable as marriage partners, neighbours and co-workers etc. Racially different groups such as Blacks and Orientals were relatively less desirable. Aboriginals were ranked near the bottom. In a study which used a different methodology, a sample of over 2,000 Torontonians were

---

45 Edward D. Boldt, "Maintaining Ethnic Boundaries: The Case of the Hutterites," in R.M. Bienvenue and Jay Goldstein (eds.), *Ethnicity and Ethnic Relations in Canada*, 2nd ed., (Toronto: Butterworths, 1985), p. 93.

46 Herberg, *op. cit.*, pp. 149-152.

47 Leo Driedger, *The Ethnic Factor: Identity and Diversity*, McGraw-Hill Ryerson Limited, 1989, pp. 341.

asked about the prestige of a number of ethnic groups.[48] The results largely paralleled the Winnipeg study. British and European groups ranked highest. Visibly different groups and Aboriginals ranked lowest. Somewhat surprisingly, most groups agreed with the majority in assessing the prestige of their own group.

In yet another study members of the two charter groups were asked to rank a list of 27 ethnic groups in order of similarity to themselves.[49] French and English respondents ranked each other quite highly and they also seemed to agree about the positions of most of the other groups. In general the same pattern prevailed as to European and Non-European groups. Their were only a few differences from the study mentioned above, most notably in the relatively higher rankings given by all respondents to Natives and Blacks. Insular religious groups (Mennonites, Hutterites and Doukhobors) were ranked at the bottom by both charter groups.

This kind of research suggests that there are perceived ethnic divisions in Canadian society. There also seems to be broad agreement about, at least, the relative importance of these cleavages with respect to various groups. Such perceptions and attitudes obviously affect the integration of immigrants. They are inevitably associated with their ethnic group in the mind of the broader public.

Ethnic endogamy

Another measure of ethnic enclosure is the rate of intramarrige or endogamy. Ethnic endogamy refers to the tendency of members of an ethnic group to marry or choose mates from within their group as opposed to outside it. Some indication of past rates of endogamy can be gleaned from the number of people who report mixed ethnic origins on the census. Over 28 percent of Canadians claimed to be members of more than one ethnic group in 1986. "Groups with the highest propor-

---

48   Jay E. Goldstein, "The Prestige Dimension of Ethnic Stratification," in R.M. Bienvenue and J.E. Goldstein (eds.), *op. cit.*, pp. 188-189.

49   J. Berry, R. Kalin and D.M. Taylor, *Multiculturalism and Ethnic Attitudes in Canada*, (Ottawa: Minister of Supply and Services, 1977), p. 96.

tion of multiple response were the Welsh (84 percent), Irish (81 percent), Swedish (79 percent) and Scottish (78 percent). Those groups with the lowest proportion of multiple response were Koreans (7 percent), Cambodians (12 percent), Filipinos (13 percent) and the Chinese (13 percent)."[50] Low numbers could be indicative of a tendency toward ethnic enclosure but more likely they simply reflect how long members of the group in question have been in the country. More direct measures of endogamy taken in 1981 indicate relatively high rates of marriage within the group for Asians and Jews.[51] When controls are introduced for the proportion first generation immigrants in each group, however, Jews and Asians no longer stand out as having particularly high levels.[52]

Ethnic endogamy rates in Canada have generally been falling since 1931.[53] The rates for Jews have been falling especially sharply. The rates for East Europeans, Germans, Scandinavians and the Dutch have always been low and they continue to decline.

Residential segregation

Some groups are residentially or territorially segregated, though it should be remembered that spatial segregation is partially confounded with income and social class.[54] A study based on 1981 Census data found that Greeks, Portuguese, Italians and Jews exhibited the highest rates of residential concentration in Canada's three largest metropolitan areas. Surprisingly, given most assumptions about the social distance between groups and the possible existence of racial discrimination in housing

---

50 Statistics Canada, "Profile of Ethnic Groups: Census Canada, 1986," *Dimensions*, Catalogue 93-154, February 1989.

51 Edward N. Herberg, *Ethnic Groups in Canada: Adaptations and Transitions*, Nelson Canada, 1989, pp. 186-187.

52 Ibid., pp. 296-297.

53 Herberg, *op. cit.*, p. 191.

54 T.R. Balakrishnan, "Immigration and the Changing Ethnic Mosaic of Canadian Cities," report for *The Review of Demography*, (Ottawa: HWC, October, 1988), p. 45.

markets,[55] visible minority groups did not appear to be as concentrated.[56] As a partial explanation, some researchers note that the Asian and Black minorities are actually more diverse in terms of language, religion and culture than are the Mediterranean groups. Montreal seems to be the centre with the highest rates of concentration for almost all ethnic groups. This may be due to the fact that many groups do not speak French. Western cities in particular seem devoid of identifiable ethnic concentrations.[57] Overall, researchers agree that "it is scarcely sensible to talk of 'ghettos' in Canadian cities."[58]

Parallel institutions

Immigrant and ethnic groups do not seem to rely on the social structures of their own community for long periods after their arrival or over generations. In 1981, researchers studied the utilization, by Toronto ethnic groups, of their own ethnic media and vacation facilities, as well as their attendance at ethnic functions.[59] Italian immigrants exhibited the highest degree of enclosure. They were followed by Ukrainian and Black immigrants and, more distantly, by Jewish, British, Portuguese and Chinese immigrants, in that order. When second and third generation members of these ethnic groups were looked at, Jews appeared to

---

55 Frances Henry, "Housing and Racial Discrimination in Canada," *Multiculturalism and Citizenship*, August 1989.

56 T.R. Balakrishnan and John Kralt, "Segregation of Visible Minorities in Montreal, Toronto and Vancouver," in Leo Driedger (ed.), *Ethnic Canada: Identities and Inequalities*, (Copp Clark Pitman Ltd., 1987), p. 156.

57 L.S. Bourne, A.M. Baker, W. Kalbach, R. Cressman and D. Green, "Canada's Ethnic Mosaic: Characteristics and Patterns of Ethnic Origin Groups in Urban Areas," (Centre for Urban and Community Studies, University of Toronto, July 1986), p. 31.

58 John Mercer, "Asian Migrants and Residential Location in Canada," *New Community*, 15:2, January 1989, p. 198.

59 W.W. Isajiw, *Ethnic Identity Retention*, (Centre for Urban and Community Studies, University of Toronto, 1981), pp. 26-35.

Table 10-4: Persons granted Canadian citizenship during 1989

World Area of Former Allegiance	Number of Persons Granted Citizenship	Average Number of Years Since Immigration
U.S.A.	1,853	15.7
Western Europe	21,898	14.5
Eastern Europe	6,441	6.2
Caribbean & Latin American	15,558	6.9
Asia	29,268	4.9
Africa	2,432	5.1
Others—Australia, Oceania	8,842	5.3

be the most cohesive group while Italians and Ukrainians had clearly fallen away from their ethnic networks.

In general it appears that immigrant and ethnic groups maintain their respect for Canadian institutions and perceive them as fair and impartial. Research indicates that ethnic groups are quite prepared to rely on the organizational structures of the broader society, even in order to redress problems like discrimination. Minority groups with origins in the Third World, as represented by the Chinese and West Indians, were especially reluctant to rely on their own communities. According to a 1979 survey conducted in Toronto, a majority favoured Canadian agencies and institutions to protect them from discrimination.[60] Immigrants from the Third World also take out Canadian citizenship and avail themselves of the protection and rights thus afforded more quickly on average.

---

60 Raymond Breton, *op. cit.*, 1990, p. 221.

With regard to the political process, preliminary research suggests that immigrants and ethnic minorities generally have high rates of participation in Canada regardless of the political tradition from which they come.[61] Moreover, their participation rates and political interest levels apparently reach Canadian norms very quickly.

Criminality

Immigrants who turn to crime or are criminalized are plainly not integrated. There is an obvious disjunction of values and behaviour. Perhaps the institutionalization of immigrants for criminality is the clearest indicator of alienation and failure in the integration process.

Crime is apparently not rampant in Canada's immigrant communities. Research utilizing the records of the country's most serious criminals clearly indicates that, while some groups may have problems, the foreign born overall are under represented among inmates of Canada's federal prisons. Immigrants account for approximately 19 percent of the total Canadian adult population but only about 10.3 percent of the federal prison population is foreign born.[62] The non-aboriginal visible minority population is also under-represented among the federally incarcerated.

The offence patterns of immigrant criminals does differ from that of the native-born criminals, however. Immigrants tend to be imprisoned for black market offences such as narcotics and gambling.[63] Basically the pattern could be indicative of differing moral values or analogous social structures in the form of organized gangs. It is interesting to note that among Canadian-born visible minorities, who can be expected often to be the children of immigrants, the pattern of criminality conforms very much to the Canadian-born norm as opposed to the

---

61 Jerome H. Black, "The Practice of Politics in Two Settings: Political Transferability among Recent Immigrants to Canada," *Canadian Journal of Political Science*, December 1987.

62 Derrick Thomas, "Criminality among the Foreign Born," EIC, in progress.

63 John Samuel and Ron Santos, "Canadian Immigrants and Criminality," (forthcoming).

immigrant norm. This suggests that patterns of criminality among immigrants and minorities are not rooted in a persistent subculture and are not perpetuated over generations.

Cross-cutting versus reinforcing cleavages

The divisions or cleavages between groups can be cross-cutting or reinforcing. Cross-cutting cleavages exist when individuals attach themselves to different groups depending on which interest or issue is at stake. They may ally themselves with members of their own faith on religious issues, with those who speak their language on linguistic issues and with those who supply or demand the same factor or product on economic issues.

Cleavages reinforce each other when individuals feel that ostensibly different interests are actually connected or parallel. They may rely on the same group to defend their religious, linguistic, cultural, social, economic and other interests. All interests appear as collective interests. Society seems always to break down into the same insular groups on every issue.

Cleavages are most dangerous when they reinforce each other. If group members share many or all interests, if there are no interests in common between groups or which cut across groups then the viability of the larger society will be called into question. One can even envision a kind of national paralysis in which all issues assume an ethnic dimension and are weighed in terms of how they affect the power of each group in question. In effect, all issues become ethnic issues. "The available evidence . . . suggests that the chances for stable democracy are enhanced to the extent that groups and individuals have a number of crosscutting, politically relevant affiliations."[64]

---

64 S.M. Lipset, *Political Man: The Social Basis of Politics*, (Garden City: Anchor Books, 1963), p. 77.

Socio-economic status, a potentially reinforcing cleavage

In his famous 1965 analysis of social class and power in Canada, John Porter argued that status was ascribed, at least partly, on the basis of ethnicity.[65] Based on occupations he identified ethnic strata. British groups and Jews were at the top, followed by the French, West and North Europeans. East and South Europeans were somewhat lower. Japanese and Chinese were near the bottom of the hierarchy.[66]

Today, many members of visible minorities still feel that "Canadian society is in reality a 'vertical mosaic' with some pieces raised above others."[67] Measures of social distance suggest a stratification among ethnic groups. Certain groups are more preferred as neighbours and mates and are seen as enjoying more prestige.

As can be seen from the tables of Appendix I, the overall foreign-born population clearly does not constitute an underclass in Canada. On the whole the foreign born earn higher incomes, are wealthier, and are more often managers, owners and employers than the native born. They typically have lower unemployment rates and those of working age are also less likely to collect social assistance from government.

There are, however, important differences among the various immigrant groups on the above mentioned measures of status. In Table 1 of Appendix I groups have been ranked according to their performance across the available indicators of economic status. The method employed is admittedly crude, but, it is illustrative to note that the hierarchy observed conforms in its essential characteristics to that observed by Porter in the sixties. Third World immigrants or racially different immigrants seem to be at some disadvantage vis à vis immigrants born in the traditional source countries. Different groups fall below the norm on each measure. Third World groups, however, are fairly consistently

---

65 John Porter, *The Vertical Mosaic*, (University of Toronto Press, 1965), p. 69.

66 Porter, *op. cit.*, p. 81.

67 Canada, House of Commons, *Equality Now*, (Report of the Special Committee on Visible Minorities in Canadian Society, March 1984), p. 5.

at the bottom of the list. At least one important researcher feels that the shorter time which they have spent in Canada does not adequately explain the relatively poor performance of our non-traditional immigrants.[68]

Part of the explanation may also be found in the fact that Canadian employers, professional associations and accreditation bodies are not in a position and do not have the incentive to assess the prior learning or experience of immigrants. This is especially true of Third World immigrants.[69] We cannot, however, wholly reject good old fashioned racism and discrimination as an explanation for the relatively poor performance of non-traditional immigrants.

Members of non-aboriginal visible minority groups earn marginally lower incomes,[70] have higher unemployment rates and are underrepresented in management occupations.[71] This despite the fact that visible minorities are better educated than the Canadian norm.[72] Indications are that the situation is worst among visible minorities who are foreign born.[73] In comparison to other groups a lower proportion of visible immigrants are in non-manual occupations. The fact that many ethnic minorities have relatively elevated levels of participation in

---

68 George J. Borjas, *International Differences in the Labour Market Performance of Immigrants*, (W.E. Upjohn Institute for Employment Research, 1988), pp. 61, 97.

69 Ibid., p. xiii.

70 T. John Samuel, "Immigration, Visible Minorities and the Labour Force in Canada: Vision 2000," (November 1987), p. 3.

71 Employment and Immigration Canada, *Employment Equity Act Annual Report*, (Minister of Supply and Services Canada, 1984), pp. 51-52.

72 R.S. Abella, Commissioner, *Equality in Employment: A Royal Commission Report*, (Ottawa: Supply and Services Canada, 1984), pp. 143-144.

73 Fernando G. Mata, "Visible Minority and Immigrant Status: Education Credentials, Occupations and Incomes," (DPAR: Multiculturalism, Draft, April 1990).

higher education[74] indicates that this discrimination operates not in the education system but in the labour market.

Evidence of discrimination in the Toronto labour market was detected in a 1985 study which found that, given equivalent qualifications, white job applicants were three times more likely to receive a job offer than were black applicants.[75] This implies that blacks had to look three times harder or three times as long to obtain work. These findings may underline the need for employment equity and anti-discrimination programs. A 1989 repeat of this study seems to indicate that the situation has improved with respect to visibility if not with respect to those who speak with certain accents.[76]

Conclusions

A clear socio-economic hierarchy exists among immigrant groups. It is reflected both in the attitudes of Canadians and in the measurable income and wealth of the different groups. The so-called traditional groups for the most part exceed the Canadian norm while other groups sometimes fall below it.

Non-traditional groups of course contain a larger proportion of younger people and recent arrivals who may not have fully adapted to life in Canada. This at least partially accounts for their relatively poor economic performance. It seems, however, that the attitudes of Canadians will also have to undergo change before these groups can really be integrated into our society. Failure on the part of immigrants and

---

74 "Participation of Different Ethnic Groups in Postsecondary Education," (Canada, Secretary of State, Multiculturalism Branch, April 1987).

75 Frances Henry and Effie Ginzberg, "Who Gets the Work? A Test of Racial Discrimination in Employment," (Toronto: The Urban Alliance on Race Relations and The Social Planning Council of Metropolitan Toronto, January 1985), p. 52.

76 F. Henry and E. Ginzberg, "Who Gets the Work in 1989?" (study commissioned by The Economic Council of Canada, 1989 [in progress]). An effort was made to control for the effects of tighter labour markets which prevailed, especially in Toronto, during this follow-up study.

Canadians to make these adjustments could have dire consequences for Canada.

It has been argued that Canada's racial problems may be only a generation away. According to pessimists, Canada does not differ from societies which have experienced race riots in terms of the level of racism which is present but only in terms of the amount of conflict which has taken place.[77] First generation immigrants often measure their economic well-being in relation to conditions which prevailed in their country of origin. Their children, on the other hand, may feel economically deprived relative to other Canadians and may attempt to rectify the situation through violence or crime.

To the degree that the existing system is perceived as unfair or illegitimate immigrants will turn to their own resources in order to redress the situation. More segregation and increased racial and ethnic conflict could result. Yet, there is little evidence that this is happening. Immigrants and especially non-traditional immigrants seem to value Canadian citizenship and trust Canada's institutions. Canadian society seems also to be adjusting and there is evidence of improvement in the areas of job discrimination and racism.

Perpetually segregated enclaves do not seem to have formed so far in Canada. Many researchers argue that most ethnic groups simply lack the social structures to preserve their culture.[78] They cannot "effectively restrict their members' exposure to alternate norms, values and behaviours." In general, they become even less residentially segregated, they learn an official language, they cease to speak the ethnic language, they are no longer involved in the ethnic community and they feel less social distance from other groups. The result is that only the "symbolic" or "affective" ethnicity detected in the Census survives beyond one or

---

77 Jeffrey G. Reitz, "Less Racial Discrimination in Canada or Simply Less Racial Conflict?: Implications of Comparisons with Britain," (Centre for Industrial Relations and Department of Sociology, University of Toronto, November 1987).

78 Lance Roberts and Rodney Clifton, "Exploring the Ideology of Multiculturalism," *Canadian Public Policy*, VIII, Winter 1982, p. 89.

two generations.[79] The higher the level of education, the more this pattern of assimilation is likely to hold.

Third World groups have been in Canada for much less time than have the traditional ethnic groups, but already they exhibit a trend away from ethnic group cohesion. The newer immigrants are not significantly concentrated residentially. Their rates of language retention and the extent of religious monopoly are also low.

Even though a socio-economic stratification based on ethnicity exists in Canada, we have, thus far, been able to avoid most of its negative consequences. Incidents of ethnic conflict involving immigrants have not been absent, but Canada has had no experience of ethnic or race riots for scores of years. Similarly there is no evidence that alienated and ghettoized immigrants are resorting to criminal activity in disproportionate numbers.

Some immigrant groups or more accurately some immigrants are segregated in some ways but overall there is no evidence of a serious, persistent or insoluble problem. It appears that, in so far as society-wide institutions are perceived as impartial and cleavages are not reinforced by other social barriers or underclass status, Canada will have little to fear from its growing diversity.

Canada's practice of selecting immigrants on labour market criteria has helped ensure that not *all* newcomers are confined to the lower strata of society, even if they are not always rewarded commensurate with their skills. This policy may help to attenuate racial conflict because it provides role models and demonstrates the possibility of mobility. The fact that Canadians have no racially or ethnically defined national identity may also have helped. Canada's commitment to respect minority cultures, equal treatment and universal human rights is also helpful.

Problems of intergroup relations have a long history in Canada. These problems will obviously remain critical. The outcome is by no means guaranteed but success could position Canada well in the world of the future.

---

79 Morton Wieinfeld, "Myth and Reality in the Canadian Mosaic: 'Affective Ethnicity'," in Bienvenue and Goldstein, *op. cit.*, 1985, pp. 71-72.

Appendix 1

Table 10A-1: Measures of economic performance or status by country of birth ranked on these measures (mean # wks/yr worked)

Country of Birth	% unemployed	mean # wks/yr worked	% managers & profs.	% manual workers	mean employment income	mean total income	% main income investments	% main income transfrs	% employ others	% self-employed	% own home	% home over $99K
Southern Africa	7.2	42	38.0	19.2	$24,440	$24,319	3.0	1.7	9.6	3.1	69.1	60.9
Austria	5.7	44	32.5	33.0	$23,427	$19,433	2.2	4.0	10.2	9.6	80.2	46.8
Ireland	3.2	45	39.3	24.3	$24,114	$20,474	.7	2.8	5.4	6.9	69.1	53.9
Northern Africa	10.7	44	45.5	16.3	$24,026	$20,898	1.4	3.3	8.1	5.7	55.9	59.8
Germany	6.8	45	29.7	34.0	$23,017	$19,367	1.8	3.8	8.2	8.2	77.7	45.0
Netherlands	4.1	45	28.5	39.9	$23,317	$18,788	2.0	4.0	10.2	10.3	81.7	37.5
Hungary	7.6	44	29.5	38.8	$24,132	$19,661	3.2	4.0	9.1	9.8	70.5	47.9
UK	6.6	44	35.8	23.3	$23,360	$19,290	1.6	2.8	4.3	4.8	70.7	44.1
Eastern Asia	8.1	43	28.9	21.1	$17,668	$14,614	2.1	2.7	9.1	5.4	77.6	63.0
Italy	6.3	44	13.2	55.2	$20,755	$17,189	1.2	2.9	7.9	3.9	89.9	64.3
USSR	7.3	43	30.2	36.4	$22,175	$16,120	3.4	4.7	8.2	8.2	79.2	43.4
Belgium & Luxem.	8.2	43	35.9	35.2	$22,745	$19,154	1.6	4.8	8.3	10.3	71.3	31.3
Czechoslovakia	8.6	42	36.0	29.9	$22,093	$19,037	2.4	4.8	5.6	7.5	71.6	44.4
Other Europe	7.4	43	26.4	37.5	$21,254	$17,371	1.3	3.3	7.2	10.2	71.8	45.7
France	8.9	43	40.5	24.3	$21,919	$19,584	2.0	3.4	4.5	5.9	61.3	34.9

Table 10A-1: *continued*

Country of Birth	% unemployed	mean # wks/yr worked	% managers & profs.	% manual workers	mean employment income	mean total income	% main income investments	% main income transfrs	% employ others	% self-employed	% own home	% home over $99K
Yugoslavia	7.7	44	15.6	53.2	$20,642	$17,529	1.3	3.1	6.7	5.4	82.4	53.4
USA	8.9	40	40.6	22.7	$20,407	$16,681	2.2	3.8	5.4	8.6	65.8	38.8
Poland	7.0	43	23.9	42.9	$20,123	$16,379	3.5	3.9	7.6	7.5	74.2	42.5
Greece	9.3	44	12.9	37.8	$16,818	$14,937	1.4	4.2	13.4	6.6	76.5	64.0
Other	10.6	41	31.6	24.3	$19,126	$16,880	1.7	2.7	4.1	4.5	68.0	57.0
All Immigrants	8.2	43	27.4	34.5	$20,208	$16,897	1.5	3.4	6.0	5.4	70.5	49.9
Western Asia	13.7	41	33.0	26.0	$16,902	$13,568	1.6	3.8	11.0	9.3	51.9	56.9
Other Africa	11.1	41	33.6	19.6	$17,660	$14,882	1.2	2.9	5.6	6.0	55.2	54.2
Portugal	6.5	43	6.7	57.7	$16,570	$14,113	.7	3.0	2.9	2.2	75.8	51.2
Canadian Born	10.2	41	26.4	32.0	$18,190	$15,718	1.2	4.4	4.0	5.1	68.0	28.3
Caribbean	10.8	42	26.5	32.0	$16,560	$14,417	.3	3.7	2.1	2.5	47.3	54.1
Southern Asia	13.0	40	26.7	39.9	$18,556	$15,966	.7	5.5	3.3	3.3	70.5	51.1
South East Asia	10.3	42	24.1	35.9	$15,869	$12,634	.4	3.3	2.3	1.9	49.1	45.1
S. & C. America	11.7	40	19.4	40.9	$15,598	$12,387	.2	4.1	2.9	2.0	47.0	48.7

Source: Public Use Sample Tape, 1986 Census of Canada prepared on 5 Jan 91.

Table 10A-2: Measures of human capital & factors affecting performance by country of birth ranked on performance measures

Country of Birth	Median Age	% Male	% Married	Mean Family Size	% with University Degree	% Under Grade 9	% No Official Language	% Urban	% Arrived 1978-86	% Came before 1945	% Visible Minority	% in Labour Force	Mean # hrs/wk worked
Souther Africa	38	54.4	59.6	3.4	27.2	3.6	0.0	79.2	31.4	1.9	19.1	71.0	41
Austria	55	52.4	71.2	2.6	9.8	22.5	.7	70.8	5.1	16.3	.5	56.9	40
Ireland	47	48.7	67.9	3.0	11.7	10.3	0.0	74.7	13.4	11.2	1.4	66.3	39
Northern Africa	40	56.4	65.7	3.1	30.4	9.7	2.1	93.7	19.1	.5	55.9	72.3	39
Germany	48	48.5	72.8	2.7	9.5	11.4	.8	64.8	6.8	4.4	.7	68.4	40
Netherlands	49	51.4	81.3	3.2	6.9	22.2	.3	46.5	5.2	2.8	.6	65.2	42
Hungary	56	54.4	69.9	2.3	12.6	25.1	3.0	74.5	6.2	14.3	.3	61.2	41
UK	50	46.2	65.0	2.6	10.4	10.7	0.0	67.1	8.5	20.6	2.8	58.7	39
Eastern Asia	38	49.1	64.2	3.4	19.2	22.3	21.5	90.8	37.2	1.8	98.0	66.4	41
Italy	48	53.0	82.6	3.4	3.8	56.6	13.5	86.6	2.1	2.5	.1	66.0	40
USSR	65	47.5	66.5	2.2	9.5	42.6	4.0	73.7	6.3	30.2	1.4	36.5	39
Belgium & Luxem.	48	50.7	69.6	2.7	14.7	24.1	0.0	51.6	8.0	11.3	.4	64.6	42
Czechoslovakia	49	48.7	64.5	2.6	18.5	18.3	3.1	74.4	17.9	20.9	.5	64.4	40
Other Europe	49	52.2	69.6	2.8	10.2	23.5	2.1	66.6	13.3	15.3	1.6	61.6	41
France	42	50.9	61.0	2.7	21.3	9.0	0.0	75.9	12.8	4.3	1.9	73.2	40
Yugoslavia	46	51.8	75.2	3.0	6.0	34.3	3.5	78.0	5.9	5.8	.6	70.2	41

Table 10A-2: *continued*

Country of Birth	Median Age	% Male	% Married	Mean Family Size	% with University Degree	% Under Grade 9	% No Official Language	% Urban	% Arrived 1978-86	% Came before 1945	% Visible Minority	% in Labour Force	Mean #hrs/wk worked
USA	41	42.8	57.3	2.8	22.6	13.7	.2	53.4	18.3	28.4	5.0	57.4	39
Poland	60	50.2	68.8	2.4	9.6	39.7	4.1	75.3	18.5	24.3	.1	49.2	39
Greece	45	51.5	79.2	3.4	4.4	51.6	11.5	91.5	4.9	1.6	.6	71.1	43
Other	35	48.0	57.4	3.2	14.9	8.8	2.0	77.0	26.5	2.9	40.3	76.7	38
All Immigrants	44	49.0	66.0	3.0	12.2	23.3	5.5	76.0	18.6	10.2	28.1	64.7	40
Western Asia	33	54.3	55.5	3.4	20.3	17.0	5.8	89.5	45.9	1.2	81.5	65.6	40
Other Africa	33	53.2	59.6	3.3	19.6	8.3	2.2	90.9	32.9	.2	86.1	77.4	41
Portugal	37	50.8	72.6	3.5	1.6	51.7	19.6	85.7	12.5	.3	.2	74.4	40
Canadian Born	28	49.4	44.6	3.2	8.9	14.8	.1	48.6	0.0	0.0	2.6	67.5	39
Caribbean	36	45.1	49.0	3.2	9.2	10.2	.6	93.3	23.6	.8	97.5	77.7	39
Southern Asia	35	52.8	68.4	3.4	25.2	13.2	7.3	82.6	33.5	.5	94.6	74.5	39
South East Asia	31	47.2	50.0	3.6	19.7	16.7	9.1	88.2	66.5	.2	97.0	73.6	38
S. & C. America	31	47.1	54.4	3.6	9.4	16.6	5.8	83.5	41.5	1.0	64.6	73.2	38

Source: Public Use Sample Tape, 1986 Census of Canada prepared on 5 Jan 91.

Table 10A-3: Occupations by country of birth ranked on performance measures

Country of Birth	% Managers	% Professional & Tech.	% Clerical Sales	% Service	% Manual & Trade	Sample n	n over 15
Southern Africa	14.2	23.8	30.7	12.3	19.2	366	331
Austria	14.6	17.9	20.6	14.0	33.0	607	591
Ireland	14.7	24.6	25.8	10.5	24.3	499	478
Northern Africa	19.1	26.4	28.3	9.9	16.3	776	750
Germany	14.1	15.6	25.1	11.1	34.0	3735	3649
Netherlands	13.7	14.8	21.6	10.0	39.9	2563	2527
Hungary	11.1	18.4	19.3	12.5	38.8	1234	1222
UK	15.4	20.4	29.9	11.0	23.3	15435	14948
Eastern Asia	11.1	17.8	25.6	24.4	21.1	4765	4452
Italy	7.1	6.1	17.4	14.2	55.2	7268	7227
USSR	12.5	17.7	22.1	11.3	36.4	2189	2167
Belgium & Luxem.	15.0	20.9	18.6	10.3	35.2	450	435
Czechoslovakia	12.1	23.9	22.0	12.1	29.9	829	793
Other Europe	11.1	15.3	23.6	12.5	37.5	2642	2551
France	13.6	26.9	21.5	13.6	24.3	1018	983
Yugoslavia	7.1	8.5	16.8	14.4	53.2	1788	1759
USA	12.9	27.7	27.2	9.6	22.7	5037	4620

Table 10A-3: *continued*

Country of Birth	% Managers	% Professional & Tech.	% Clerical Sales	% Service	% Manual & Trade	Sample n	n over 15
Poland	8.5	15.4	19.0	14.1	42.9	3047	2951
Greece	8.4	4.5	14.3	34.8	37.8	1708	1677
Other	9.6	22.0	27.7	16.4	24.3	665	592
All Immigrants	10.8	16.6	23.7	14.4	34.5	76462	72853
Western Asia	14.8	18.2	28.3	12.6	26.0	1522	1367
Other Africa	14.5	19.1	32.8	14.0	19.6	1124	1057
Portugal	3.3	3.4	15.9	19.7	57.7	2806	2681
Canadian Born	10.2	16.2	28.7	12.8	32.0	74861	56475
Caribbean	6.6	19.9	26.0	15.4	32.0	3954	3735
Southern Asia	9.4	17.3	21.5	12.0	39.9	3164	3006
South East Asia	4.9	19.2	21.0	19.1	35.9	4330	3717
S. & C. America	6.8	12.6	23.8	15.9	40.9	2941	2587

Source: Public Use Sample Tape, 1986 Census of Canada prepared on 5 Jan 91.

Table 10A-4: Sectors of employment by country of birth ranked on performance

Country of Birth	% Primary Industry	% Manuf. Constr.	% Trans. & Comm.	% Whole-sale	% Retail	% Fin. & Business Services	% Gov. Educ. Health	% Housing & Food Services	% Other Services
Southern Africa	1.9	20.7	4.6	6.9	9.6	16.1	27.2	8.0	5.0
Austria	4.7	28.0	6.0	4.1	12.9	13.2	16.5	7.4	7.1
Ireland	4.2	23.4	6.9	3.6	8.7	11.7	32.4	4.5	4.5
Northern Africa	.7	18.9	5.5	9.0	13.1	13.6	24.1	8.5	6.5
Germany	6.1	29.0	7.2	5.5	12.7	10.5	17.6	5.0	6.4
Netherlands	15.0	25.9	6.0	4.7	12.3	8.8	18.3	3.1	6.0
Hungary	7.1	31.9	4.7	4.6	10.9	11.7	16.5	4.8	7.8
UK	3.1	23.1	6.9	4.5	11.5	14.7	24.9	4.8	6.7
Easter Asia	1.7	20.1	5.3	4.1	14.7	12.5	13.4	21.8	6.2
Italy	1.2	48.4	5.9	3.8	11.8	6.1	10.6	5.4	6.7
USSR	7.4	30.6	5.3	4.1	11.6	11.3	19.5	3.5	6.8
Belgium & Luxem.	-6.6	21.3	7.0	2.3	9.0	7.6	21.9	5.6	8.6
Czechoslovakia	4.5	25.9	6.2	4.3	9.3	15.9	20.0	7.8	6.2
Other Europe	7.5	28.0	6.6	4.3	11.7	10.2	18.0	6.6	7.1
France	3.8	20.2	6.7	2.8	11.0	9.2	28.9	8.5	8.9
Yugoslavia	3.5	47.8	4.5	3.5	10.9	6.3	12.4	6.4	4.7

Table 10A-4: *continued*

Country of Birth	% Primary Industry	% Manuf. Constr.	% Trans. & Comm.	% Whole-sale	% Retail	% Fin. & Business Services	% Gov. Educ. Health	% Housing & Food Services	% Other Services
USA	7.2	14.9	5.7	3.9	11.0	12.8	28.4	5.9	10.1
Poland	6.8	34.0	4.8	4.1	10.8	9.3	17.9	5.7	6.6
Greece	.9	32.5	2.9	2.6	9.5	5.7	7.1	30.3	8.5
Other	3.6	15.6	5.5	4.7	11.5	13.4	26.4	7.9	11.3
All Immigrants	4.1	29.6	5.7	4.2	11.4	11.0	18.8	7.9	7.2
Western Africa	1.6	20.8	5.5	5.5	21.2	10.3	16.9	11.8	6.4
Other Africa	2.4	15.9	6.9	4.6	17.5	14.5	20.5	8.0	9.8
Portugal	3.3	48.8	4.6	3.2	9.7	7.5	6.7	5.9	10.3
Canadian Born	7.6	21.3	7.8	4.7	13.0	10.4	22.3	6.4	6.6
Caribbean	.8	28.3	5.8	3.7	9.1	12.1	24.8	7.4	7.9
Southern Asia	7.3	32.3	6.4	4.1	8.5	12.3	16.7	7.4	5.0
South East Asia	2.4	33.5	3.4	3.9	8.4	10.1	19.4	11.1	7.7
S. & C. America	3.9	34.5	4.5	4.9	10.5	10.7	15.2	7.6	8.2

Source: Public Use Sample Tape, 1986 Census of Canada prepared on 5 Jan 91.

Appendix II

Data source and definitions of indicators

The data used in the tables of Appendix I and others throughout this report came from the Public Use Microdata File on Individuals. The file, provided on 9 track computer tape by Statistics Canada, is a product of the 1986 Census of Canada. The sample was drawn from among the 20 percent of Canadians who completed the Census long form. It represents about 2 percent of all 1986 Census respondents or about 500,000 individuals. Records for over 78,000 foreign born persons are available. Since a detailed country of birth breakdown was not available for the Atlantic provinces or the Territories these areas are not represented in the tables of Appendix I. Records on all foreign born and records on a random sample of just under 75,000 Canadian born individuals from the rest of the country were used.

Definitions of the various measures employed in the tables are provided below. Readers who find these definitions inadequate should consult the "Documentation and User's Guide" for the 1986 Census Public Use Microdata File on Individuals or the 1986 Census Dictionary (Catalogue No. 99-101E).

Country of Birth: Refers to the specific country of birth according to boundaries at the Census date for those born in Europe or the USA. Those born in the countries of Asia, Africa, South and Central America, the Caribbean and elsewhere are grouped by area as described in the documentation provided with the Microdata File.

Percent Unemployed: Refers to the proportion of labour force participants 15 years of age or over in each group who reported they were unemployed during the Census reference week.

Mean Number weeks/year worked: Refers to the average number of weeks worked in 1985 by members of each group who were 15 years old or more. Only those who had worked at least 1 week are included.

Percent Managers and Professionals: Refers to the proportion of those 15 or over in each group whose reported occupation was classified in 1980 SOC Major Groups 11, 21, 23, 27, 31 or 33. Occupations are present occupation for those employed on the Census date or most common occupation between January 1, 1985 and the Census date for those not employed.

Percent Manual Workers: Refers to the proportion of those 15 or over in each group whose occupation was in Major Groups 71, 73, 75, 77, 81-83, 85, 87 or 91.

Mean Employment Income: Refers to the average income earned from employment in 1985 for those 15 and over in each group who earned at least some employment income in that year.

Mean Total Income: Refers to the average income from all sources for all those 15 and over in each group. Mean Total Income is less than Mean Employment Income due to the larger denominator used in its calculation.

Percent Main Income from Investments: Refers to the proportion of those 15 and over in each group whose most important source of income in 1985 was from investments.

Percent Main Income from Transfers: Refers to the proportion of those from 15 to 64 in each group whose most important source of income in 1985 was from pensions, unemployment insurance benefits, government transfers, credits or allowances.

Percent Employ Others: Refers to the proportion of those 15 and over in each group who were mainly self-employed between January 1, 1985 and the Census date and had paid help.

Percent Self-employed: Refers to the proportion of those 15 and over in each group who were mainly self-employed and did not have paid help.

Percent Own Home: Refers to proportion 15 or over in each group who live in a home owned by a member of their household.

Percent Home Over $99,999: Refers to the proportion 15 or over in each group who live in a home owned by a member of their household for which the owner would expect to receive over $99,999 if it were sold. We have no direct information about the existence of mortgages and hence about the amount of real net equity.

Median Age: Refers to the median age in each group.

Percent Male: Refers to the proportion of each group who are male.

Percent Married: Refers to the proportion of those 15 and over in each group who were currently married on the Census date.

Mean Family Size: Refers to the average number of persons living together in the same dwelling as a Census family for all individuals in each country of birth group.

Percent With University Degree: Refers to the proportion of those 15 and over in each group who had attained at least a bachelor's degree on the Census date.

Percent Under Grade 9: Refers to the proportion of those 15 and over in each group whose highest level of schooling attained was less than grade 9.

Percent No Official Language: Refers to the proportion of those over 5 years old in each group who reported that they were unable to speak either official language.

Percent Urban: Refers to the proportion in each group who lived in a Census Metropolitan Area on the Census date.

Percent Arrived 1978-86: Refers to the proportion of those in each group who immigrated to Canada between January 1, 1978 and the Census date.

Percent Arrived before 1945: Refers to the proportion of those in each group who immigrated to Canada before 1945.

Percent Vismin: Refers to the proportion of those in each group who are members of a non-aboriginal visible minority.

Percent in Labour Force: Refers to the proportion of those 15 and over in each group who indicated that they were labour force participants employed or unemployed.

Mean Number of Hours/Week Worked: Refers to the average number of hours worked by those 15 and over in each group in the week prior to enumeration. Only those who had worked that week are included.

Occupations: Refers to those 15 and over in each group whose reported occupation of employment or usual employment were classified in the 1981 SOC as follows:

Managers: includes Major Group 11

Professional & Technical: includes Major Groups 21, 23, 27, 31 & 33

Clerical and Sales: includes Major Groups 41, and 51

Service: includes Major Group 61

Manual & Trade: includes Major Group 71, 73, 75, 77, 81-83, 85, 87 and 91.

Industries: Refers to those 15 and over in each group whose reported industry of employment or usual employment were classified in the 1980 SIC as follows:

Primary: includes divisions A, B & D;
Manufacturing and Construction: includes divisions E & F;
Transportation and Communications: includes divisions G & H;
Wholesale: includes division I;
Retail: includes division J;
Finance & Business Services: includes divisions K, L & M;
Government, Education and Health: includes divisions N, O & P;
Accommodation & Food Services: includes division Q;
Other services: includes division R.

Ranking

The overall ranking of the groups by country of origin was obtained by ordering them according to the sum of their ranks on all of the indicators reported in Table 10A-1 of Appendix I. Note that there are two indicators for overall labour market access (columns 2 & 3), two indicators for occupation (columns 4 & 5), two for income (columns 6 & 7), three indicators for relationship to the means of production (columns 8, 10 & 11), two indicators of ownership and wealth (columns 12 & 13) and a measure of state dependency (column 9).

Tied ranks at the indicator level were given the mean value of all of the positions they occupied so that the total range of rank values was the same for each indicator. Some indicators were, of course, ranked in order of ascending value and others in order of descending value. (e.g. For "percent unemployed" the lowest value received the highest rank while for "total income" the highest value received the highest rank.)

This process is a rather crude one and the inclusion of different indicators or the use of a slightly different method could affect the position of individual groups. Virtually any method will yield the same basic stratification with respect to traditional and non-traditional groups, however. Explanations can be sought among the indicators in Table 10A-2 of Appendix I. Median Age and Percent Married are significantly and positively correlated with the overall rank score. Percent Vismin and Percent Arrived after 1978 are negatively correlated with it at a significant level.